why we hate us

why we hate us

AMERICAN DISCONTENT IN

THE NEW MILLENNIUM

Dick Meyer

CROWN PUBLISHERS   NEW YORK

Copyright © 2008 by Richard Meyer

Published in the United States by Crown Publishers, an imprint of the
Crown Publishing Group, a division of Random House, Inc., New York.

www.crownpublishing.com

CROWN is a trademark and the Crown colophon is a registered trademark of
Random House, Inc.

Grateful acknowledgment is made to the following for permission to reprint previously
published material:

Alfred Publishing Co., Inc.: excerpt from "Once in a Lifetime," words and music by
David Byrne, Chris Frantz, Jerry Harrison, Tina Weymouth, and Brian Eno, copyright © 1980
by WB Music Corp., Index Music, Inc., and E.G. Music Ltd. All rights on behalf of itself and
Index Music, Inc., administered by WB Music Corp. All rights reserved. Reprinted by
permission of Alfred Publishing Co., Inc.

Alfred A. Knopf and Faber and Faber Ltd.: excerpt from "Of Modern Poetry" from
The Collected Poems of Wallace Stevens by Wallace Stevens, copyright 1954 by
Wallace Stevens and renewed 1982 by Holly Stevens. Rights in the United Kingdom
administered by Faber and Faber Ltd., London. Reprinted by permission of Alfred A. Knopf,
a division of Random House, Inc., and Faber and Faber Ltd.

The Wall Street Journal: excerpt from "Prole Models" by Charles Murray (*The Wall Street Journal,*
February 6, 2001), copyright © 2001 by Dow Jones & Company, Inc.
All rights reserved worldwide. Reprinted by permission of *The Wall Street Journal,*
administered by the Copyright Clearance Center.

Library of Congress Cataloging-in-Publication Data
Meyer, Dick.
Why we hate us : American discontent in the new millennium / Dick Meyer.
p.   cm.
Includes bibliographical references.
1. United States—Civilization—21st century. 2. Political culture—United States. 3. Popular
culture—United States. 4. United States—Social conditions—21st century. I. Title.
E169.12.M49 2008
973.93—dc22   2008007053

978-0-307-40662-0

Printed in the United States of America

Design by Leonard Henderson

1 3 5 7 9 10 8 6 4 2

First Edition

To Jill
For Lily and Daniel

Contents

Preface

THERE'S SOMETHING ROTTEN in the state of America.

It is something phony, belligerent, and toxic in the culture. We are mad as hell about it, but we keep on taking it. We keep electing partisan phonics we can't stand. We keep watching loudmouthed pseudo-news shows on cable and keep yelling back at the television. We get furious at liberal bias and right-wing slant. We watch television for three hours a day and complain that there's nothing to watch. We whine about the ads and then buy the beer, the plasma-screen television, and the "bottomless bowl" at Olive Garden. We pay two dollars a bottle for water and feel like suckers. We commute ninety minutes a day in our SUVs and complain about gas prices. We read *People* magazine and then get irritated by the hypersexual ads and fawning coverage of celebrity skanks and himbos. We watch Paris Hilton on *Larry King Live* the day after she gets out of jail for drunk driving and feel like dopes for watching. We get furious at the loud cell-phone talker in the waiting room as we bang out e-mails on BlackBerries with our angry thumbs.

Americans are down on America. There are wide patches of the cultural landscape that we just plain hate.

We're often aware of this social self-loathing, but that doesn't relieve it. The trust and confidence Americans have in the country's major institutions and leaders have been at historic lows since the early 1970s and are staying low in the first decade of the twenty-first century. We are disillusioned and repelled by the polluted social and cultural environment we live in. We perceive it as toxic, and we are wary. The values we have as families and individuals aren't reflected in the collective culture. This threatens our individual happiness and our collective ability to get things done in politics and in communities. The recipes of self-discovery and do-it-yourself spirituality we have used to replace more traditional religions, social codes, and worldviews aren't working. The planned communities we have built to replace real ones are hollow. Technology isn't making us happier. If America were put on the couch of popular psychology, the diagnosis would be obvious: low self-esteem. Our society is successful and admirable in so many ways, but we don't feel either pride or satisfaction in any sustained fashion. We would benefit from a better understanding of why we hate us.

This isn't a job for social science alone. Polls, focus groups, and brain scans can't prove that we hate us or explain why. So there won't be a lot of charts and graphs ahead. This book is not a political book. It isn't liberal or conservative. It avoids the hot-button issues of the chattering political elite because those repetitive arguments are sources of interminable heat but no light. Instead, I hope to swipe smart ideas from smart people who think about culture and history and mix them together in a useful way. I make no claims to originality and thank all the people I quote at the outset. This book came out of columns I wrote for CBSNews.com and the blunt, generously open responses I received from readers. They taught me much about what we hate, and they taught me that it is impossible to have a friendly, open-minded conversation about our complaints, flaws, and foibles without a sense of humor.

In chapter 1, I will describe what we hate most, what that says about us, and why it's important to pay attention. Chapter 2 sorts our antipathies into some basic categories such as bullshit, belligerence, and boorishness. The next two chapters deal with "why?" I pin much of the blame for our crankiness on a disorienting one-two punch of rapid societal change; the combination of the moral, intellectual, and civic transformations that came after the sixties; and the disruptive social fallout from the revolution in technology at the turn of the millennium. After that I'll go into what I think is the emblematic malady of our times: phoniness. Then I'll dig into some specific areas of public life: politics, the gargantuan soul-sucking creature I call OmniMedia, its black sheep cousin OmniMarketing, and then character and manners.

At the end, I'll explore ideas we might use to hate us less and, importantly, to produce less that is hateful with our own lives and work. In life, you give and you get. The problems and discomforts I write about are not reparable by legislation, political platforms, or social programs. We are deluged by people and ideologies that claim to have the cures for what ails us. I belong to no intellectual team or ideological faction, and I am not making a political argument. I don't have answers. In times as cynical and skeptical as these, even making helpful suggestions is risky business. But I'll take that risk in the final chapter.

The sorts of complaints I'll be writing about come only to societies that have abundance, and ours has more than any nation has ever had. Our discontent in the face of such plenty is a puzzle. Obviously, too many people in America don't share in the country's prosperity and relative peace. But people of all sorts, I learned from my readers and reporting, do hate what has happened to the country's public culture—to "us"—and they are the "we" I am talking about. We might hate different things, at different times, in different ways. Politics and media exaggerate our differences and disagreements. I do not think we hate one another. Still, everyone hates something about "us," our collective work, our culture. We do have that much in common. And we do fight back. That's the good news.

My ambition for this project was well expressed by Daniel Boorstin in 1961. He prefaced his wonderful book *The Image: A Guide to Pseudo-Events in America* this way: "I remain confident that what dominates American experience today is not reality. If I can only dispel some of the mists, the reader may then better discover his own real perplexity. He may better see the landscape to find whatever road he chooses."

Washington, D.C.
JANUARY 2008

why we hate us

Chapter One

LAND OF THE FAKE

THE CASKET WAS WRAPPED in an American flag, bright in the sun reflected off the marble Tomb of the Unknowns at Arlington National Cemetery on a May morning in 1998. A military band played the old hymn "Going Home" as an honor guard lifted the casket and carried it to the waiting hearse. During the night, the coffin had been taken out from under the heavy stones of the tomb. It had rested there since Memorial Day 1984 when President Ronald Reagan led a ceremony to finally honor the soldiers of the Vietnam War by putting one of their own into the Tomb of the Unknowns. Who was he? What was his story? Where was his family? "We will never know the answers to those questions about his life," Reagan said that day. For fourteen years that casket protected an unknown soldier from the Vietnam War, guarded around the clock by the Army's Old Guard at the country's most solemn war memorial. On May 14, 1998, the disinterred casket was loaded into a black hearse and taken away.

Everyone at the ceremony that day knew that the human remains under the flag were not unknown. They were the remains of Air Force 1st Lt. Michael Joseph Blassie, who was shot down over An Loc on May 11, 1972. Jean Blassie, Michael's mother, knew it, as did his brother and

1

his sisters, who watched from the steps above the tomb. I knew it, as I watched from a press stand.

Astonishingly, Pentagon officials knew it back in 1984.

I remember the moment during the ceremony when I realized the Tomb of the Unknowns was literally a fake on a monumental scale. A deliberate fake. A false monument.

The hearse drove away to take the remains to a laboratory for DNA testing. On June 30, the Pentagon announced that the Vietnam War remains in the Tomb of the Unknowns were officially not unknown anymore. They were the remains of Jean Blassie's son, Michael. Two weeks later, Michael Blassie was buried for good near the family's home outside St. Louis. "My brother deserves to be known," Blassie's younger brother, George, said that day.

I had been working on this story for months with two colleagues from CBS News, correspondent Eric Engberg and Vince Gonzales, a tenacious reporter who had unlocked the key secrets of the tomb. A series of stories we produced for *The CBS Evening News* had shown beyond any doubt that it was Michael Blassie, not an unknown soldier, in the tomb. The Reagan administration had been under tremendous pressure in 1984 to honor the most poorly treated soldiers in American history, the veterans of the Vietnam War. But technology had gotten so sophisticated that there simply weren't many remains from that war that hadn't been identified. Still, the pressure went down the bureaucratic food chain to the military identification laboratory in Hawaii. The Pentagon brass wanted unidentified remains to be buried at a presidential ceremony at the Tomb of the Unknowns on Memorial Day, and they intended to get them. One of the few sets of possible remains at the Hawaii lab had been labeled X-26. Those bits of human bone, however, had been clearly identified back in Vietnam as Michael Blassie's. Blassie was shot down during a daytime bombing run on North Vietnamese artillery positions that were pulverizing South Vietnamese troops and a handful of U.S. advisers at a place called An Loc. That night, Col. William Parnell sent out a patrol. They found bodily remains, Blassie's ID card, and other personal gear. Through some later screwup, the remains were separated from the identification card and eventually given the X-26 reference. But there was a clear paper trail. Witnesses were available to clear up any confusion. Military officials knew all of that when they sent the X-26 remains off to Arlington National Cemetery in 1984.

Our reports forced the Pentagon to reopen the case and exhume the remains. There is no soldier from the Vietnam War within the tomb today. But for years that monument was defaced by a fraud. It was another casualty of Vietnam. The memorial was insulted by the kind of stagecraft that the Reagan administration brought to Washington and that has flourished ever since. For me, it was an initiation into the land of the fake.

After the disinterment ceremony, I became even more of a phoniness vigilante than I had been. I have no special claim on authenticity or sincerity. But I'm fairly well trained to spot fakery and fraud in the public realm. My job back in 1998 was to produce a segment called "Reality Check" for *The CBS Evening News*. I was a professional bullshit hunter, and in those days Washington was loaded with big game. That was the year of the president and the intern—that woman, Ms. Lewinsky. President Bill Clinton was put through an impeachment trial essentially for philandering and some of his most zealous and righteous prosecutors were exposed as cheaters as well—Speaker of the House Newt Gingrich; his designated replacement, Bob Livingstone of Louisiana; and two powerful Republican committee heads, Henry Hyde of Illinois and Daniel Burton of Indiana. The hypocrisy rose to trophy levels. The hunting was easy.

Trust and confidence in government sank to Watergate-era lows. Wise people worried that "civility" had vanished from public life and that government was in perpetual "gridlock." Two commissions of academics and statesmen convened to ponder the civility crisis, the Council on Civil Society and the National Commission on Civic Renewal, and both issued dire reports.

Unfortunately, civility can't be commissioned, morality can't be legislated, and money can't buy you love. Despite levels of peace and material abundance on a scale this nation had never before seen, the mood grew even more sour. The election of 2000 between Vice President Al Gore and Texas governor George W. Bush was bitter and venal. But it was nothing compared to the battle that erupted after the disputed re- sults in Florida. The conventional über-narrative of American politics then (and now) was the story of polarization, red versus blue, right against left. But it seemed clear to me that this wasn't anything like the extreme, violent polarization of the Civil War, Prohibition, or the 1960s. This was very different and didn't run nearly so deep. Soon after the 2000 election, columnist Lars-Erik Nelson died. A tribute quoted him as once saying, "The enemy isn't liberalism. The enemy isn't conservatism. The enemy is bullshit." I immediately cut it out and taped it to my desk. I was in the trenches of the bullshit wars. I even had a motto.

"One of the biggest reasons I left Elkton Hills was because I was sur- rounded by phonies," said J. D. Salinger's Holden Caulfield, the greatest enemy of phonies of all. I felt like a grown-up Holden, surrounded by phonies, and it felt crummy, as he would say. In the very last month of the twentieth century, I changed jobs and went to work on the Internet, as an editor for CBSNews.com. The dot-com bubble burst a few months later. Terrific timing on my part.

Do We Hate Us?

PART OF MY new job meant regular travel between Washington, D.C., where I live, and New York City, where Satan lives. One Tuesday a few months after the Battle of Florida ended, I was headed to a 9:30 a.m. Delta shuttle at Reagan National Airport. The lawyers, investment bankers, lobbyists, and media types like me who are shuttle regulars lined up as usual about a half hour before the flight, barely looking up from our PalmPilots and *Wall Street Journals*. As the first passengers entered the ramp to the plane, the gate agents turned them around and said there was a delay at LaGuardia Airport in New York. Someone on a cell phone said they heard that a small plane had crashed into the World Trade Center. I called my newsroom and they confirmed that *something* had happened but didn't know much more. It was about 9:15 by then and the gate agent said all the New York airports were closed.

I ran to my car parked in the nearby short-term lot. It was past 9:30 when I pulled onto the George Washington Memorial Parkway along the Potomac River, listening to radio reports that the planes that hit the World Trade Center appeared to be commercial airliners. I tried to get the newsroom back on my cell phone. As I drove near the Pentagon from the southeast, I saw a mass of dark smoke rise up from behind the building.

After 9/11, the whole bullshit-detection business seemed trivial. A good deal of the news I had covered over the years and many of the stories I had worked so hard on now struck me as frivolous. The entire country felt like it had been naïve and immature. Americans were stunned and disoriented; the terrorism they watched stalking foreign lands on television had come to their own country, bringing real blood and real death. A few weeks after 9/11, *Newsweek* magazine set out to answer an essential question with a cover story headlined "Why They Hate Us."

"Everything has changed" was a common platitude at that time. But of course everything hadn't changed.

Certainly politics had not changed. A little more than a year later, the debate in the Senate over granting the president authority to invade Iraq smelled more of posturing than statesmanship. A year after the invasion of Iraq, polarization was again the Big Idea that pundits used when describing the country. Civic distemper was back, with the exaggeration and animosity common to fresh disenchantment. An unpopular war, a corporate crime wave, and an economy that was great for the rich and hard for the rest combined to put the country in a foul humor. Revelations about sexual abuse by Catholic priests spread disillusionment and cynicism; was there no corner of society left that we could look at with innocence and uncomplicated respect? The attention we lavished on *American Idol*, Lindsay Lohan, and Anna Nicole Smith proved we could be every bit as superficial as we were before some 2,700 Americans were murdered in a single day. But there was something new: a sense of civic embarrassment bordering on shame. The sort of phoniness discovered at the Tomb of the Unknowns was rampant and alienating, but it was a subset of something much bigger. Americans were down on themselves, and for good reason, it seemed. We needed a new cover story to explain this new condition. We needed to figure out why *we* hate us.

"National pride," the philosopher Richard Rorty wrote in *Achieving Our Country*, "is to countries what self-respect is to individuals: a necessary condition of self-improvement." Our lack of national pride—our lack of social self-respect—makes all society's problems harder to solve.

What We Hate

THE "HATE" WE need to understand is not the bomb-throwing kind of hate. It's not the diseased paranoia of Timothy McVeigh, the Weather Underground, or the Unabomber. It is a mood of social self-loathing. The country is suffering from low self-esteem and is acting out. Everybody doesn't hate everything. We don't hate one another in the flesh. Often we hate abstractly. But from little things to big, everyone hates something.

My friend Mo hated it when a young man at the table next to him at a coffee shop clipped his fingernails. He hated it more when the kid was oblivious to the dirty looks Mo sent his way. Mo was livid when he explained to the guy that sending shards of dead protein and cuticle around a place where people eat food is impolite and unappetizing and was met with a blank slacker stare that was the nonverbal equivalent of "Fuck you." Snip.

My brother didn't like it when an angry cow kicked him in the back and cracked several vertebrae. But he also didn't like it when he was watching CNN while recovering in a rural hospital in central Missouri and a nurse looked up at a news story about gay marriage and said it was a sign that Satan was sending America straight to hell. And I imagine the nurse hated that there were gay people on the news and that they wanted to get married. "Worlds collide," in the words of *Seinfeld*'s George Costanza.

My sister hated hearing the story of a man who didn't want his kid to go to camp with a bunch of other rich kids so he paid a "lifestyle management consultant" $15,000 to find an appropriately downscale summer camp that cost $5,000.

My colleague Danny hated it when a girl sitting next to him on the subway attached her false eyelashes and Q-tipped her waxy ears. My wife doesn't like seeing Bentleys on the road. She went on Google and discovered most Bentleys cost over $300,000.

My friend Jeff was grumpy when he had to call Verizon to report a problem and found himself talking to a computerized voice. But he got really angry when the voice, having determined that Jeff had an actual problem, said, "I am sorry to hear that." How could "you" be sorry to hear that? "You" are not a person but a machine. How absurd, how insulting, to be forced to pretend to be having a human interaction with a machine. What was Jeff supposed to say? "And I'm sorry that you are just a machine because you seem so sensitive"?

I don't like people who go to the Holocaust Memorial Museum wearing T-shirts that say "Eat Me." True story.

When you write an Internet column about things like this, as I do, and your e-mail address is at the bottom of every column, as mine is, you hear about what people hate loud and clear, over and over. I can report definitively that people hate columnists who hate things. They loathe snails who drive slowly in the left lane. They don't like people who talk full volume about the heartbreak of their psoriasis on cell phone headsets in restaurants and quiet bookstores. They don't like that more and more stores are chains, the same everywhere, mostly with lousy service from blasé employees, even if prices are lower and choice is more plentiful. They hate it when big multinational corporations have advertisements that say "We care about you," because corporations can't care, and besides, they don't really know you that well. They don't like it when they're talking with someone who starts thumbing their little digital personal device to answer an e-mail from someone five hundred miles away. They don't appreciate being bumped into at airports or on sidewalks by people with white earbuds crammed in their ears, oblivious to their human surroundings. They don't like oversold flights.

I don't care for Marilyn A. Mitchell. I haven't actually met her, but she's a "personal coach" who sent me literature promising "a refreshing way to look at making necessary changes in your life." I didn't even know I had to make changes. She told me to "Make changes that will nourish your desire, spark your enthusiasm, provide sensitivity to realize *your* true gifts." Actually, I hate her—sensitively, though. I'm pretty sure I don't have any true gifts.

These are little things in some respects. They're not global warming or genocide. But they don't feel little. They cramp up everyday life. Is this happening more than at other times in history? I have a thick file of polls that indeed say most people do think America is ruder, more vulgar, and more inconsiderate than it used to be. But people almost always think things used to be better and are getting worse. What is important is that these kinds of irritations are shared by virtually every person I have encountered in the past several years. The big song in *Avenue Q,* a popular Broadway musical, is called "It Sucks to Be Me." We can be whiny, too.

Culture Hate

ONE THING THAT is certainly unique to our times is that you don't have to leave the house physically to be in the outside world. "The media" vividly brings the world to you—at least a represented, mediated version of the world. We spend hours and hours a day with electronic media: television, the Internet, radio, music devices, phones, and gadgets. By 2006, Americans on average spent forty hours a week in front of television or computer screens. Most of how we experience what I call "public culture" is through media, which is ubiquitous and inescapable—unless you're a hermit or Amish. So public culture is omnipresent in a way it never has been. We worry so much about the quality of media culture that we overlook the sheer quantity. We are overexposed to a culture that is dangerous. In the early 1960s Newton Minow said television was a "vast wasteland." Now it's a vast minefield.

One part of that minefield many young people see every day is the AIM Today Welcome Screen, the computer page that pops open every time an AOL instant message user logs on. The screen always features four pop news items, and I collect the most inane ones ("The Biggest Party Girls: See Which Celebs Have a Degree in Party-ology," "Friends with Benefits: Have You Ruined Your Chance for a Relationship?"). But

I have one headline that isn't so inane: "TV's Most Hated: There is So Much Hate We Had to Make a Second List."

There certainly is. One night, I was clicking around and came to a show I'd never seen before called *Wicked, Wicked Games*. It's a prime-time soap opera targeted at young women and girls. Two bikini-clad hotties were talking poolside about how one of them could get a guy interested. The advice-giving friend suggested her pal ring the guy's doorbell completely naked under a trench coat. Hottie Number Two agreed that would prove she was "a nasty little slut." Okay, so how can you not hate having teenage girls watch that? By the way, there's a "S.L.U.T." line of cosmetics. And go into any high school or junior high in the country and you'll see girls dressed up as "nasty little sluts." Probably in clothes bought by their parents. We permit it, enable it, and hate it all at once. It spreads.

The world is filled with "nasty little slut" moments. The things that set us off don't necessarily have to involve sex, vulgarity, or violence; there's a big menu of creepy irritations. They're like cultural fingernail clippings flying into our latte. My friend Martha is observant and organized. She keeps a file she calls "Disgusting Examples." Newspapers, websites, magazines, and television provide a barrage of disgusting examples. I am perennially irritated with the Sunday *New York Times*. Supposedly it's the Magna Carta of liberal bias. What I see week after week polluting some of the best remaining journalism in the country is the worship of great wealth. Every Sunday they display and celebrate the weddings and parties of the megarich. The business section always profiles a mogul of some sort. The news section almost always features a trend story about the Hamptons, Martha's Vineyard, or Nantucket. The whole back of the magazine is filled with pictures of $1 million cottages and one-room apartments, $5 to $10 million apartments and suburban four-bedrooms, and $15 to $20 million estates and palaces. In the summer of 2007 there was a two-page ad for a $47.5 million apartment. This is real estate pornography. It's a subset of wealth porn.

Readers have sent me hundreds of disgusting examples. They don't like dumb beer ads aimed at dumb young men. They don't like driving by McMansions. They don't like cars that blast music so loud the bass jiggles their livers. They don't like strip malls and traffic jams in exurbs far away from cities. They don't like stupid, legalistic warnings on every possible consumer product. They don't like feeling like they have to make informed choices about seventy-five different kinds of toothpaste when all they want is some goddamn toothpaste. And they hate not being able to carry toothpaste on airplanes because of a bureaucratic, cover-your-ass, Potemkin village stunt to create the illusion of safety.

Readers hate reality television shows about has-been or out-of-control celebrities and semi-celebrities like Paula Abdul, Carmen Electra, Jessica Simpson, Tommy Lee, and Britney Spears. They kind of hate themselves for sometimes watching and liking these shows and other stuff they sort of hate. They don't like cable news shows where people yell at one another and pretend they are creating high journalism.

There are lots of famous people they don't like. They hate Barry Bonds because he's a cheater who broke Hank Aaron's home run record. They don't like Mark Foley, the former Florida congressman and cochair of the Congressional Missing and Exploited Children's Caucus who got caught sending raunchy e-mails to young male pages. He promptly announced that he had been abused by a priest as a child and was an alcoholic. Then he disappeared into rehab. They don't like the "abuse excuse." They don't like Lizzie Grubman, the New York publicity agent who backed her father's Mercedes SUV into a crowd of sixteen people at a swanky Hamptons nightclub after calling a bouncer "white trash" when he asked her to move her vehicle. She served a month in jail, cried in public, starred in her own MTV reality show called *PoweR Girls,* and resumed a fabulous high-profile PR career. (Yes, you, too, can pay top dollar for public relations advice from a woman who drove her truck into a crowd in a hissy fit.) They hate that there is always a Lizzie Grubman in the news and that most of them make money off their infamy.

Readers don't like another Grubman, Jack Grubman, who is reportedly related to Lizzie. His claim to infamy was that he improperly upgraded his investment bank's rating of a stock so that a mogul named Sandy Weill would help get Grubman's child into the "in" Manhattan preschool.

This is the kind of cultural contact that feels poisonous and that many parents want to keep their kids away from, whether they're fundamentalist Christians, urban lefties, rural nuts-and-berries types, Catholic dads, suburban soccer moms, African-American Baptists, corporate nomads, or single lesbian mothers. It is a paradox that our society creates so much cultural product that so many people consume so gluttonously but also dislike so ferociously. It's a cultural obesity syndrome.

Meta-Hate

SO FAR I'VE talked about typical complaints we have about everyday life and popular and commercial culture. In these arenas, you can control your exposure to some degree. You can turn off the television or throw it out the window. You can leave the cell phone at home or never go online unless you must for work. You can ignore any movie and any news story you want. But you can't pay your taxes to a different government. You can't control the health coverage your company gives you, if it gives you any. You can disengage from the non-media real world. You can ignore politics, as many do. That doesn't help your community, though, and so in the end it doesn't help you.

On this broad level, America has had a disheartening experience similar to the one I had with the Tomb of the Unknowns. Trust in the major institutions in America is at a historic low. In 2006, a Gallup Poll showed that less than 40 percent of the public had confidence in the medical system, public schools, organized labor, the press, the justice system, and big business. A CBS News poll taken in July 2007 revealed that just 19 percent thought the country was going in the right direction, the lowest percentage in the history of that poll.

A long-running Harris Poll shows that the way Americans view society's leaders parallels how they see institutions. Compare the percentages that expressed a "great deal of confidence" in the leaders of major institutions in 1966 and 2007.

CONFIDENCE IN LEADERS: 1966, 2007
HARRIS POLL

	1966	2007
Military	61 percent	46 percent
Universities, Colleges	61	37
Medicine	73	37
Supreme Court	50	27
Organized Religion	41	27
Executive Branch	41	22*
Major Companies	55	16
Organized Labor	22	15
The Press	29	12
Congress	42	10

* *In 2007, the question referred to the White House, not the executive branch.*

The public's trust in government is barely half of what it was throughout the 1940s (the starting point for reliable data) through the late 1960s. The plunge began with Vietnam and Watergate, and we're still waiting for the recovery. Low points came in 1974, 1980, 1994, and 2007. A Gallup Poll in August 2007 found Congress's approval rating was the lowest it had been since Gallup first separately tracked public opinion of Congress in 1974. Just 18 percent of Americans approved of the job Congress was doing, while 76 percent disapproved.

Politics has been the poster child for American phoniness. The consequences have been severe. Government cannot be ambitious or effective without a minimum level of public trust. The governments that delivered the New Deal, the Great Society, and the landmark civil rights legislation of the 1960s enjoyed that basic trust. Since it was lost in the 1970s, no Congress or administration has been able to put together comparable accomplishments. Nor has any other institution in society been able to fill that vacuum.

So Who Hates Whom?

I MET CHRIS Eads at a Mexican restaurant in Sterling, Virginia, about twenty miles outside of Washington, D.C. Sterling is in Loudoun County, the fastest-growing county in the nation. At thirty-seven, Eads is already the senior pastor at CrossCurrents Ministries, an evangelical church of about three hundred people, mostly in their late twenties or thirties, many just starting families. Eads has a goatee and preaches in jeans and a T-shirt. Sunday services are held at Eagle Ridge Middle School in a development called Broadlands, where town houses sell for around $400,000 and detached houses for closer to $700,000. CrossCurrents is what's called a "seeker targeter" ministry, serving people who are Christians but who haven't yet found that combination of church, community, worship style, and message that makes them feel at home.

Eads says his congregation is struggling with life in the suburbs. "They are filled with genuine anxiety," he said. "Like 'If I can't provide my children with all the external things—a home, a minivan, big yards'—it's all that stuff that genuinely deep down they believe they *have* to provide to be good parents. But that's what's so insidious, because they really are trying to be good parents. That's what causes the stress."

Eads grew up in the Washington suburbs, too. His father worked for the government. Eads's upbringing was secular but he was born again when he was fifteen. His father, his stepmother, and his sister are all close to him but not to his religion. "My family feels like 'you Christians' want to take over the country," Eads said. "Now, I'm unique in that I don't feel more and more threatened by the prevailing culture, but 80 or 90 percent of evangelical Christians do. They think the whole world is collapsing all around them. They think the prevailing culture is an enemy to be defeated."

I imagine that when Eads mentioned the "prevailing culture," readers who are not evangelical Christians assumed he was talking about things such as gay marriage, abortion, opposition to prayer in school, and government-funded stem-cell research—the dread pillars of "secular humanism." But he wasn't. He was talking about the materialism of suburban life, the emptiness of it, and, importantly, the messages his congregants get from the media—news, entertainment, and advertising. He was also talking about politics, the narrow-minded nastiness he sees there on all sides, including his. Yes, his congregants oppose gay marriage and the agenda of "you liberals," but they don't think that's really at the very heart of the prevailing culture, either. It's bigger than the hot-button issues. Members of Eads's family are just as appalled by the "nasty little slut" moments as Eads and his congregants are. They might use different vocabularies, but they also use common sense. In what "we" hate, ironically, there is common sense and common cause.

That common cause is nearly invisible to our society right now because so many groups, so many reds and blues, appear to be at one another's throats. On one level they are. Chris Eads's father, Larry, really does believe "you Christians" are trying to take over the country, and so do a lot of other people. The night before I first met Chris Eads, I happened to have drinks with a dedicated, idealistic government lawyer who was talking about "you Christians" taking over the Department of Justice under John Ashcroft and Alberto Gonzalez. She was angry that I wasn't outraged. Her outlook wasn't unusual. She believes extreme conservatives and politicized Christians have more cultural and political power than liberals, feminists, intellectuals, and people who focus on the perceived needs of minorities and the disadvantaged. She does believe "you Christians" and conservatives are an enemy threatening her moral sensibilities and what she holds dear. But she also knows that religious fundamentalism and political conservatism are just some of the threads in a prevailing culture that she and her social set are wary of: They also see the power and greed of Wall Street, the dishonesty of establishment politicians of all stripes, the vulgarity and violence of Hollywood, and the bias and incompetence of the news media as equally serious threats. But in politics, there are teams. It's easier to get personal and mean.

Similarly, people in Eads's congregation believe the prevailing culture is an "enemy to be defeated." Gay marriage and abortion are parts of the dominant, powerful majority culture they oppose, just like "you Christians" are for the liberals. But they are not the core. The core is, yes, the power and greed of Wall Street, the dishonesty of establishment politicians of all stripes, the vulgarity and violence of Hollywood, and the bias and incompetence of the news media. All the sides (and there are many more than two) demonize the others. The real culprit is that very real but impersonal prevailing culture. We attribute malice to the intentions of our perceived enemies—reds, blues, and now greens; traditionalists or progressives; urban or rural people; gays or straights. This is not polarization. It is not multiculturalism. It is Balkanization. Politicians and the press exploit it. Society is losing the tools to overcome it.

Larry Eads told me, "People just seem to talk past each other now. We're polarized but there are multiple dimensions to that. It's not just religion and politics, it's lots of things." Like his son, Larry Eads has strong beliefs combined with the ability to get out from under his own perspective. "We don't have the right vocabulary to talk to each other when we talk about extremes. The bottom line is we don't trust each other."

That really is the bottom line. Americans don't trust our institutions or one another. Without trust, without a shared vocabulary, without community, we feel endangered. The social environment is polluted. Americans really don't hate one another. But they do hate "us."

As parents, patients, consumers, and citizens, we are careful and suspicious. We perceive other Americans as belligerent in arguments, boorish in manners, vulgar and violent in entertainment, greedy in business, ostentatious in style, and phony in a big way. We've come to embody the caricature of the "ugly American" in our own American minds. The times cry out for Holden Caulfield in all his sophomoric splendor and snarkiness. But the fight against phoniness and alienation is not trivial and sophomoric anymore.

Who Are "We"? Are We "Us"?

WHEN I SAY "we hate us," I imagine many people rightfully think, "Speak for yourself, Buster." Well, I do and I admit it. I implicate myself in almost all of the catty things I say about people and culture in this book. I am part of the media. I have a BlackBerry and other vile yuppie toys. But for all my carping, I would like to think "we" share more than we give ourselves credit for; it's just that part of what we have in common is negative. It is like the saying "The enemy of my enemy is my friend." The prevailing culture is a common enemy. Obviously, everyone doesn't hate everything all the time. But everyone hates something sometimes. "We" share that, and that is what I mean by "we." And that prevailing culture is "us." We all contribute to it and consume it. We're all implicated.

But when "we" hate "us," it is not a hatred of American ideals. It is not unpatriotic.

Of course, there are many people so bad off in society they don't have the luxury of these kinds of worries. They can't afford to indulge in social self-loathing. And some people are still so marginalized by prejudice that a book like this may seem quaint or parochial. But ours is not just an upper- or middle-class malaise. Nor is it just a snotty habit of carping by culture snobs. There is no demographic subset, no socioeconomic cohort that gives high marks to the government, the media, corporations, and the prevailing culture.

Think about it this way: Everyone is part of a counterculture now. Society is a new and radically pluralistic bundle of real and virtual social pods battling a faceless, dominant prevailing culture that virtually no one takes credit for or defends. Even the people we think of as the most conservative—the bastion of what is supposed to be countered by a counterculture—are rebelling against the mainstream, according to sociologist Alan Wolfe:

> The popular idea that Americans are attracted to conservative Christianity because they are traditionalists at heart who want to return to the morality prominent in the United States before the 1960s runs into the complication that evangelical Protestantism is anything but traditional in its outlook on the world. If I had to invent a term that meant the exact opposite of "traditional," I would use the phrase that evangelicals apply to themselves: "born again." To be traditional is to be born into a world shaped by one's parents and grandparents and to feel an obligation to pass that world on unchanged to one's children and grandchildren.

In this regard, most Americans are born again in some way; no one feels "born into a world shaped by one's parents and grandparents" or obliged to "pass that world on unchanged." An evangelical is part of a counterculture just as much as a New Age woman in Big Sur struggling to find herself and her angel, or a middle-aged executive laid off from a company in Canton who wants to reinvent himself for the second act of his career, or a woman in Tulsa struggling to come out of the closet. Everyone in Chris Eads's family runs counter to the culture. So does my brother, a Jew who left the Chicago suburbs for a cattle ranch in the Ozarks. So does his nurse, who sees Satan in the news. So does Martha of the disgusting examples. So do I, though I have worked in the dreaded mainstream media.

Modern society forces all of us to figure out a way to be born again. There isn't much of an alternative. There is no longer much vibrant, living tradition and community to be born into, to inherit, or to bequeath.

So the lack of trust Americans have in our systems and institutions forces us to counter the culture. We're wary of it, wittingly or not. Rod Dreher is a columnist for *The Dallas Morning News* and the author of *Crunchy Cons: The New Conservative Counterculture and Its Return to Roots.* He also writes a blog, where he posted this:

> We need to in some tangible and consequential sense set ourselves apart from the mainstream, for the sake of raising our children. . . . It's my view that our culture is pretty messed up in some fundamental ways, and I know that my wife and I can't raise our children without community. We are learning how to creatively resist the consumerist values of mainstream culture. I am not confident that this can be done successfully, but I am utterly confident of my obligation to try, and to try as hard as I can.
>
> Broadly speaking, the best ways we've found to do it is to form communities of like-minded people—who are usually Christian, but I know quite a few Jews (and I've even recently met some Muslims) who I consider fellow travelers/fellow dissenters from our consumerist paradise. I've also found it important to turn off the television, and not only to protect them [children] from the usual pop-cult crap, but also to teach them to love good books, good art, good culture.

Dreher sounds more like a liberal than a religious conservative by the measure of today's labels. And liberals sound conservative or even Puritan when they rant against materialism or sexploitation in entertainment and advertising. Disillusionment is widespread and people protect themselves. Not everyone is as deliberate about it as Rod Dreher, obviously. Yes, there are plenty of people who mindlessly watch four hours of television a day, rarely read a book, buy more things than they can afford, and don't ever use the word "culture." But it doesn't follow that they are "pro-culture," happy in the mainstream, and full of trust and respect for their hometown, Washington, D.C., Hollywood, Madison Avenue, and Wall Street. Is *anyone* like that?

Why Do We Hate Us?

IN 1955, THE population of America was 165,931,202. In 2005, it was 296,410,404. The number of people in our country nearly doubled in just five decades. Those raw numbers reflect extraordinary changes in every imaginable dimension: demographic, social, religious, geographic, economic, cultural, and mundane. The sixties were Phase One. That brief period of time spawned an enduring shift in the ways society viewed mores and manners, relations between races and genders, rights and duties. Phase Two came at the end of the twentieth century. This was a technological revolution that dramatically altered the pace of daily life, wildly expanded everyday access to information and media, and transformed our business, errands, entertainment, gossip, health care, time wasting, sports, news, and socializing.

We are morally and existentially tired, disoriented, anchorless, and defensive. That is why we hate us.

For an allegedly soft and self-absorbed country, we have actually underestimated the effects of all this change on our ability to garner happiness, character, fellowship, and empathy—things that actually sustain human beings through the decades, "in sickness and in health, for better and for worse." We have argued ad nauseam and ad infinitum over whether the changes the sixties brought were good or evil. We are at the start of the same argument about the Information Revolution. There are teams and hardened positions in these debates, which just makes it harder to see that all sides are thin-skinned and undernourished by the social and cultural times.

"A society in rapid change inevitably produces confusions about appropriate modes of behavior, taste, and dress," Daniel Bell wrote in his 1976 classic, *The Cultural Contradictions of Capitalism.* "A socially mobile person has no ready guide for acquiring new knowledge on how to live 'better' than before." These are not words to be taken lightly. Only those with great hubris think they don't suffer without a "ready guide." But hubris was at the core of the sixties project of liberating free spirits from the shackles of convention and conformity. We have now discovered that for all too many grown Aquarians and their children, liberation degenerated into narcissism. What matters most is Me: the sacred, discovered, reinvented center of the universe—Me. It is selfism.

It didn't start that way. In 1968, Theodore Roszak coined the term "counterculture," calling it "the effort to discover new types of community, new family patterns, new sexual mores, new kinds of livelihood, new aesthetic forms, new personal identities on the far side of power politics, the bourgeois, and the Protestant work ethic." But getting rid of the old proved easier than creating the new. Hungry capitalism wrought as much or more social disruption as liberation movements. The culture didn't toss out just the destructive and oppressive customs. Useful social mores and ties suffered, too, especially when it came to that uptight bourgeois word "moral." Many "have tos" began disappearing: Men didn't have to hold the door for women. Companies didn't have to consider the welfare of workers on a par with stockholders. Couples didn't have to be in committed relationships to have sex or be married to have children. Children didn't have to care for elderly parents. There were a million "have tos" to argue about. But the cumulative effect was an erosion of socially shared ways of treating others respectfully, the ties that make community possible. A new selfism trumped everyday moral impulses. But without community, it didn't make selves any happier.

William Geohegan, who taught Introduction to the Study of Religion in my freshman year of college, talked memorably about history's "*weltanschauung* shifts"—great changes in "worldviews." It's tough to get through life without a good, solid worldview. But Americans pursuing the new creed of selfism have been shifting their *weltanschauungs* constantly since the sixties, picking and choosing among religions, therapies, ideologies, and lifestyles.

This is the essence of what Bell meant by being "socially mobile." Virtually everything about both Phase One and Phase Two has made Americans more mobile. Our mobility comes in several forms: in the obvious, geographic way, fewer and fewer people live near close relatives or have multigenerational relationships and lifelong friends, perhaps to a degree unparalleled in history; mobile in that, compared to most other societies at most other times, people can move around among classes, professions, social roles, and religions; mobile in the sense that this is a society that truly and deeply believes the "self" is something autonomous yet malleable that can be "found" or "reinvented" or "discovered"; mobile in ethnic and racial diversity, constantly changing demographics, and the sheer number of heritages and traditions that collide daily (we're not Norway); mobile in that our lives and activities are portable to a degree unimaginable a generation ago and we can take our phone calls, e-mails, file cabinets, and music library with us everywhere and anywhere; most important, society's "dos and don'ts" are dizzyingly mobile compared to the past. Our rules have become fluid, weak, and relativistic in parts of life as different as entertainment, etiquette, and ethics. All that motion creates friction, which rubs and burns and makes us cranky.

Perhaps the most underestimated societal change has been the waning of stable, natural, intergenerational communities of family and intimates who live nearby. Increasingly, Americans live without deeper forms of what we now casually call "support networks" that help and nourish us, both practically and emotionally. Worldviews or "ready guides" come primarily from community, teaching, and example, not from the Internet and journeys of self-discovery. Lacking that, we must forge our own identities and social roles, something that is quite new in human history. For most of us, this isn't an option or a choice, but a necessity. There aren't assigned seats in life anymore. This, of course, is the mark of freedom, but it can be a burden as well. It is difficult to find a traditional path in life that has depth, endurance, and authenticity. But it is difficult to create an untraditional one, too.

The prevailing culture—media culture, political culture, and all the culture we hate—replaces little of the good in what has been lost. Finding the good bits is difficult on one's own. At the funeral for a family friend who was a brilliant computer scientist and freethinker, the rabbi noted, "Peter was a person of incredible moral character and deep principle, all of which were based in his own reasoned view of the world. He simply did not need any religious tradition for a frame of reference—but he had enormous respect for wisdom, whatever its source." Few Americans are so well equipped to reject religious or secular tradition yet sustain moral character and appreciate wisdom.

Today's culture preys on those who are adrift. We experience the prevailing culture as a dangerously rough sea, and we have discarded the old "ready guides" over the past fifty years. Into those choppy waters comes an enemy ship, the Information Revolution. We become more lost, frazzled, and overloaded.

The simple equation is this: Social change plus technology revolution equals American brain goes boom.

These changes are not unambiguously good or bad, but they are intrinsically disorienting and difficult to navigate. On the collective, public level, the result is a prevailing culture that seems to have no effective standards or authority—one that we are not proud of and that we don't trust. We hate it.

Nostalgia?

LET ME ANTICIPATE one criticism: I am not arguing that because change, social and cultural, has harmful aspects, things were better in the olden days of June Cleaver and Andy Griffith. But I will offer a confession: I am nostalgic and melancholy by temperament. I will attempt to fight that geezerish impulse at every juncture, but be forewarned.

When a society changes substantially, there are trade-offs. But each transformation is amorphous and mysterious, not deliberate. Being free to leave your hometown, your family, your job, or your adopted town is a liberty few had centuries or even decades ago. It is a fundamental part of the American identity—the pioneer, the frontiersman, and the explorer. But pioneers do *leave behind* valuables: loved ones, community, a place, belonging, and tradition. Generations of immigrants and seekers discovered this. Being materially, culturally, and morally "self-made" is a great freedom people don't have in repressive, primitive, or closed societies. Few in the Western tradition would willingly choose to forgo such freedoms, as some Muslims do. But there are costs. We have underestimated our modern mobility. Replacing tradition, community, religion, and social cohesion is difficult. Freedom doesn't equal happiness.

America before World War II or before the sixties was no utopia, and the idea of re-creating it is silly. Yes, there were more rooted communities then, but they could be conformist and smothering, especially for many who were not conventional or privileged. Many people needed to escape. Much of America was blatantly discriminatory toward women, minorities, and gays. Communities can still be cruel and closed, but the sixties inspired a period of extraordinary progress. The point is to be honest about what has been lost and what has been gained. And just as it is important not to be nostalgic or even reactionary, it is essential to resist the impulse now popular in academia to always blame rotten oppressors and paint the past black.

The Agony of Abundance

A CRUCIAL BUT puzzling aspect of our distemper is that it comes at a time of extraordinary peace and prosperity by any historic measure. We are as safe, well fed, cleanly sheltered, long-lived, free, and healthy as any people who ever roamed the planet. We hate us at a time of abundance. It's as if our plenty has freed us to act out and behave poorly. We have the extra time and safety to invent all sorts of head problems. The question of why we hate us is perhaps just part of a bigger conundrum: Given our blessings, why aren't we happier?

Our material well-being, health, and safety aren't proportionate to our psychic or emotional well-being. As a *statistical whole,* the nation is less "happy" than it was a half century ago. This has been a topic of considerable research by social scientists over the past few years. Gregg Easterbrook synthesized much of it in his book *The Progress Paradox:*

If you sat down with a pencil and graph paper to chart the trends of American and European life since the end of World War II, you'd do a lot of drawing that was pointed up. Per-capita income, "real" income, longevity, home size, cars per driver, phone calls made annually, trips taken annually, highest degree earned, IQ scores, just about every objective indicator of social welfare has trended upward on a pretty much uninterrupted basis for two generations. Many subjective graphs would also show steady upward trends: personal freedom, women's freedom, reduction of bias against minority groups.

But your graphs would lose their skyward direction when the topics turn to the inner self. The trend line for happiness has been flat for fifty years. The trend line is negative for the number of people who consider themselves "very happy," that percentage gradually declining since the 1940s. And the trend line would cascade downward like water over a falls on the topic of avoiding depression.

Battling for survival settles many existential questions. Material comfort gives people the opportunity to be angst-ridden and self-absorbed. But there is more to the connection between abundance and unhappiness. Political scientist Robert E. Lane studied modern discontent from an empirical perspective in *The Loss of Happiness in Market Democracies*. He used a "malnutrition model" to explain the disconnect between material and emotional well-being:

My hypothesis is that there is a kind of famine of warm interpersonal relationships, of easy-to-reach neighbors, of encircling, inclusive memberships, and of solidary family life. There is much evidence that for people lacking in social support of this kind, unemployment has more serious effects, illnesses are more deadly, disappointment with one's children is harder to bear, bouts of depression last longer, and frustration and failed expectations of all kinds are more traumatic. Thus, the malnutrition model explains why the search for increases in objective hardships will fail, for the causes lie not in the rise of objective traumas but in the increased vulnerability of the public.

People without "social support" and "warm interpersonal relationships" are grumpy and inclined to hate the world.

Social scientists have now documented how Americans have lost what can best be called "belonging": belonging to a church, a neighborhood, a PTA, a choir, a softball team, or even to a family. A well-known account of this is Robert Putnam's book *Bowling Alone: The Collapse and Revival of American Community*. Putnam quantified just how much membership in groups like bowling leagues declined in the second half of the twentieth century. These kinds of memberships, the sense of belonging they create, are crucial sources of what Putnam calls "social capital." Like Lane, Putnam thinks Americans are starved.

We are susceptible to over-attaching and toxic attachments as ways of compensating. I've always thought part of the appeal of the television series *The Sopranos* was a perverted envy and admiration for Tony Soprano: a thug, but a guy who really belonged to something. In his case it was the New Jersey mob—"this thing of ours." He had pals who wouldn't just take a bullet for him, they'd shoot someone. He had a pretty solid, if mildly unconventional, family life. Face it: The man had a ton of social capital. And today we can be jealous of anyone who belongs, even a fat, violent mobster. If audiences can cling to the mob as an appealing community, imagine the allure of religious fundamentalism, virtual community, political partisanship, ethnic solidarity, or even fanatic sports fandom.

Defensive Living

PEOPLE TAKE SOCIAL attachment where they can find it. Frank Bascombe is a more typical New Jerseyean than Tony Soprano. He lives in a town called Sea-Clift on the Jersey Shore. He's a character in Richard Ford's 2006 novel, *The Lay of the Land*. Set in 2000, this is Ford's third novel about Bascombe. Facing prostate cancer and possibly a second divorce, Bascombe works with some success as a real estate agent, but not in the place that feels like his real hometown, Haddam. In all three novels, he makes hapless, misanthropic attempts to fit in and belong—to something, anything.

In *The Lay of the Land,* he volunteers with a group generically called Sponsors. "The idea of Sponsoring is that many people with problems need nothing more than a little sound advice from time to time. These are not problems you'd visit a shrink for, or take drugs to cure, or that require a program Blue Cross would co-pay, but just something you can't quite figure out by yourself, and that won't exactly go away, but that if you could just have a good common-sense conversation about, you'd feel a helluva lot better." Someone can just call up Sponsors and have a one-time conversation with someone they don't know. Someone like Frank Bascombe. "Anybody with a feet-on-the-ground idea of what makes sense in the world can offer advice like this. Yet it's surprising the number of people who have no friends they can ask sound advice from, and no capacity to trust themselves."

It is surprising, in other words, how many people don't belong and are unattached. Social scientists study this. They have found that Frank Bascombe was exactly right. In June 2006, the *American Sociological Review* published a rare piece of headline-making social science, a report that loneliness in America has grown dramatically in the past twenty years. Sociologists Miller McPherson, Lynn Smith-Lovin, and Matthew Brashears wrote "that the number of people saying there is no one with whom they discuss important matters nearly tripled" from 1985 to 2004.

The authors tried to describe empirically how socially connected Americans were by asking them questions like "Who are the *people* with whom you discussed matters important to you?" They did this through the General Social Survey, face-to-face social surveys that have been conducted almost every year since 1972. In 2004, the survey team precisely replicated questions about social networks (essentially the number of "confidants" a person has) that had not been asked since 1985. In 2004, 24.6 percent of those surveyed—one in four Americans—reported they didn't have any confidants at all, no one in their family and no one outside their family. On top of that, another 19.6 percent said they had just one confidant. So that meant 43 percent of Americans reported having either no confidants or just one. That number doubled since 1985.

More than half, 53.4 percent, didn't have any intimates outside of family. Back in 1985, 80 percent had at least one confidant who was not family. The bottom line: "We have gone from a quarter of the American population being isolated . . . to almost half of the population falling into that category."

It's not just bowling alone, it's living alone.

So I sat alone in a poorly lit room and wrote a short column about the study. Over the next week, there was a deluge of surprising e-mail. Roughly half the e-mails declared, in essence, "I'm lonely by choice and damn proud of it!" These were not heart-tugging missives from isolated nebbishes. These were assertive and clearly argued position papers about why avoiding other featherless bipeds was a smart move in dumb times.

"U.S. citizens are isolated because it is unhealthy to risk contact with one's fellow citizens," wrote Holly from Midland, Texas. "When bullies are free to act out their aggression and disdain for others—threatening behavior, in other words—road rage, cell phone calls at the top of their lungs, shoving in grocery stores are just a few examples—then others will act to limit their exposure to these people. Humans wish to survive. It is healthier to be lonely than to risk contact with a society without decency and without mores."

Isolation, for some, is evidently more tolerable than contact pollution. "I am one of the people in the 'no confidant' category that twenty years ago had a network of friends and confidants that I no longer have to rely upon," a woman named Sheri e-mailed. "Today I avoid as many people as possible. Why? I am tired. Tired of rude people. Tired of angry people. Tired of people who have no pride in their homes, their neighborhoods, their jobs. Tired of people who disregard how they affect others. Tired of people with no patience, no compassion, no understanding. Tired of people who have no tolerance at all."

"It is normal for the people to be isolated more during this phase we are in. People have become more politically polarized and less willing to have a discussion," said S.T. "Intelligent people don't really want to talk to people that can't reason. That's healthy."

Some lonely-and-proud-of-it correspondents said their decisions to isolate themselves stemmed from the political climate, especially the frustration of not being able to find polite common ground with people of different philosophic bents. "I am, according to Meyer, 'lonely,' but it comes from a conscious decision on my part," wrote Ron Vida, from the conservative side. "Political correctness is a direct cause of our current plight. We speak of blue and red states, but that is too over-generalizing. The colors change from house to house and sometimes within a house. . . . For me, it is safer to be a loner than to chance 'offending' some sensitive soul who will lash out against me with a lawsuit if I speak what I believe. We've all heard of 'defensive driving.' The current social environment is so potentially chaotic that we resort to 'defensive living.' "

I was reminded of Herman Melville's famous short story "Bartleby the Scrivener: A Story of Wall Street." In the unnatural caverns of Wall Street, an untouchable, affectless ghost of a man named Bartleby responds to every request, day after day, in the same way: "I would prefer not to." His detachment, his defensive living, was so total that he disappeared at the end of the story.

The people who wrote to me were obviously not typical. They were reaching out to me, a stranger. Still, despite American society's abundance and freedoms, there is much defensive living within a hostile culture.

Isolated or Lost?

AMERICANS INCREASINGLY LIVE among strangers. I've been running my own informal polling operation for a couple years as I've tried to figure out why we're so cranky. Every time I speak to college students, I ask the same question: How many of you grew up within easy driving distance of relatives who weren't parents or siblings? I don't think more than 10 percent of the students ever raised their hands. They usually think it's a weird question. After the follow-up questions, they get it.

Growing up, did you know any of your friends' grandparents or aunts and uncles? Well, not really. Were your parents involved in local civic activities like school boards, town councils, parade committees, or community groups? Some kids said their parents were involved in their schools (when they were still attending them), in their sports activities, and sometimes in their churches or synagogues. But that other stuff? No, not really. Did they know many people who worked in the stores where they shopped by name or by sight? Duh, of course not.

I asked the same question to groups that could have been the parents of the college kids I speak to. One was a group of technologists from the top of government, academia, and business. Out of about forty-five people, two hands went up. Only two people in the room lived within driving distance of any relatives except their children. The group was quite surprised. I'm not sure why. The room we met in was in a new hotel in a new mall in a newly developed, sprawling exurb that was a cornfield thirty years ago.

Lunch with Frank, Art, or Tommy

I LOST MY patience with this alienated, unattached world at lunch. My salvation came after lunch.

Several years ago I was waiting to get a sandwich at a place near work called Au Bon Pain. It's a chain, it's cheap enough, it's fine. I was in a bit of a hurry. I eat late and the place was empty. There was no one in line but I obediently stood in the proper place between the stanchions and waited to be told to approach the counter. Two sandwich makers were talking to each other behind the counter. They looked up, I stepped forward meekly, and they continued their conversation. Fine, I waited. And waited. They laughed, I presume at me. I gave the customary attention-seeking cough and laser stare. Eventually one of them asked what I wanted in a surly tone and with a put-out look. The other guy slowly made the sandwich. I went back to my office to eat. The sandwich had tomato on it. I asked for no tomato.

I vowed to never, ever buy lunch on a workday from a stranger again. It was a solemn vow that I break only under drastic circumstances. So now I get lunch from Frank, Art, or Tommy, guys I have come to be

friends with who run three different places. I like them. I think all three
are funny, and they usually laugh at my jokes, which is key. I don't see
them except for lunch, but that's fine. I enjoy spending money where I
know the proprietor and the people. And now I love getting lunch. It is
always a little social part of my day, and I feel like I work in a real neighborhood, which it really isn't. I love being a regular. I love purposefully
limiting my choices instead of expanding them. Most of all, I think that
I enjoy being loyal just for the sake of being loyal.

I consider lunch one of my greatest triumphs.

Creating Character

FINDING A GOOD lunch spot takes work. The places that are easy are
too much like that sparkling new hotel in the ritzy mall in the new ring
of exurbs around an old city. It should be good, but it isn't. The portions
are big, the linens crisp, and shops are conveniently next door. But
it's clean to the point of being sterile. It is barren. With all our riches
and freedoms, we have assembled what we thinly call "lifestyles"—
assemblages of recreation, work, consumer goods, freely chosen beliefs,
family arrangements, and a great deal of media. Our new arrangements
are not providing the nourishment we need, the warm relationships and
ready guides. The older, organic connective tissues of American life are
fraying, and the new, artificial ones are weak.

Against this current, the old American ideal of being self-made endures. Americans still earnestly believe they can go out and create an
identity, that they can be born again or reinvented. It's a job they tackle
with can-do spirit and ingenuity. Late in life, ensconced in a fresh New
Jersey setting, Frank Bascombe in *The Lay of the Land* is still at it. He
wants more than Sponsors. He is thrown for an existential loop when his
bout with prostate cancer leads him to wonder about exactly what in his
life is enduring and solid.

> Very little about me, I realized—except what I'd already
> done, said, eaten, etc.—seemed written in stone, and all of that
> means almost nothing about what I might do. I had my history,
> okay, but not really much of a regular character, at least not an

inner essence I or anyone could use as a predictor. And something, I felt, needed to be done about that. I needed to go out and find myself a recognizable and persuasive semblance of a character.

Go out and find yourself a character. Find yourself a place to eat lunch. It's not easy in the Land of the Fake.

Chapter Two

EARLY TWENTY-FIRST-CENTURY

IRRITANTS

IN 2006, the dictionary publisher Merriam-Webster awarded its "word of the year" honor to a new verbal concoction, "truthiness." It was a perfect choice. "Truthiness" was a fake word invented by a comedian, Stephen Colbert, portraying a fake right-wing talk show host named Stephen Colbert, on a fake news talk show, *The Colbert Report*. "Truthiness" was actually Colbert's "word of the day" on his very first show, a sign to me that he had nailed the zeitgeist. "Face it," Colbert said, "we are a divided nation. Not between Democrats and Republicans, or conservatives and liberals, or tops and bottoms. No. We are divided between those who think with their head and those who *know* with their heart. . . . That's where truth comes from—the gut."

Webster's has now sanctioned truthiness with two definitions (so we don't need to give it quotation marks anymore): "truth that comes from the gut, not books" and "the quality of preferring concepts or facts one wishes to be true, rather than concepts or facts known to be true." At the end of the truthiness routine, Colbert said, "I know some of you may not trust your gut yet. But, with my help, you will. The truthiness is, anyone can read the news to you. I promise to feel the news *at* you."

How We Hate Us

TRUTHINESS: THERE COULDN'T be a better word for the times. We get a whole lot of news and views "felt at us" these days, never mind the outright lies and deceptive spin from advertisers, marketers, public relations artists, and politicians. American culture is unimpressed by truth—absolute, perennial, or moral. That means all truth is relative, right? Right. This is why there is strong market demand for a word to replace truth, which has become obsolete. Truth is just another consumer good: Pick it. "You think global warming is a myth? That's cool, that's your truthiness." "You think the U.S. government secretly conspired to cause 9/11? Fine." The founder of one of the country's largest public relations agencies was quoted as saying, "In this era of exploding media technologies there is no truth except the truth you create for yourself." YouTruth .com. Truth 2.0.

In the words of George Costanza, "Jerry, just remember, it's not a lie if you believe it."

You can pick the facts and concepts you wish to be true. Go forth and blog! In a perversion of classic American ideals, picking what truth to believe in is now considered a basic right, the very thing individuals *ought* to do if they are making their own free and honest choices and creating their authentic identities. Objective truth is medieval.

There's one problem with truthiness: We hate it.

And it deserves to be hated.

Truthiness adds to our isolation, to living in our own bubbles or virtual communities. It's a barrier to communication. On the surface, the posture of accepting anyone's truthiness is kindly and tolerant. Below the surface, it is dismissive. That's because truthiness is solipsism. It can't be shared.

We're actually skilled at detecting truthiness in its several variations: lies, bullshit, and sincerely held falsehoods. That colors how we see the world—skeptically and defensively. A few weeks before truthiness was so augustly honored, a CBS News–*New York Times* poll showed trust in government was at the lowest level the poll had ever recorded. Mistrust is our default position.

So we're clued in to phoniness and spin. We are good at decoding.

We can deconstruct a campaign ploy, spot the marketing angle, parse the doublespeak, and unravel the subliminal suggestion. But it is an exhausting posture that treats the world as an enemy.

As facile as we've become at decoding the world, it remains difficult to decode ourselves. Perhaps the phonies we're having the most trouble spotting are the phonies within. It's hard to spot our own truthiness. And that makes sense; to be a modern grown-up, we have to make many basic life choices that were not options for our forbears: where to live, whether to marry, how many kids to have, whether and how to be religious, what career to pursue, and when to retire. Then there are the ever-so-urgent consumer decisions: blue jeans or black? Plasma or LCD? Apple or PC? Blond or brunette? It would be odd if our confidence were not occasionally rattled by all these decisions, if we weren't sometimes worried about choosing out of character, striking a false note, or, in short, being phony. Perhaps that is why we're so unforgiving about spotting inauthenticity in others. We fear our own choices are phony.

Mistrust makes it difficult, if not impossible, to find bullshit spotters and truth tellers that we rely on or respect for very long. Our critics, pundits, journalists, public intellectuals, and politicians are quickly dismissed as phonies. Many popular social critics are make-believe—not only Stephen Colbert, the fake right-wing pundit, but also Jon Stewart, the fake news anchor, and Borat, the fake reporter from Kazakhstan. Somehow in a world where we select the truths we like, it has become too easy to dismiss "straight" commentary and criticism. Maybe it's too threatening; maybe it isn't ironic and cynical enough to be credible. If it's not self-consciously fake, we don't believe it. Give me Velveeta, not the real stuff.

The Internet is a fabulous enabler of truthiness. Virtually anyone with the will and know-how can be an online publisher. Purported facts and factoids online look and smell like facts and figures in government reports, news broadcasts, or newspapers. The same is true of cable argutainment. However low your regard for what is now sneeringly referred to as "mainstream media," it generally does try to maintain some old-fashioned verification procedures. Web evangelists say "citizen journalists" and the wisdom of crowds will seek and destroy bad facts and falsehoods. Maybe. But this strikes me as just as naïve as the belief that financial markets are perfect and just.

Facts that come out of conventional journalism have a different dynamic online. Consider a simple story about a factory fire. Police first report two deaths at 10 a.m. At noon they announce two more deaths. At 5 p.m. the police say the final death count is six. The local news Web site has reported all this as it unfolded, so there are stories in cyberspace that report variously two, four, and six deaths. These separate stories can all turn up through Internet search engines like Google. Even though the early reports may have been properly qualified and hedged (with language like "initial police reports say . . ."), reports of two and four deaths are now factoids in cyberspace. Television and radio will have reported all the same information at the same time, but that information is ephemeral and not as easy to retrieve as online material. Jason DaPonte, an executive at the British Broadcasting Corporation, calls this "truth decay." On the Web, he says, truth has a "half-life."

Newstruth

IN 2006, IF you wished to believe that the war in Iraq was righteous, there were myriad blogs and sites that would deliver news and information from that angle. There was a parallel universe of information slanted and sifted from the other direction. Both purported to be objective and said that facts are facts. This gave people ammunition that helped rationalize simply seeing what they wanted to see—or didn't want to see. To a stunning degree now, different sides take totally different meanings from a single "fact" or report, and they do so with total and ferocious conviction.

For example, in 2006 I wrote a column in which I said it was hypocritical when President George Bush said flat-out in an interview, "We don't torture," when on that same day, the Pentagon announced it was discontinuing prior interrogation "techniques" and would follow international guidelines in the future. I wrote, "The president's statement here is beyond doublespeak and above spin. It's untrue, it's egregious. The Pentagon's backhanded, long-delayed, and uncourageous acknowledgment that torture was used also repudiated what the president has been telling citizens for years. We've been lied to and we are still being lied to. By the president."

I was instantly swamped with e-mail condemnations for not calling out Bush's lies earlier and more aggressively. I was an administration "pimp," "apologist," "lackey," "butt boy," "stooge," and other names not printable in a family-style polemic. Many e-mails used the exact same language. The technique of bombarding an enemy with e-mail is called flaming. I was on fire.

The next night on *The O'Reilly Factor*, Bill O'Reilly attacked from the opposite flank, calling my column "inflammatory." "And he is a bomb thrower," O'Reilly said. "We have fifteen left-wing quotes from this guy going back years." Fifteen left-wing quotes! Egad. Only one conclusion was possible: "Meyer would not appear on the *Factor* to explain. Thus, I can only conclude that he is an irresponsible partisan who should not be running any responsible news organization's website." It was my McCarthy-lite moment.

Two months later, after the Republicans lost control of the House and Senate in the midterm election, I wrote a tongue-in-cheek column that said it was my considered judgment that Newt Gingrich, Dick Armey, and their posse were a bunch of "weirdos." Blogs on the right condemned me for liberal bias; blogs on the left skewered me because I hadn't reported my psychological findings when the Republicans still controlled Congress. You get the idea. People assert their own truthiness, and they do it with a vengeance.

I actually am not a partisan and hold the two parties in equally low regard. I am not a liberal or a conservative, I do not lurk in any particular wing, and my views are inconsistent. In all my writing, I try to be unpartisan and avoid doctrinal argument. But I know that a large group of people will never believe me and will slot me into the pigeonhole of their choice. Thus are the times.

In everyday life, truthiness is a source of irritation. Truthiness in high places, however, is dangerous. President George Bush's most vehement detractors, the most rabid Bush-haters, accuse him and his administration of being insanely drunk with truthiness. Their smoking gun was a 2004 article by reporter Ron Suskind in *The New York Times Magazine*. Suskind described a meeting with a Bush aide in 2002:

> The aide said that guys like me were "in what we call the reality-based community," which he defined as people who "believe that solutions emerge from your judicious study of discernible reality." I nodded and murmured something about enlightenment principles and empiricism. He cut me off. "That's not the way the world really works anymore," he continued. "We're an empire now, and when we act, we create our own reality. And while you're studying that reality—judiciously, as you will—we'll act again, creating other new realities, which you can study too, and that's how things will sort out. We're history's actors . . . and you, all of you, will be left to just study what we do."

The phrase "reality-based community" has become a rallying cry for those who believe the administration's policies on science, public health, Iraq, and many other issues are based on fact-transcending truthiness. The motto of a blog called "The Reality-Based Community" is "Everyone is entitled to his own opinion, but not his own facts."

Selfism

SOCIOLOGICALLY, TRUTHINESS IS a first cousin of selfism, which is American individualism redefined by the age of marketing, self-help, moral relativism, and belief that the "self" is something that can be deliberately found or made. The ethos of selfism was most famously described by Tom Wolfe in the essay that stuck the label "the Me Decade" on the 1970s: "The old alchemical dream was changing base metals into gold. The new alchemical dream is: changing one's personality—remaking, remodeling, elevating, and polishing one's very self . . . and observing, studying, and doting on it. (Me!)"

The difference between the 1970s and early 2000s is that the Great Me Project is now even more mainstream (reinventing yourself is now a recognized corporate skill taught by human resources departments and personal coaches) and thus more commercialized and marketed (see the self-help aisle of your bookstore). Selfism is different than regular old narcissism and egomania because of this commercialized, mass-market aspect. It is different than the older, can-do, self-made-man American spirit because it substitutes feeling for doing.

Bullshit

AT THE SAME time "truthiness" was the word of the year, an unlikely bestselling book was a short, challenging work of philosophy called *On Truth*. It was written by Princeton University philosopher Harry Frankfurt, the author of the surprise bestseller of 2005, *On Bullshit*. "One of the most salient features of our culture is that there is so much bullshit," wrote Frankfurt. "Everyone knows this. Each of us contributes his share. But we tend to take the situation for granted."

Unlike regular lying, bullshitting entails an attempt to finesse the truth, to somehow stop short of perpetrating a black-and-white falsehood. As Professor Frankfurt noted, bullshitting is about "trying to get away with something." Bullshit often comes with a certain unspoken complicity on the part of the listener, the person being "bullshat." Generally you know when you're hearing bullshit, but it isn't worth the effort to protest it. Of course, when you're hearing bullshit on television, talking back is not very satisfying. The proliferation of media vastly expands the opportunities for bullshit; if you were limited to face-to-face interactions, bullshit would be infrequent; if you added just telephones and letters to the mix, it would be slightly more frequent; add modern media, and you can be bullshat 24/7—by strangers.

It is almost un-American to presume to tell an American anything new about bullshit or detecting it. We're all trained professionals here. We know what "downsizing" really means. We know the phrase "high-net-worth individual" means filthy rich. We know why products are still priced at $9.99 instead of $10.00, a trick some dumb cluck invented a hundred years ago and that dumb clucks everywhere still use. Nobody believes for a second that dog food, toilet paper, plastic wrap, and breakfast cereal are really "new and improved." Americans are connoisseurs of this stuff. We invented it. We know to beware of sentences that begin with the words "To be perfectly honest."

To be perfectly honest, politics is the gold standard of bullshit. One of my favorite books about American politics is *Roscoe,* part of William Kennedy's cycle of novels about Albany, New York. On V-J Day, Roscoe Conway, the brain behind Albany's Tammany Hall–like political machine, has news for his crony, Elisha.

> "I'm a fraud," Roscoe said. "I've always been a fraud."
> "Nonsense. Nobody ever believes anything you ever say about yourself."
> "Even when I'm lying?"
> "No, never."
> "What if I said I was quitting the party?"
> Elisha stared at him, inspecting for fraudulence.

If the politician wants to cleanse his soul of fraud—of bullshit—he must quit the party.

While political bullshit is ancient, there is more of it today simply because there is so much more campaigning and there is more media to carry the bullshit to the masses. Today, President Bill Clinton is considered a master bullshit artist even by his fans. In January 1998 he uttered one of the most famous lines of BS in American history: "I did not have sexual relations with that woman, Ms. Lewinsky." Somewhere in the tawdry recesses of his high-IQ brain, the president of the United States thought he wasn't technically lying, because by "sexual relations" *he* meant sexual intercourse and he didn't do that with that woman, Ms. Lewinsky. He just had oral sex. Abracadabra, no lie, just a little Arkansas bullshit. Furthermore, everyone knows it's bullshit, so what's it matter? Did anyone in the United States believe Bill Clinton that day? President Clinton topped himself a few months later with his classic locution before a federal grand jury, "It depends on what the meaning of 'is' is." A classic of the genre.

Bullshit doesn't occur just through the spoken word. Bush the Younger has proved that for the ages. The epitome of bullshit in his presidency was the phrase "Mission Accomplished," even though Bush never actually uttered those words. On May 1, 2003, the president put on a pilot's jumpsuit and landed on the USS *Lincoln* in a navy jet, something no sitting president had done, because it was thought to be too risky. He then gave a speech under the dramatic backdrop of an enormous banner declaring "Mission Accomplished." What the president actually said was, "Major combat operations in Iraq have ended. In the battle of Iraq, the United States and our allies have prevailed." That, of course, turned out not to be accurate either.

But the bullshit from that day that will be remembered was the event as a whole—the bravado, the stagecraft, and the cavalier proclamation of "Mission Accomplished" when the greatest bloodshed of the war was just beginning. There was already ample reason to think—to know—that there would be much more tragedy ahead in Iraq. There was no good faith; it was bullshit. And now we know, of course, that the administration's case for the war was less than honest, built with twisted and misleading evidence and blinkered analysis. Doubts about whether Iraq had weapons of mass destruction and direct ties to al-Qaeda were suppressed in order to market administration policy. There was an honest case to be made, one that treated voters as adults. But it contained uncertainties and gambles. That was jettisoned for a more marketable set of arguments. That was bullshit on a tragic scale.

Bullshit is not trivial. The deceptions and half-truths of Vietnam set trust in government on a downward tack that has never altered. The deceptions of the Iraq War have done irreparable harm to the possibility of restoring trust and legitimacy to government and public servants anytime soon. We need to consider whether ingesting so much mundane, nonlethal, commercial-grade bullshit weakens our capacity to spot and battle the more dangerous lies. What complicity do we have as citizens?

Categorizing the various forms of contemporary political bullshit would take a team of cyber-scriveners. Congress lives on the stuff. A simple example: Every summer when gas prices rise, politicians of both parties spout bullshit. They demand investigations of whether there has been a price-fixing conspiracy by Big Oil, even though this has been investigated repeatedly since the 1970s with no findings of guilt. They de-

mand the president "do something," even though there is nothing realistic that the president can do about gas prices. And, of course, they ignore the fact that Americans pay less for gas than almost any other
country in the world that isn't a giant oil producer. Americans happily
pay more for bottled water than gasoline.

Some political bullshit does still remain hidden from plain view. The
story of Sal Risalvato has always stuck with me. When I encountered
Risalvato while working on a story for *The CBS Evening News,* he owned a
Texaco station in New Jersey. A funny, well-spoken guy, Sal was just the
kind of "real person" a politician would want at his side at a press conference or a hearing. At the 1996 Republican National Convention, the
governor of Connecticut (John Rowland, who has since done ten
months in federal prison), introduced Risalvato to the crowd and cameras as "a real, live small business owner." It turned out that Sal Risalvato
was a serial "real person," practically a professional. If there were a central casting agency for politics, Sal would be in the Rolodex, filed under
"GOP, small business, any angle, salt of the earth, can do testimony Q&A
and improv." Sal had already testified before Congress about twenty
times, by his count, on "small business" issues ranging from health insurance to environmental regulations to safety. He had even starred in a
radio ad. Press conferences were small potatoes.

Now, Sal did own a gas station. He said he was never paid for any of
his political appearances. And I have no doubt he expressed his genuine
political views. He was an honest person, I suppose. But he was used in
a dishonest way. He was falsely portrayed as a random Joe who happened
to be having special trouble with some dumb government program.
What wasn't mentioned was that he had testified or spoken out about almost every possible dumb program. He was an experienced, sophisticated, trained, and polished "real person." Sal saw his future not in retail
gas, but in politics. That is all fine and good for Sal. But posing Sal as a
"real person" is spin and show business.

The press uses "real people" just as manipulatively. Cries of "I need
a real person" are ubiquitous in newsrooms. A reporter assigned to do a
daily story on Medicare will be told by his editor to find a "real person."
Depending on the angle, the reporter will call the AARP, the pharma-

ceutical industry trade association, a labor union, or the local chamber of commerce, and the public relations people will produce a "real person" on deadline. Some of those real people are fake real people like Sal. Some journalists retain an odd belief that a twelve-second sound bite or a nineteen-word quote from a "real person" will make a news story more credible and gripping. But unless the individual's story is told in some nuanced detail, the technique is superficial and perhaps misleading, another form of getting away with something.

So beware of real people. Stick with the fake ones; they're more honest.

Bullspotting

ONE OF THE anomalies about political bullshit is that society is hyperconscious of it, yet it flourishes. Like the newest super-bug bacteria, it's immune to anti-bullshit medication. *The Onion* is a humor outfit that doses out some of the best political antibiotics on the market. Early in the 2008 primary process, they did a mock newscast about the state of political bullshit:

> *Anchor: As the 2008 presidential race heats up, a new survey finds that again this year the number one issue among voters is bullshit. And joining us now to discuss the survey is the director of political polling at the Shuttleworth Research Center, Kip O'Leary. Mr. O'Leary, now we all know that bullshit is the deciding factor in most elections and this poll says that this election will be no different.*
>
> *O'Leary: That's right. When it comes down to electing the leader of the free world voters look to issues like a candidate's relationship with their ex-wife, did they ever smoke, where do they vacation, what's their exercise regimen. These are the kind of core bullshit issues that people really care about.*
>
> *Anchor: Now in the past, whether the candidates are photogenic has been of key importance to voters who care about bullshit. Is that still the case today?*
>
> *O'Leary: Oh, yes. And also what a candidate wears at public appearances is very crucial to the bullshit-conscious voter.*

You get the idea. Calling out bullshit is a growth industry. The job is interminable, like the task of Sisyphus, the mythical Greek king who was condemned in the afterlife to push a huge boulder up an impossibly steep hill. Every time it rolled back down, he started again, eternally. The press is supposed to expose bullshit in politics and government; blogs and press critics hunt for bullshit in the media; blogs call out one another, and press critics expose bullshit in blogs; comedians search for it everywhere. In the end, the boulder rolls down. Revealing the fake is never deeply satisfying in the way creating or discovering something genuine or honest is. But often, it is the best we can do.

Alan Sokal, a professor of physics at New York University, perpetrated a classic exposé a few years back. He wrote an article titled "Transgressing the Boundaries: Toward a Transformative Hermeneutics of Quantum Gravity" and sent it to a leading academic journal of cultural criticism, *Social Text* (postmodern, structuralist, that kind of thing). Sokal's central claim: "In quantum gravity, as we shall see, the space-time manifold ceases to exist as an objective physical reality; geometry becomes relational and contextual; and the foundational conceptual categories of prior science—among them, existence itself—become problematized and relativized. This conceptual revolution, I will argue, has profound implications for the content of a future postmodern and liberatory science." The article was, of course, a parody. It was mischievous gibberish. But the editors of *Social Text* remarkably thought it was a serious academic paper and published it. Apparently they were so duped by their own bullshit, they didn't recognize Sokal's. Controversy ensued.

In his paper exposing and explaining the hoax, Sokal quoted *Science and Relativism* by Larry Laudan, a philosopher of science: "The displacement of the idea that facts and evidence matter by the idea that everything boils down to subjective interests and perspectives is—second only to American political campaigns—the most prominent and pernicious manifestation of anti-intellectualism in our time." I think that pulls together quite nicely the bonds of bullshit, selfism, and truthiness, and the special place of politics in the culture of bullshit.

Belligerence

WHEN DISTINCT TRUTHINESSES collide or when two bullshit artists meet, pointless arguments generally follow. (The '85 Bears were the best football team ever; no, the '72 Dolphins were. Soccer is better than football. We must protect the sanctity of marriage; civil marriage is a civil right.) There are two basic attitudes toward passionate worldview collisions. One is a hard-fought truce, "Let's agree to disagree." The other is "You just don't get it," "You're biased," or, commonly, "Shut up and die" or "Fuck you." We know which temperament is more prevalent lately. Belligerence flows from bullshit.

Obviously, truthiness and selfism are just some of the sources of heightened social crankiness. The classic symptom of contemporary belligerence is probably road rage, which has precious little to do with social and epistemological theory and everything to do with the growth of commuting times and the general congestion of our space *and* time. Unconsciously, many go through the mundane chores of life with a looming fear of blowups in the style of road rage. How many people would now confront a mother or father with an out-of-control kid in a grocery store? Not many, because we're scared that the parent will go postal. Understandably so. My children live in mortal fear that one day in a restaurant I'll ask some slob to take off his hat or stop yelling into her cell phone. We face floating aggression constantly in the real world and the mediated world; it is distinct from truthiness-based animosity, but not unrelated. This is stressful and we hate it.

Linguist Deborah Tannen nailed this escalated aggression in her popular 1998 book, *The Argument Culture: Stopping America's War of Words*. She wrote, "Our spirits are corroded by living in an atmosphere of unrelenting contention—an argument culture." She detected "a spirit of demonography" in the climate, both public and private. The "argument culture" is displayed, celebrated, and exploited in public arenas of all sorts, far more now than when her book came out and not just in news and politics. There are more loud talk-radio and cable television news shout-shows—much more, much louder. We have a strange new genre of entertainment—reality television—that Tannen didn't have to contend with; part of the allure of reality TV is the voyeuristic thrill of watching real people fight and melt down—and the performers deliver. (Of course, it is all bullshit because the situations are staged and the "real people," like Sal Risalvato, are playacting or they are already celebrities.) Game shows goad contestants into catfights. We enjoy watching the naked aggression of exhibitionists. We find it entertaining, even soothing.

This enters our daily lives in new ways. On the Internet, belligerence can be anonymous, faceless, and hence risk-free. In schools and offices, for example, the Web is a problem, because parents and workers say nasty things in e-mail that they would never say in person. Chat rooms, blogs, and online comments are clogged with vitriol and hate-mongering. Even the genteel world of academia is apparently infected. "Philosophy is now more adversarial and argumentative than it used to be, but I do not think that it is pursued at a higher intellectual level," said philosopher Richard Rorty. Tannen made a similar point. "The standard way of writing an academic paper is to position your work in opposition to someone else's, which you prove wrong," she wrote. "This creates a need to make others wrong." Indeed, the idea to write *The Argument Culture* came to Tannen because of the distorting and hostile attacks her academic colleagues made on a prior book after it became a bestseller.

The need to make others wrong has turned into an addiction. The argument culture has ceded to a belligerent culture. The word "argue" stems from *arguere,* the Latin word meaning "make clear, prove, assert, accuse." "Belligerent" comes from the Latin word *belligerare,* to wage war. Our vocabulary for public life has become warlike. We're in the midst of a culture "war." Politicians promise to "fight" for Medicare. They campaign using "attack" ads. They "seize the offensive." Harsh words are "grenades" or "rockets." Surprises are "bombs." Advertising campaigns are "blitzes."

Publicly sanctioned belligerence has a profound impact on private life. We imitate it. It fills a vacuum. Tannen said the argument culture was closely "related to the breakdown of a sense of community."

"Our lives are populated more and more by strangers, less and less by people we know," she wrote. "This surely plays a role in the increasing level of aggression and hostility we experience, just as advances in technology enable new ways to express that hostility." The strangers in our lives are not just people we see in the flesh every day, but people we watch on TV or pay attention to through other media. Indeed, we probably spend more time with virtual or media strangers than with real-life strangers. Human beings are essentially wary of strangers. Many people and groups feel like spotted owls, endangered by the environment as well as by predators. Belligerence is a natural response.

Again, politics is the poster child for belligerence. Political belligerence (like bullshit) is more pervasive than it used to be simply because there are so many more media outlets to convey it. The floor proceedings of the House and Senate were not always televised live. There hasn't always been live cable television news twenty-four hours a day, seven days a week. What stands out in these gargantuan currents of events is conflict. Consensus has no drama. Public figures, be they politicians or pundits, have great incentives to be belligerent.

As a result, citizens become more belligerent and more partisan, too, giving politicians further incentives to raise the volume. Rhetorical belligerence "motivates the base." It's a vicious circle. In the Bush-Clinton-Bush era, voters who said they "care a lot" about politics were more partisan and ideological than the populace as a whole. That seems obvious, because it comports so directly with our personal experience; most people who want to talk politics have unmovable positions, which makes arguing with them no fun. But this isn't inevitable or constant in history. The percentage of people who label themselves independent or moderate in polls varies over time. These voters are just as smart and well-informed as partisans.

What may be happening now is not so much a change in the overall mix of partisans and independents, but a change in intensity at the extremes. Extreme partisans are becoming more extreme. They are also more angry—or belligerent—toward their ideological opposites. One proponent of this view is Arthur Brooks, a professor of political administration at Syracuse University's business school. Brooks examined the ongoing General Social Survey and found that from 1972 to 2004, the percentage of *self-described* "extreme liberals" and "extreme conservatives" has increased 35 percent, a substantial lift. Now, only a small slice of the public ever voluntarily describes themselves as "extremely" anything. People think they are reasonable and balanced. And remember, in 1972 the country was wildly overheated over Nixon and Vietnam. So while the absolute percentages are small (6.6 percent in 2004 said they were extremely liberal or extremely conservative), this increase in extremism is significant and applies to a couple million voters, enough to swing elections. The increase was greater among liberals, by the way.

Brooks also found a higher level of what he calls "personal demonization" (the same word Tannen used) in 2004. This time he used another prestigious, long-running survey, the American National Election Survey, which gauges public opinion data using "feeling thermometers"; for example, on a scale of 0 to 100, zero being the subhuman low, how do you feel about members of Congress? Scores below 20 are very rare. Brooks told me, "No one gets zeroes, not even Hitler." But in 2004, lots of people gave out zeroes. They were—surprise, surprise—self-described liberals and conservatives, and they gave zeroes out to their ideological opposites.

Twenty percent of self-described extreme liberals gave "conservatives" zeroes, while 23 percent of extreme conservatives returned the favor. So about one-fifth of the people at the far ends of the ideological spectrum consider those they disagree with "dead to me," as Tony Soprano would put it.

This is the vanguard of the politically belligerent culture. You could also call it an insult culture. This is the target demographic for writers like Ann Coulter (*Treason: Liberal Treachery from the Cold War to the War on Terrorism; Slander: Liberal Lies About the American Right*), Bernard Goldberg (*100 People Who Are Screwing Up America (And Al Franken is Number 37)*; *Crazies to the Left of Me, Wimps to the Right: How One Side Lost Its Mind and the Other Lost Its Nerve*), and Al Franken (*Lies and the Lying Liars Who Tell Them: A Fair and Balanced Look at the Right; Rush Limbaugh Is a Big Fat Idiot*).

Anyone who has had a political conversation stopped dead in its tracks by a phrase like "you're biased" or "you just don't get it" knows that further discussion is futile. The wall of attempted reason has been hit, and there is nothing ahead except emotionally charged assertion and rationalization. Most people walk away after a good-faith effort. Those more deeply attached to the certainty of their opinions continue to wage war. Mercenaries do it for money—online, on television, and in print.

Fortunately or not, the Internet has built a marketable public forum for every would-be warrior of ideas. On sites like YouTube and MySpace, belligerence metastasizes. Anyone can create a micro–media empire. Or is that looking at it backward? Is media getting more democratized? Perhaps, but in a narcissistic way. "Everyone was simultaneously broadcasting themselves, but nobody was listening," wrote Andrew Keen in *The Cult of the Amateur: How Today's Internet Is Killing Our Culture.* Keen calls the intellectual style of Web 2.0 "infinite filibustering." This is what hardcore selfists do.

Balkanization

EXAGGERATED ATTACHMENTS TO a point of view or single issue foster a kind of cultural Balkanization. "The more people feel themselves adrift in a vast, impersonal, anonymous sea," wrote Arthur Schlesinger, Jr., in *The Disuniting of America: Reflections on a Multicultural Society,* "the more desperately they swim toward any familiar, intelligible, protective life-raft: the more they crave a politics of identity." Schlesinger is talking about multiculturalism and identity politics, the notion that we ought to reject the melting-pot ideal of America and embrace ethnic, racial, and sexual separateness or "otherness." The emphasis in identity politics is on what comes before "American": African-American, Native American, gay American, Asian-American. It is an ideology most popular in academia and on the left but pervasive throughout public education today. It is, I think, an outlook that is perpetually at risk of veering from tolerant to chauvinist, pluralist to fragmenting. It can nourish group identity and solidarity as well as perpetual aggrievement and resentment.

Today, the protective life rafts Schlesinger wrote about are not anchored only by race and ethnicity, but by ideology and interest as well. Angrier and more resentful than multiculturalism, this division is more a kind of ideological or cultural Balkanization. The Internet provides an apt metaphor.

As geographic communities have become scarcer, as Americans have become more "adrift in a vast, impersonal, anonymous sea," new forms of social networks emerged on the Internet. Virtual communities are people connected not by physical proximity but by common interests. Orbit cyberspace and you'll find a glut of blogs, social networking sites, and chat rooms. There's a cyber-place for everyone: plastic toy soldier collectors, Linux software developers, NFL draft aficionados, Catholic mothers, accordion players, Barbie doll sculptors, walleye fishermen, Wittgenstein scholars, pie bakers, hedge fund traders, orchid growers, ferret owners, skin-care fanatics, Druids, mah-jongg players, taxidermists, and dried fruit specialists. There is a community for boosters of every team, fans of every band, and practitioners of every sexual variation. Of course, some people are simply hooked on staying in touch by gadget, no matter who might be on the other end.

It won't be clear for a long time whether e-communications and virtual community can create social capital as well as physical, geographic community can. I'm a skeptic. Regardless, the Balkanization of the Web is a metaphor for society. Americans, compensating for the loss of family and neighborhood bonding, are growing more likely to over-identify emotionally with almost random objects of desire and interest: sports teams, rock bands, political factions, religion, ethnic history, or designer labels. Grasping for belonging, they are more inclined to label or brand themselves so their identifications are apparent to the outside world.

One can argue that it is a wonderful thing that the Internet has made it so easy for like-minded people in faraway places to find one another more easily. It is, in part. The danger, and the source of mass obnoxiousness, comes when people become overly attached to their interest—when it becomes a crucial source of their identity. At their worst, virtual communities can be like pods of people who share the same truthiness, are hooked on constant reaffirmation, and can't process conflicting input. People can develop attachments to interests or groups that are toxic, sort of like nonviolent cyber-gangs. Or they can just become insufferable boors.

When I arrived at college I had not spent much time with city kids. Figuring they were fast and sophisticated, I was a bit scared of them. I'll never forget meeting one guy from the Upper West Side of Manhattan who would eventually become a good friend. This guy was truly fast and sophisticated. "I'm a saxophonist," he told me. I was blown away. He didn't just *play* the saxophone, he *was* a saxophonist. I didn't know anyone who *was* an anything. I knew guys who played tennis and baseball well. Some of the girls in my high school played basketball well enough to play in college. My brother was good at skeet shooting for a while. But I had never met a kid who had the gumption to stake an identity claim so confidently early in life. I was impressed on some level, but mostly I thought he was an ass for a long time. (He did not become a professional saxophonist, by the way.)

In grown-up life, most over-identifiers are irritating. As we've become more mobile and less connected, over-identifiers have grown more common. There are fewer people who play the saxophone and more saxophonists. There are fewer Methodists and more born-again Christians. Among American Jews, Christians, and even Muslims, the more separatist and extreme strands are growing. As communal bonds weaken, tribal impulses grow stronger.

People seem to have an increased need to display badges of their own personal "Balkan states" to the world. That is part of what is going on with the whole branding concept in fashion and marketing. You don't just want a polo shirt; you want a Lacoste, Ralph Lauren, Lilly Pulitzer, Patagonia, Brooks Brothers, or Tommy Hilfiger. This is obviously more about social signaling than clothes that fit and last through many launderings. What are people trying to signal? Worth? Style? Cool? Group identity? Individuality?

Tattoos are peculiarly popular. Preppy is a self-conscious look. Some openly gay people dress in ways that announce their sexual identity. Urban African-American culture has a cultivated "ghetto" look, and it's frequently imitated by white suburban kids. Celebrities have "bling." Wealthy people adorn themselves with recognizable designer-brand hyper-luxuries to announce their privileged status in ways that would have been considered unspeakably gauche twenty years ago. They do this in everyday life, not just on special occasions. In business settings, back-to-school nights at schools in affluent zip codes, and in malls, it is typical to see men and women getting into $75,000-and-up cars, swaddled in $75,000 worth of diamonds, with a $5,000 purse, a $12,000 bespoke suit, a $50,000 Patek Philippe watch, and other forms of upmarket bling. (This is more than Balkanization; it's a form a belligerence-by-wealth.)

Geopolitical Balkanization is universally considered dangerous and unstable. So is de facto racial and ethnic Balkanization in modern cities and racial clustering in suburbs and exurbs. The Balkanization typified by the virtual communities of the Internet, on the other hand, can be socially redemptive. But there's a substantial difference between a user group for cancer patients or parents of disabled children and one for white supremacists or pedophiles. In this respect, the Web is perhaps value-neutral, as social scientists say. It will take a long time to discern whether the social connections fostered by new media are also value-neutral.

The Balkanization of politics offers a cautionary tale. People now use the phrase "my politics"—like my wardrobe, my library, or my music collection. This extreme sorting has been enabled by the proliferation of news sources and news commentary. The political consumer today can get, 24/7, news and opinion distilled into any ideological flavor. That hardens social arteries and feeds belligerence. Here's a typical example. In 2006, Deborah Howell, the ombudsman at *The Washington Post,* had a minor factual error in a story about a notoriously corrupt Republican lobbyist, Jack Abramoff. This is the correction the *Post* ran: "In a Jan. 22 article, Deborah Howell wrote that lobbyist Jack Abramoff made substantial campaign contributions to both parties. He did not. Abramoff directed his Indian tribal clients to give campaign contributions to members of Congress from both parties, but donated personal funds only to Republicans." Not a big deal, right?

Wrong! Howell was viciously flamed by highly organized left-wing bloggers and activists. WashingtonPost.com received so many obscene and threatening comments that they had to shut down the comment function on the entire website. Howell's in-box was flooded with hate mail and vile insults even after the correction ran. Liberal blogs were filled with what can only be described as hate speech. Now, these folks are part of what is considered a virtual community. That community was utterly unapologetic about its methods and took full credit for the *Post*'s simple correction, despite the fact that the *Post* would have made the correction anyway in response to a couple civil letters or calls.

Technology can be used to expand the horizon or collapse the field of vision. The Internet can explore and it can provide blinders. The narrowcasting of information by ideology or affinity can create groupthink loops. Virtual crowds form quickly and mimic real crowd behavior. They can be brilliant and well informed, or vicious and ignorant. But it simply wasn't possible before the Internet for groups of people scattered across the world to communicate and coordinate instantly. This has the potential, as they say, for good or evil. That tension shouldn't be papered over.

Boorishness

IN 1973, A high school freshman named Clint O'Connor, who just happened to be my best friend, was summarily kicked out of Mr. Howard Cohrt's Classical Cultures class for uttering the verboten word "sucks." O'Connor got over it, eventually, and is now a distinguished movie critic with a lovely vocabulary and three fine sons. But can you imagine what kind of word it would take to get kicked out of 99 percent of high school classes in America today? My kids aren't allowed to use "suck" around me. Other parents and kids think I'm a freak.

"Suck" was perhaps the gentlest word aimed at Deborah Howell during her flaming. Boys call girls "hos" in junior high classrooms and aren't punished. That's because the word is used constantly in song lyrics and on television. This is one of the least attractive ways society is using its newfound freedom from social conventions and uptightness—to be rude.

Manners, linguistic sensitivity, and respect for dignity and decorum in public space are less obvious casualties of truthiness. Though not the main cause, truthiness has contributed mightily to the erosion of common decency, a corny old concept that needs resuscitation. In his presidential campaign, Barack Obama called it "the coarsening of our culture." Society has lost the self-confidence it takes to insist on good manners and respectful behavior. The rise of boorishness and the demise of respectful social habits are critical sources of twenty-first-century irritation.

You could say that boorishness is in the eye of the beholder, but once you do, you've entered the dreaded land of truthiness. The philosophic problem is that there is no way to make a case for objective standards for either boorishness or common decency, at least no practical way in modern America. Example: I laughed when I saw a guy wearing a T-shirt that said "Beam me up, Scotty, this planet sucks." I wasn't offended, even though I side with Howard Cohrt on the "suck" issue. But I wanted to punch a meathead I saw wearing a T-shirt that said "Virgins are inexperienced sluts." (As a father of a daughter, I suppose I am particularly quick to pick up on misogyny.) In trying to adjudicate what is rude and boorish and what isn't you can just go with Supreme Court justice Potter Stewart's guidance on pornography: "You know it when you see it."

So what's a father to do? Boorishness is everywhere. It is the essence of beer ads that target young men. It is at the heart of "gross-out" movies like *American Pie*. It is the behavior that producers of reality television want their "real people" to exhibit to please voyeuristic audiences. Belligerence plus boorishness is a recipe for great Nielsens. Boorishness and vulgarity are sanctified by public culture and thus omnipresent. Donald Trump flaunts his greed, Howard Stern his misogyny, and starlets their fake boobs.

Most of the time we try to tune out boorishness. But the resentment, the offense, and the anger stew. This makes public life subtly more malignant. You silently note a tattoo of "Fuck You" on a man's pumped-up bicep. You listen to the unembarassable woman at the next table at a restaurant blather into her cell phone the details of her last gynecological checkup. You go to live theater among men in gym shorts, T-shirts, and baseball caps. At night, you hear people drive by with bass blasting so loudly that your liver jiggles. If you complain about this stuff out loud (or in print), you're a snob. Or a nut. Or a Behavior Nazi.

A beach my family loves is accessible only by walking down a very fragile, beautiful sand dune. Since it's a popular beach, a stable path has been cut into the steep dune and there are signs everywhere asking people to use the path and not to walk on the dune, which will cause it to erode swiftly. One day, I scolded a beefy man in his twenties for walking straight down the dune far off the path. My tone was not saintly, but not aggressive either. He went nuts on me. I responded poorly and came as close to getting into a fight as I ever had as an adult. Should I have not said anything? Should I have confronted him only if I was certain I could do so in a gentle and controlled way? (Yes.) Should I have clobbered him? (No comment.)

The social superego has been silenced or at least muted. Brothers have no keepers. Respectful, polite behavior can't be enforced by external, deliberate action, by vigilant etiquette and spontaneous censorship. It comes from shared boundaries and conventions, and they are disappearing. I suppose I am essentially advocating social inhibition, an idea that has become unacceptable in America. Honesty and "letting it all hang out" are the higher virtues. It is more important to be true to yourself and spontaneous than mannered and considerate. In group living, this is social cannibalism.

The Thinness of Our Skin

NOT ALL OF our irritation is related to either truthiness or my quirky metatheory of why we hate us. Some of it, as Robert Pirsig wrote in *Zen and the Art of Motorcycle Maintenance: An Inquiry into Values* back in 1974, is just "this hyped-up, fuck-you, super modern, ego style of life that thinks it owns the country." Our busy lives are overcrowded and stressful, despite the relative historic ease of contemporary life. The need for two incomes to meet expenses, the difficulties of single parents (and the dramatic rise in that population), the difficulty of obtaining health insurance, the challenges of saving for college and retirement, the increased expectations for parental involvement in children's schooling and extracurricular activities, longer commutes, and the increased cost of housing combine to fry our patience and wobble our even keels. On top of this, many of us are attached 24/7 by digital umbilical cords to our jobs or our families and friends. There's little time to let our guards down, even during supposed leisure time.

In fact, the amount of leisure time we have is shrinking—in another irony of contemporary American capitalism. This phenomenon was documented in a popular book published in 1991, *The Overworked American: The Unexpected Decline of Leisure* by Juliet Schor. "In the last twenty years the amount of time Americans have spent at their jobs has risen steadily," she wrote. "Americans report that they have only sixteen and a half hours of leisure a week, after job and household are taken care of. Working hours are already longer than they were forty years ago." This occurred despite enormous gains in productivity that theoretically could have been used to increase leisure. The work/leisure ratio is worse now than in 1991. It sure as hell feels that way.

"Tempus edax rerum," Ovid wrote and my college Shakespeare teacher constantly quoted: time, that devours all things. The pace with which our time, our days, are devoured is depressing. Schor noted that the English vocabulary for time has changed; we "spend" time, we don't "pass" time anymore. "Time is money." Our time is filled with work and obligation. Schor took great pains to show that being overworked adds to stress, leads to sleep deprivation, and taxes relationships and families. That is taken for granted today; it is acknowledged and complained about by virtually every working person, especially working women.

Consider just one aspect of the modern life hassle: commuting. A 2005 report by the U.S. Census Bureau found that the average adult worker spent over one hundred hours a year commuting to work. Most people get only eighty hours a year in vacation. There has been a marked increase in what are being called "extreme commuters," people who commute more than ninety minutes a day. In New York they were 4.3 percent of all commuters, 4 percent in New Jersey, and 3.2 percent in Maryland. In *Bowling Alone,* Robert Putnam found that for every additional ten minutes of daily commuting, a person's civic or group involvement declines by 10 percent. Social capital aside, commuting is stressful and often lonely. It's a classic example of a kind of structural change that makes everyday life a little harder to greet with a smile, even if it allows one to own a home with more square footage. It also takes away from the time we have to contemplate, think things through, and enjoy high, not just low, culture.

The Opposite of Progress

THESE KINDS OF stresses have helped turn routine parts of life into complicated, menacing challenges. Many feel they must monitor their children's TV watching today, which was unheard of thirty years ago. (What was there to monitor? Mr. Kotter's Sweathogs getting rowdy? A romance between Mary Ann and Ginger?) Working for a large company used to provide a high measure of job security, health-care coverage, a pension, and a stable retirement; none of that is true anymore. We worry constantly about what we eat and drink and how much time we spend in the sun. Abundance is adding stress.

Even life's festivities are getting gross. People complain about the commercialization of Christmas and ostentatious bar mitzvahs and Sweet Sixteen parties. Weddings even have a toxic aspect these days—not just because of garishness but because a marketing mentality has infected them. There is a new kind of monster called a bridezilla, a bride who must have a perfect, opulent, "statement" wedding. She demands that exorbitant sums of money be spent outdoing the other bridezillas with better flowers and more caviar. Weddings are now big business. There is even a reality TV show called, yes, *Bridezillas*. I've encountered a few in real life, and they're scary.

Bob Mikolitch, the catering director of a grand Washington hotel, has been in the hotel and banquet business for twenty-five years. He told me that real-life bridezillas exist but aren't common. But he does say that brides and their families have become "much more materialistic." There are ad-filled magazines and slick websites for brides. Couples create websites honoring themselves with photos, stories, and comments ad nauseam about how "Amber and Zach are so cute!" Couples allow guests to buy treats for their honeymoons on their websites—dinner at a five-star restaurant in Paris or a massage in Miami. Bridezillas are not just rich or upper-class. Couples commonly spend huge sums on a lavish wedding instead of a down payment on a house or using it to pay off student loans. A wedding must be a statement of the couples' or the parents' position or station; it is about them, not the guests. Instead of table numbers, couples will use names that refer to the great events of their epic lives:

the Venice Trip table, the Made Partner table, the Summer Camp table. Couples are like well-marketed commodities. Or narcissistic exhibitionists.

There is virtually no social protocol that guides weddings for most people, no taboos and fewer and fewer resonant traditions. "There are no rules anymore," Bob Mikolitch said. And to be perfectly honest, that's the problem.

Chapter Three

AMERICA UNTIED

HOW HAS IT come to pass that so much of America is rotten in the eyes of so many Americans? We are not a bad people compared to others. We stack up well. We try hard. But we hate us in many ways. In some regards, we are the victims of our own success. Modern Americans have an abundance of material security and flexibility that permits them to pursue an abundance of spiritual and "lifestyle" options. The old, uniquely American ideal of being "self-made" changed after the prosperity of the post–World War II era and then the radicalism of the 1960s. To Benjamin Franklin, being "self-made" meant being self-reliant and free of the Old World's monarchs, class system, professional guilds, and religious intolerance. Being "self-made" after the 1960s meant being liberated from the "have tos" of sexual roles, community expectations, etiquette, family obligations, civic duties, professional ethics, and religious observance. Americans over the past fifty years have been exhorted to choose most every aspect of their lives like great existential consumers: not just where to live, but how to live, what to believe in, how to be in a family or a relationship, which community to join or reject, and even what type of body to inhabit.

Now America has overdosed on abundance in all its forms.

For all the societal accomplishment of that period, Americans lost important community bonds and deeply rooted worldviews that helped forge satisfying, connected lives. Affluence quickly became overabundance. Having so many more options in life, ironically, made it harder to find contentment and spiritual direction. We became more confused, disoriented, and discontent. And it is no surprise that since we have trouble holding on to values in our own lives, our society—the collective "us"—has had the same problem. We dislike the culture we're producing but don't have the moral and cultural ammunition to fight it. That's why we hate us.

The torrent of social change after the sixties, what I earlier called Phase One, was fitful. Many prejudices and inequities have been addressed, and society is fairer in many ways. Yet the rise of spoiled selfism, the fragmentation of our ethical thinking, and the decline of our civic community has untied social bonds. This is all played out in our everyday lives, not just in society. The whole "Sixties: Good or Bad" debate has been politicized and calcified for a long while now. Conservatives argue that sexual permissiveness and antiauthoritarianism have destroyed marriage, weakened families, and increased crime. Liberals say poverty is more of the culprit and the liberations of the sixties have brought more humane conditions for minorities, women, homosexuals, and people trapped by society. The argument is exhausted as both sides are essentially right. And both sides are displeased with the state of America today. All sides, I should say, are displeased.

The understanding we need now is different. We need to understand things more human and concrete than "demographics" and "rights." We need to understand how the ways our lives are put together have changed and, apparently, become more challenging. And why we have lost so much trust and admiration for our own culture. And why society doesn't seem to reflect the values and standards we still have as families and individuals. Understanding those things might help us—as individuals, families, and citizens—generate less that is hateful in our own lives.

Sponsoring the Bascombes

RECALL FRANK BASCOMBE from Richard Ford's novel *The Lay of the Land,* the lonely guy who "sponsored" strangers and felt compelled to go out and find a "character" for himself. At age fifty-five, he was still looking for how to be "self-made" in the contemporary sense. Imagine the plight of his children, Clarissa and Paul. Their Mississippi-born father tried to write novels as a young man but became a sportswriter for a top magazine. He moved to Haddam, New Jersey, a suburb of New York, with his wife, Ann, who was from Michigan. They had a third child, Ralph, who died when he was a little boy. Frank's marriage to Ann couldn't withstand that blow. Ann remarried a successful architect and moved the children to Connecticut. Frank stayed in the family home in Haddam and became a real estate agent. He called that time his "Existence Period." Eventually Frank married another transplant, Sally Caldwell, who grew up in Lake Forest, Illinois. Together they moved to Sea-Clift, New Jersey, where Frank had some success as an agent and developer.

In 2000, when *The Lay of the Land* is set, their marriage is in trouble. Sally has left the house. Clarissa, four years out of Harvard, is living with Frank after breaking up with her girlfriend. She is nursing Frank through his treatment for prostate cancer. Paul, several years older than Clarissa, is settled in Kansas City, just a few blocks from where he went to college. He works for a greeting card company.

Clarissa poses a question to her father during a long beach walk: "Who do you think's turned out better, me or Paul?"

Frank, like any father, prefers not to answer, telling Clarissa, "I don't really think about you and Paul turning out, per se."

Neither kid has turned out especially well. Both are fragile, neither is flourishing. They have a low-grade anger at the world. Frank and Ann have not supplied Clarissa and Paul with many tools or "ready guides" for turning out well.

In Frank's opinion, Paul "has rigorously fitted himself in." Paul has self-consciously tried to assemble the accoutrements of a normal American guy. When Frank visited Kansas City, Paul blew up at his father, yelling, "I've sure as fuck done what you haven't done. . . . Accepted life, for one fucking thing . . . I reflect society. . . . I understand myself as a comic figure. I'm fucking normal. You ought to try it."

Understanding yourself as a comic figure is what is normal to Paul. He expresses this by getting "fat," wearing "plaid Bermuda shorts, dark nylon socks, black brogues, occasionally a beret," and procuring "a good wage and benefits package." He's a Kansas City Chiefs fan. Normal, but comically normal. He wears a costume.

Paul cannot tolerate that his father isn't normal but also isn't ironic. After all the knocks he has taken, Frank is still earnest. He tries to be a regular guy through hollow but sincere things like selling real estate and joining civic groups. "You're all about *development*. . . . You're stupid. It's a myth. You oughta get a life." Paul's efforts to be normal, by going every year to the Kansas City Chiefs summer training camp, for instance, are cool precisely because they are not earnest; they are "comic" or ironic. Paul remains essentially detached from his own life. And by the end of the Bascombe trilogy, we know that Paul is in a very bad way.

Clarissa is outwardly even more adrift. At twenty-five she has no career or plans, no home of her own, and is not certain if she is gay or straight. According to her father, she "likes to read but doesn't finally say much. . . . She maintains a great abstract sympathy for the world but, in my mind, seems in constant training to be older, like children of divorce often are. . . . Clarissa was never a 'great kid,' like the bumper stickers say all kids have to be now." She is sensitive and honest but has no passion or urgency. She skates lightly on the surface.

"We're normal enough . . . if you back away a few feet," Clarissa said to her dad.

The Disinherited

THE BASCOMBE CHILDREN are familiar kinds of characters today. Little has stayed in the train of Paul's and Clarissa's lives except psychological baggage. No family or family traditions, no religion, no community, no vocational calling, no passions, and no "being comfortable in your own skin" or "knowing who you are." They lack the nourishment they need to gain existential weight. How can people like this view the external world as anything but inhospitable, not worthy of trust, and phony? There is no way they *can't* hate it much of the time. As that manager of the posh Washington hotel told me when we were talking about bridezillas, "There are no rules." It is both immature and unrealistic to think that is a good thing.

Bascombes and bridezillas have no ready guides for navigating. They have no instructions. In 1937, Wallace Stevens, the poet who spent his career working at the Hartford Accident and Indemnity Company, wrote "Of Modern Poetry." It began:

> *The poem of the mind in the act of finding*
> *What will suffice. It has not always had*
> *To find: the script was set; it repeated what*
> *Was in the script.*
> > *Then the theatre was changed*
> *To something else.*

Our theater has now changed. In 1937, philosophy, poetry, and literature were all about "the mind in the act of finding." But for most people, "the script was set" for their approach to life. There aren't scripts anymore, for anyone. Writing your own script is no longer an esoteric parlor game for intellectuals but a common, concrete social challenge. "What do I want to be when I grow up?" People now ask that question when they're forty. Society no longer hands out guides and roles (at least in a positive way; stereotypes and prejudice endure, of course). Like the Bascombes, many drifting Americans suffer without scripts or even stage directions to work from. We're squandering our social inheritance.

Not a Trophy Life

A MODEL OF what I mean by "social inheritance," and indeed what I think a modest, realistic view of community has been and can be, comes from my mother.

Jean Gutmann Meyer was born in 1923 in Highland Park, Illinois, then an affluent village thirty miles north of Chicago on Lake Michigan. Her parents both grew up in the Hyde Park neighborhood of Chicago; both were German Jews whose ancestors had come over in the late 1840s or early 1850s. My mother moved just once growing up, to a larger house a few blocks away. Her first cousins lived in the same town, and her grandparents lived in the city with a crowd of more distant relatives. Her parents' social lives revolved around a small country club where only other German Jews were members. My mom's social life was set up the same way when she was a girl and young woman. She had few close friends who weren't the children of people in her parents' set. My mother's parents, like their parents and grandparents before them, were Reform Jews. Her home and her life were entirely secular; other Jews would say the family was "assimilated," a disapproving description. There was no Jewish education, no synagogue, and the big family holiday was (and remains) a secular Christmas. My mother went to public schools in Highland Park and college in California until the impracticalities of frequent travel during World War II led her to finish up at Northwestern University in nearby Evanston, Illinois.

My father also came from a family of German Jews who had been in the country since the 1850s, but his ancestors ended up in Richmond, Virginia. His family was acquainted with my mother's, and so when the navy sent my father to midshipmen's school in Chicago to train for the war, he was invited to their home for Thanksgiving. They married right after the war and moved into a converted dog kennel on the grounds of a fancy house owned by close friends of my mother's family. My father went to work for my mother's father, who ran the leather tannery on the north side of Chicago that his grandfather had started in 1892 (it operated in the same location until 2007). My dad worked there until the day before he died. My parents settled in Glencoe, the town right next to Highland Park, and then stayed put. My mother died before my grandmother and never lived more than a few miles away from her. My mother's brother and his family lived one town over. A bunch of second cousins lived nearby. Our aunt and her family moved to Fargo, North Dakota, which was sad for my mom and my grandmother.

Nearly all of my mother's friends were pals from childhood. Her very best friend has stayed close to my family for at least thirty years after my mother died. My mother, of course, made other friends and close acquaintances as an adult, but the heart of her social life was the old gang.

And when I was little, my friends were the children of her friends. The whole time I was growing up, Mom did volunteer work twice a week with kids who had mental disabilities. She had a cast-iron identity as a Jew, her orbit was Jewish, and she felt Jews were marginalized people in society. But she was not at all observant. She was a devoted mother who made people feel very comfortable around her; she ran a house that kids' friends always wanted to play at. She lived a life that felt very natural to her.

On Thursdays, my mom went to the beauty parlor and to the Jewel grocery store. She drove a station wagon with that funny fake wood paneling on the side. Her life was regular and common, though certainly privileged. Few women in her world needed to work, though some certainly did. The world my mom spent her whole life in was not exemplary in any way or especially worthy of mourning. It was a social world where it was hard to be different, though one that was tolerant of personal idiosyncrasies and eccentricity within her crowd; it was homogenous and unwelcoming to people who weren't white and heterosexual, though it did have a sort of "don't ask, don't tell" policy.

My mother wasn't a shining star or moral rebel in that conformist world. She wasn't a joiner or energetic do-gooder. Mom was shy and didn't like parties and big groups very much. She wasn't on the school board; she didn't organize amazing volunteer projects, entertain passing political candidates, or have a passionate avocation. She wasn't beloved by local orphans or widows. She truly and honestly didn't try to keep up with the Joneses, and that was a deliberate choice. Her head wasn't turned by what other people had or did. She didn't strive for her children to achieve and lead trophy lives. She never found occasion to reinvent herself.

My mother was not a strikingly happy or driven person. She had some family problems, like most people. She had cancer for a very long time and died from it when she was only fifty-three. She is buried at Rosehill Cemetery in Chicago, in a family plot that includes great-great-grandparents, great-grandparents, grandparents, parents, and, sadly, a great-grandson. There are friends, cousins, aunts, and uncles all over the old cemetery.

Life's challenges did not rattle my mother's sense of herself, the meaning of her life, and what my father called her "way of going." I think this was because her world—the people, the proximity, the authenticity, the traditions, and the permanence—quietly helped her.

Social Inheritance

MY MOTHER HAD a social inheritance. That was her real privilege.

Her North Shore, German Jewish world was not idyllic. It wasn't a Vermont hamlet with high-toned town meetings or a Mennonite village where townsfolk pitch in to build red barns. It wasn't Hillary Clinton's kind of village. It was the kind of twentieth-century American life and setting dissected by so many novelists, such as Sinclair Lewis, Sherwood Anderson, John O'Hara, Ralph Ellison, Philip Roth, Harper Lee, John Updike, and Richard Ford. Our lives and towns today have even less nourishment for the soul.

Most of the social capital in my mother's life was inherited. She didn't earn it, nor did she squander it. She was not able to bequeath it to her children, however. We had to create it, though we had an easier time than the Bascombes. Our parents were from a different era than Frank and Ann Bascombe.

The most important element of my mother's inheritance was simple physical proximity to a stable community that spanned generations. She benefited not only from the affection, acceptance, and attention of her nuclear family, but also from her extended family and the extended families of her friends and her parents' friends. She learned good manners. She witnessed human character unfolded over generations of families, over lifetimes, like long novels, not just episodes. She saw families that worked and families that didn't; she saw the connection of emotional success to values, priorities, and how people lived—and also to luck. Her "ethics" or her "value system" didn't have a proper name; it wasn't conventionally Jewish; it wasn't a straight American brand of the Protestant work ethic; it wasn't bohemian; it wasn't Ayn Rand; and it wasn't super-mom. Maybe it was bourgeois. Whatever it was, it was steady, clear to her, and, importantly, shared by the people in her life.

If my mother had been in her thirties and forties closer to the turn of the twenty-first century, what would have been different socially? She might have found it easier to work full-time if she had wanted to. Cancer wouldn't have been such a taboo subject to talk about. She might have had help from people through the Internet or support groups, as well as through friends and family. There would have been more divorce in her world, some for all the right reasons and some for all the wrong reasons. She wouldn't have known many people at the country club. She would have known fewer of the merchants in Glencoe. She'd have spent way more time in the car schlepping her kids to travel soccer and "play dates." (We didn't have play dates; we just played.)

My three siblings and I all live in very different worlds from our mother. None of us stayed in that Chicago German-Jewish world, which barely exists any longer. We don't live near one another. Only one sister still lives in Chicago—a Chicago my parents didn't know—and her grown children live in North Carolina. I am the only one of the four of us who is married to a Jew. None of us live in suburbs; we live in cities or the country. None of us has ever remotely considered joining a country club. We each have a few friends from childhood, but they aren't in our daily lives except through the phone and e-mail. Luckily, I think the four of us did inherit my mother's fundamental moral sensibility and a love of her family traditions. That is part of a social inheritance. But most aspects of our outward lives resulted from very free and deliberate decisions, almost like consumer choices. Our mother was free to make such choices in theory, but they would have seemed weird, affected, and unnatural to her. We had no alternative. We had to earn our social capital. Most people do now.

Sociological Modernism

SOCIOLOGISTS CALL THE demise of the social inheritance my mother enjoyed "modernism." The idea is captured in a religious and philosophic memoir called *Taking Hold of Torah: Jewish Commitment and Community in America* written in 1997 by Arnold Eisen, who was a professor of mine in college. Though it's a book about Judaism, I think it applies to all of society. Trained in the sociology of religion, Eisen was a professor of religious studies at Stanford for many years. In 2006, he was appointed chancellor of the Jewish Theological Seminary, America's preeminent institution for educating Conservative Jewish scholars and ordaining rabbis. Eisen writes:

> The loss of integral Jewish community has meant that Jewish commitment is a matter of choice. That is nowhere more true than in contemporary America, where the freedom to participate fully in the life of the larger society is in every respect greater than it has ever been before, indeed is nearly absolute. We are living, moreover, in what is very likely the most mobile society that has ever existed on the face of the earth, or exists today . . . aided and urged on by a culture that is profoundly individualist. It is no wonder that the Jewish community in this situation has to argue for every single Jewish soul, compete for every pledge of allegiance against an ever-increasing wealth of beckoning possibilities. . . .
>
> Our freedom to choose Judaism, or not choose it, has exacted a terrible cost. . . . It constitutes the most visible example of the effects wrought by modernity's disintegration of traditional community.

"Our freedom to choose . . . has exacted a terrible cost." This observation is not something Americans swallow easily. Freedom is supposed to be an unqualified virtue. But the freedom, say, to take the wrong medicine may not be such a virtue. Freedom when there is too much to choose from is frustrating.

"Modern culture is defined by this extraordinary freedom to ransack the world storehouse and to engorge any and every style it comes upon," wrote Daniel Bell in *The Cultural Contradictions of Capitalism.* "Such freedom comes from the fact that the axial principle of modern culture is the expression and remaking of the 'self' in order to achieve self-realization and self-fulfillment." And our modern culture is dismissive of inherited wisdom. As a result, our social inheritance is thin and insipid.

American modernism, Eisen said, disintegrated traditional community and, Bell said, discombobulated the traditional ways people steered their lives. It believed in the idea that a self can and should be willfully constructed apart from tradition, community, and society.

But there is a problem. We hapless moderns have discovered that the much-hyped self can't just create itself and get happy. Human beings are not amoebas. It is not at all clear to us anymore what an invented or discovered self is to be forged *from*. Our communities have been neutered, and our traditional, inherited moral, religious, and aesthetic sensibilities have been discredited. The philosopher Charles Taylor talks about the "sources of the self." Well, what "sources of the self" have authority and credibility anymore? We're good at organizing self-centered lives, with faux chateaus, wealth, nostalgic kitchens, and sensitive therapy talk. We create what have come to be called "lifestyles." A lifestyle is thinner than a life. We hate not having something more.

So how did this exaggerated selfism come about? How did the Me Decade become the Me Era?

The World Is My Mirror

PROSPERITY AND SECURITY are necessary conditions of head problems like we have. But they are not sufficient conditions. Christopher Lasch, a historian and social critic, was one of the first to worry that the worldview revolutions of the sixties could truly threaten people's ability to build and lead productive, unselfish adult lives. "American confidence has fallen to low ebb," Lasch said in his 1978 book, *The Culture of Narcissism: American Life in an Age of Diminishing Expectations*. "Society seems everywhere to have used up its store of constructive ideas." The culprit, he said, was selfism, or narcissism.

Looking at a family like the Bascombes, Lasch would say they suffer because their self-centeredness, as it does with too many post-sixties people, has blinded them to what life is really about. They lack a sense of their place in their spiritual and intellectual ancestry, in history, and in community. They lack what I call "social inheritance." More, they don't have what we would now generically call "life skills." Lasch believed authentic and enduring life skills don't come from how-to books or innate people smarts but from teaching, tradition, and imitation. They come organically, not deliberately, from parents and grandparents, from religion, from how people in the neighborhood live and act, from high culture, and from high-quality popular culture. They come with rules and duties, not just smiley faces. Lasch says, "The atrophy of older traditions of self-help has eroded everyday competence, in one area after another." Paul and Clarissa lack everyday competence. It shows in their inner and outer lives.

Someone more sympathetic to the spirit of the sixties might see Clarissa and Paul's floundering as earnest attempts to liberate themselves from the conformity and stifling bourgeois values that messed up their parents' generation. They are trying to cut their own paths through life, like the old American adventurers Ben Franklin, Natty Bumppo, Tom Sawyer, the pioneers, the self-made man, Emerson and his *Self-Reliance*, Jay Gatsby. Aren't Clarissa and Paul just people on the same American adventure in modern times? Lasch would say no, they are simply lost. Not only don't they have any ready guides, they have nothing to replace them with. What they have is a weak new religion that preaches that finding the self is the key to life and happiness. Lasch would say that quest is futile and selfish.

"For the narcissist, the world is a mirror, whereas the rugged individualist saw it as an empty wilderness to be shaped to his own design," Lasch wrote. There is nothing new to be seen in a mirror. Narcissists are obsessed with pictures of themselves, as the minister Chris Eads put it. They care mostly about how they appear to others and, after that, how they feel. The cruel irony is that this self-centeredness is actually the ultimate form of dependence; the narcissist's pleasure and peace depend on appearances and what others think. So they rely on building the biggest McMansion on the block, wearing the biggest diamonds, blasting the loudest music, or being the most politically correct person in town. This helps create the public environment we hate.

The Limits of Me

SELF-AWARENESS, SELF-REALIZATION, SELF-ACTUALIZATION, and self-fulfillment have become the measures of emotional and existential health—"the triumph of the therapeutic," as sociologist Philip Rieff called it. But being so self-centered is a retreat. And in the 1970s, Lasch saw "selves" retreating from religion, politics, hometowns, high culture, and even history—from duty and have-tos.

Americans have also lost touch with what Lasch called "historical continuity" and think little about how they fit into past and future generations of their families, communities, and country. A simple example now is prime-time television; there are no historical shows on anymore, shows such as *Bonanza, Gunsmoke, Hogan's Heroes, Little House on the Prairie, McHale's Navy, Bat Masterson, Combat, M*A*S*H,* or *The Untouchables.* Historical movies—Westerns, war movies, *Gone with the Wind*—once were the staple of Hollywood. Now they are rare. We don't see ourselves as belonging anywhere, in history or in community.

If we don't feel that we belong, the million-dollar question becomes where does one look for one's authentic self and contentment? Feelings and therapy? Genetics? A fourth husband or wife? The self help aisle at Borders? What exactly is there to mold a self from besides bits and pieces of the family, culture, and community you came from, things that have been discredited as suffocating, oppressive, inauthentic, and, yes, phony? What are the "sources of the self"?

When everything becomes about your own self, the game is over.

That's the cruel part of Lasch's argument. The whole enterprise of selfism is doomed. The epic myth, the big lie, of modern America, Lasch argued, is that deep character and a core identity can be intentionally made in near isolation. They can't. Culture has transformed a sensible concept of the "pursuit of happiness to the dead end of a narcissistic preoccupation with the self."

The double irony is that indulging your self now trumps doing for others in our culture. But the surest path to your self, to pride and contentment, is through others. In the acknowledgments to his second book, my friend Marc Fisher reminded his children that "listening well is the path to one's own voice."

We have stopped listening well. Three decades after Lasch added the "culture of narcissism" to our vocabulary, we can easily recognize phony-

baloney self reinventions, new identities, and other more or less sophisticated versions of "Hey, it's a whole new me!" This is obnoxious in others though hard to spot in ourselves.

The entrepreneurial spirit has provided us with brand-new off-the-
rack identities for years now. Identitywear: It's a whole new fashion line.
A clownish example of this that Lasch used came from the autobiography of Jerry Rubin, a radical celebrity in the sixties who was a founder of
the yippies and one of the Chicago Seven charged with conspiring to
riot at the 1968 Democratic National Convention. In a famous passage
from *Growing (Up) at 37*, Rubin wrote: "In five years, from 1971 to 1975,
I directly experienced est, gestalt therapy, bioenergetics, rolfing, massage, jogging, health foods, tai chi, Esalen, hypnotism, modern dance,
meditation, Silva Mind Control, Arica, acupuncture, sex therapy, Reich-
ian therapy, and More House—a smorgasbord course in New Consciousness." He wasn't trying to be funny. In the end, he claimed he had found
himself.

Robert Bellah, a sociologist specializing in religion, cowrote a popular book in 1985 called *Habits of the Heart: Individualism and Commitment
in American Life.* In it, Sheila Larson, a young nurse, told Bellah, "I believe in God. I'm not a religious fanatic. I can't remember the last time
I went to church. My faith has carried me a long way. It's Sheilaism. Just
my own little voice." It sounds so innocuous now. But Sheilaism became
something of a mocking code name for the rejection of spiritual authority in favor of milky, uncommitted, touchy-feely, selfish spirituality.

Broadcast Yourself

PEOPLE LIKE JERRY Rubin and Sheila Larson are all over the place
now. They don't seem wacky anymore because there is a mainstream
business of the self. At a dinner party, a brilliant young woman, a lawyer
at one of Washington's finest law firms, told me that I should start to
keep an "I'm awesome" file. She had one after she got the idea from
Oprah. This was sincere, well-meaning advice. So, yes, you encounter
mainstream selfists at parties and hear them on *The Oprah Winfrey Show.*
You hear them preaching. Your company brings them in as consultants
or motivators. You know damn well which ones are phonies and which

are sincere. The sincere ones may or may not be wise or effective, but sincerity and authenticity—the absence of blatant phoniness—count for a lot these days.

Feeling awesome now trumps accomplishing awesome things. The culture of narcissim bred this. It is seen in the culture as the triumph of celebrity and fame for its own sake over accomplishment, virtue, or craft. "What a man does matters less than the fact that he has 'made it,' " Lasch wrote. That is why politicians care more about getting elected than governing. It is why actors care more about being famous than making good movies. It is why CEOs at underperforming companies get gargantuan bonuses. It is why there are people who are famous for being famous. Lasch called it the "eclipse of achievement." It is precisely this part of public culture we hate. But somehow we love watching it from afar, and we slop it up.

This same mix of exhibitionism and narcissism blends profitably in the Internet hit YouTube, which has as its tagline "Broadcast Yourself." Every MySpace and Facebook page is a version of Marketed Me. Everyone can now create their own fifteen minutes of fame, no need to wait for Big Media to bestow it. As bad as Lasch thought things were, I am not sure he could have imagined *Time* magazine's declaration that the 2006 Person of the Year was "You." "We made Facebook profiles and Second Life avatars and reviewed books at Amazon and recorded podcasts," the cover story said. "And for seizing the reins of the global media, for founding and framing the new digital democracy, for working for nothing and beating the pros at their own game, *Time*'s Person of the Year for 2006 is you."

Lasch would be so proud.

Safe to Be Selfish

IT IS NATURAL for a society's values to change as their material conditions change. In *America's Crisis of Values: Reality of Perception*, sociologist Wayne Baker says that like most prosperous Western societies, America has moved from emphasizing "survival" values to "self-expression" values —the sorts of values Lasch calls narcissistic. With basic security and material needs met, people focus more on self-realization than self-preservation; political fights are more likely to be about cultural disputes than crime and national security. Self-expression values are a luxury.

The common conservative take on America is that we suffer from a shortage of values. Baker says that's wrong, it's just that self-expression values aren't the sort of values conservatives admire. In most Western countries that have moved from survival to self-expression values, "traditional" values have given way to "secular/rationalist" values. But this hasn't happened in America, he argues. In Europe, traditional values form around religion, nationalism, language, and ancestry. In America, traditional values are based on an idea of the "American Way"—on a constitution, political system, work ethic, and sense of common mission. Unlike Europeans, Americans have not retreated from their traditional values. Despite our contentious debate about so-called family values, they are not the traditional American Way. They are just one contemporary, fleeting agenda. The American Way endures.

But there is a conflict, Baker says, between traditional and self-expression values. We embrace both, so we are disoriented and confused. For example, many born-again Christians speak the language of selfism; they clearly have orthodox, doctrinal values, but they also share the culture's individualistic worldview. Similarly, at the synagogue my family belongs to, there is an "egalitarian Orthodox" group. Their religious observance is very strict and old-world, except when it comes to the role of women. They speak the language of contemporary self-expression values and individualism as they keep kosher. Among wholly secular people, I see this often in post-baby-boom brain workers, who are aggressively ambitious for the "traditional values" of money and status but who talk in the jargon of selfism about creativity, personal fulfillment, and private goals. They rarely talk about the good of the group—the company, colleagues, or project.

So there is a tension now between the kinds of values we have and hold. But we are not a polarized nation, Baker says. It isn't that one-half of America has traditional values and one-half has self-expression values. That's what the politicians, pundits, and consultants preach, but it just isn't true. We share basic civic values. But we all juggle the contradictions in our own thoughts and beliefs. Narcissism battles the call of something bigger and traditional, be it religious, artistic, political, or family oriented.

Worlds Collide

CONFLICTS OF VALUES and moralities are the specialty of philosopher Alasdair MacIntyre, a transplanted Scot whose 1981 book, *After Virtue: A Study in Moral Theory,* made an enormous intellectual splash. Christopher Lasch once complained that scholars and philosophers "no longer pretend to tell us how to live." MacIntyre's book essentially responded that of course we can't tell you people how to live, you are living amid so many different ethical, religious, ethnic, and values traditions or anti-traditions that it's chaos.

In MacIntyre's view, the irascibility of our arguments and conflicts stems precisely from this wild diversity of competing values and cultures. Those who subscribe firmly to traditional, well-defined belief systems collide with believers in other orthodoxies: an evangelical meets a high Episcopalian meets an Orthodox Jew meets a Buddhist meets a Reform Jew meets a Muslim meets a radical feminist meets a secular humanist meets a libertarian meets a Marxist meets a committed Green meets a Mormon. Add to the mix the Jerry Rubins of the world, the pickers and choosers who select their own personal goods, truths, and commandments à la carte. And then there is the more temperate majority, people who are simply eclectic and not systematic, following paths that seem sensible and well-meaning but that certainly aren't consistent.

Americans became more ethnically and racially diverse in the last part of the twentieth century, and this meant becoming more morally diverse. The rise of self-expression values compounded this explosion of diversity.

That creates challenges. Separate moral spheres are bound to be in constant conflict. And there is no court of appeals, nowhere to turn to for objective or even authoritative adjudication. "There seems to be no rational way of securing moral agreement in our culture," MacIntyre wrote.

This sums up the moral and political arguments we have in America today. Without shared assumptions and a common vocabulary, there is no way to settle an argument. Thanks to the rise of self-expression values, the culture of narcissism, and the legacy of the sixties, we have fewer shared assumptions. There is less common ground and more private property. At some point, arguments degenerate into someone putting up a sign that says "No Trespassing." This helps explain what is now called our "incivility." It breeds belligerence, one of the key reasons why we hate us.

The idea of choosing goods and values individually, by taste and preference, is what truthiness is all about. It actually has a philosophic pedigree. It is called "emotivism," a term resurrected by MacIntyre from early nineteenth-century British philosophy. In *After Virtue,* MacIntyre defines it this way: "Emotivism is the doctrine that all evaluative judgments and, more specifically, all moral judgments are nothing but expressions of preference, expressions of attitude or feeling." So in this view there is no difference between saying "the death penalty is wrong" and "I don't like the death penalty." "Gay marriage is immoral" is just another way of saying "I don't like gay marriage."

Emotivism and truthiness are first cousins of the "everything is relative" outlook of the sixties. While one can make a coherent argument for moral relativism, our lazy contemporary version is a triumph of feelings over logic or any moral imperative. It is narcissism or selfism. The truthiness/narcissism axis of evil is now supported in mainstream ways by therapies, quasi-religions, and self-help entrepreneurs that encourage people to discover "my god" (Sheilaism) and "my truth" (Stephen Colbert). There is also a kind of group narcissism sanctioned by multiculturalism; any once-aggrieved group automatically gets a moral trump card.

This is an impossible environment for productive argument about important things. And as Daniel Bell said, "One can quarrel with judgments, one cannot quarrel with feelings." "I feel it is okay to watch pornography" is a very different statement than "Pornography is morally acceptable." You can only have a rational conversation about the second statement.

That is MacIntyre's key point. Where emotivism prevails, moral arguments become "interminable." There are simply no agreed-upon, common criteria for evaluating moral truth or judgment. There is no rational way to end an argument. "I like the death penalty; you don't." The abortion debate is a classic example of an interminable debate in which the two opposing camps draw on philosophies that not only are in conflict but are on different philosophic planets; they have no shared vocabulary or basic values and assumptions. Neither side is trivial or insincere; both sides reason clearly from their basic premises (taking life is always wrong versus it is my right to determine what happens to my body).

One would think that this relativism-lite would foster a laissez-faire, live-and-let-live spirit of tolerance. But it does just the opposite. It generates insurmountable frustration. When there are no shared assumptions, no basic common ground, even the most trivial and ephemeral arguments become irresolvable. People don't like to acknowledge their own emotivism; most all of us think our judgments are fact based and reasoned, not emotional. It's the other guy who's emotional.

This is ubiquitous in the real world today. You have been the victim of emotivism every time you've been told to shut up with the omnipresent locution "You just don't get it!" That's the trump card in modern moral argument: "You just don't get it!" There are certainly other versions, as we've seen. "You're just biased" is one of them. Cartoonish liberals and conservatives act this out on talk radio and cable news all day long, persuading no one and preaching angrily to their agitated choirs. This is another reason why we hate us.

The Dictatorship of Relativism

MACINTYRE'S INTENTION IS not to rescue us from this descent into incoherence by arguing for absolute or divine truth. He advocates what has come to be called "virtue morality." The idea is that there are clear and absolute moral virtues, but only within the context of enclosed communities that have shared vocabularies, heritages, assumptions, and traditions. One doesn't *select* virtues as we moderns wish; one *submits* to them. They have rules and absolutes. There are Catholic virtues and Jewish virtues. There are virtues for diplomats, judges, and journalists. To be able to act with virtue, to be able to end arguments rationally, to overcome relativism and emotivism, and to have an actual community, one must make a radical existential choice to embrace a tradition and community and submit to their authority. This means acknowledging that all virtues are not compatible or combinable but picking anyway. It means limiting choice. It means accepting that other people may respect virtues you do not and resisting the impulse to denigrate them. The virtues necessary to be a good Catholic are not necessarily compatible with the virtues of a good statesman. A Catholic and statesman may conflict without resolution, or that conflict may be within one soul. Modern Americans hate that kind of irreconcilable conflict as much as they hate submission to moral authority.

After Virtue ends with a dark, ominous proclamation of this idea. It has become a famous philosophic passage, if there is such a thing today:

> What matters at this stage is the construction of local forms of community within which civility and the intellectual and moral life can be sustained through the new dark ages which are already upon us. And if the tradition of the virtues was able to survive the horrors of the last dark ages, we are not entirely without ground for hope. This time however the barbarians are not waiting beyond the frontiers; they have already been governing us for quite some time. And it is our lack of consciousness of this that constitutes part of our predicament. We are waiting not for a God, but for another—doubtless very different—St. Benedict.

St. Benedict was the founder of Western monasticism. It is fascinating to me that the next pope after this was written called himself Benedict. In his very first homily, Pope Benedict XVI said:

> How many winds of doctrine have we known in recent decades, how many ideological currents, how many ways of thinking . . . ? Today, having a clear faith based on the Creed of the Church is often labeled as fundamentalism. Whereas relativism, that is, letting oneself be "tossed here and there, carried

about by every wind of doctrine," seems the only attitude that can cope with modern times. We are building a dictatorship of relativism that does not recognize anything as definitive and whose ultimate goal consists solely of one's own ego and desires.

Lasch and MacIntyre would agree with Pope Benedict here. But can Benedict's warning against the "dictatorship of relativism" have any meaning or relevance for secular Americans? What is the alternative to relativism? Are there any plausible sources of moral authority? Can there be a modern moral community?

Untied States

THIS KIND OF talk is often dismissed as nostalgic. There aren't absolutes, so get over it. Believing in absolute truths leads to crusades, inquisitions, and jihads. Good riddance. Besides, you have a romantic image of what community used to be.

In the early 1990s, Harvard political scientist Robert Putnam was one of the skeptics. He did wonder if all the mourning over the American community of yesteryear was mere nostalgia. Curious, Putnam decided that his job as a well-trained social scientist was to "count things." The result was a book whose title instantly conjures up a whole social theory—*Bowling Alone: The Collapse and Revival of American Community*.

Putnam assembled a team of scholars and grad students and counted every kind of group, association, and membership he could find for as far back as records allowed: Rotary clubs, parent-teacher associations, poker games, Kiwanis clubs, churches and temples, chambers of commerce, bridge clubs, Boy and Girl Scouts, book drives, Masons, League of Women Voters, Lions, Elks, collectors' clubs, trade unions, family dinners, softball leagues, town bands, 4-H clubs, the Grange, garden clubs, church choirs, and—of course—bowling leagues.

He found that instead of bowling in leagues, Americans were bowling alone: "For the first two-thirds of the twentieth century a power tide bore Americans into ever deeper engagement in the life of their communities, but a few decades ago—silently, without warning—that tide reversed and we were overtaken by a treacherous rip current. Without at first noticing, we have been pulled apart from our communities over the last third of the century."

Attendance at religious services went way down in this period. The exceptions were the more energetic, new, and often fundamentalist strands like Christian evangelicals and ultra-Orthodox Jews. Putnam shows these groups interact less with other groups than traditional religions and thus generate smaller circles of connectedness.

Political participation also declined: voting, handing out leaflets, staying well informed. Only the numbers of people on political mailing lists went up. Some argue that political participation is back because of the Internet; others would argue that blogging and its cousins are just techno-Sheilaism. Either way, trust and confidence in government plummeted after the sixties and have remained down. People are also less likely to socialize and form softball teams with coworkers than their World War II–generation parents. Perhaps most startling:

> Across a very wide range of activities, the last several decades have witnessed a strong diminution of regular contacts with our friends and neighbors. We spend less time in conversation over meals, we exchange visits less, we engage less frequently in leisure activities that encourage casual social interaction, we spend more time watching . . . and less time doing. We know neighbors less well and we see old friends less often.

This meshes with the dramatic study on social isolation we looked at in chapter 1. As Robert Lane said in *The Loss of Happiness in Market Democracies,* we face social malnutrition.

Authority That Doesn't Suck

PUTNAM'S PORTRAIT OF society was statistical and empirical, but his purpose was deeper. Putnam wanted to see what was happening to

Americans' sources of "social capital." Social capital, to Putnam, is a necessary ingredient of personal well-being. It is interpersonal nourishment, and it lubricates social life. Of course, it is not necessarily good; the classic example of malignant social capital is the Ku Klux Klan. Though not a guarantee of civic virtue, social capital is essential to creating effective social norms and rules. Without social capital, people don't know to give up their subway seats to old people. Drunken fans don't know not to use the foulest of language when they're sitting next to a little boy at a football game. Without social capital, the dad (me) doesn't ask the drunks to cool it because he doesn't have the confidence that he won't just inspire more bad behavior or get punched. Without social capital, people who become network executives are so disoriented they think it's smart to glorify "nasty little sluts" in prime-time television shows. They don't blow the whistle on a colleague who is embezzling.

Social capital is a source of teaching and social inheritance. When there is a deficit of social capital, there is a shortage of guidance for young people learning how to live and act. Today that vacuum is often filled by a media that is saturated with "nasty little slut" moments. Without social capital, generations cannot pass down their collective wisdom, perspective, stories, and manners. Public culture, high and low, loses the ability to instruct and inspire; it becomes easier to get an audience by exploiting fear, voyeurism, exhibitionism, and pure escapism than through something "uplifting."

Here's how this can play out. *Newsweek* magazine has a regular feature written by readers called "My Turn." In the summer of 2007, Lisa Segelman of Randolph, New Jersey, wrote a "My Turn" called "The Family Road Trip in a Digital Age." Segelman wanted to re-create for her three kids the great journeys her family had in its '67 Cadillac. She wanted her kids to learn to enjoy the scenery, sing stupid songs, and even fight. Her family enjoyed none of this zany road-trip bonding. They were too plugged in to their electronic devices. The Segelman family brought a two-screen DVD player along for the ride, as well as "two computers, three MP3 players and three cell phones, which meant we connected to a lot more than the scenery." And the mom was terribly disappointed.

"For much of the vacation drive time, I was in my own virtual reality," she wrote. "I had no one to talk to, no one to share whatever meager experiences I-95 had to offer."

This is a story about the evils of technology, right? That's why *Newsweek* ran it. Well, no, this is a story about the lack of authority and confidence. Why didn't the Segelmans simply refuse to let their kids use these contraptions? Okay, Mom made a mistake by packing the gizmos. Once she figured it out, why didn't she just say no or FedEx them back to Randolph? Was she worried the kids would melt? Or get mad at her? Or not like her anymore? The truth is that, like many parents, she is probably in the habit of using her authority rarely and mostly when there isn't conflict.

Here is a slightly bigger example. My wife was with a group of women who all had kids in different private schools around Washington. Some of the mothers were griping about a big "rave" held at a fancy boys' school in the city, St. Albans. Hundreds of kids showed up, including the children of the complaining mothers, some of whom were high school freshmen. They went with their parents' permission and probably got rides from them. The dance was apparently poorly supervised and over-crowded. There was drinking, grinding, and who knows what else. Toward the end, boys were parading around in their boxer shorts. And these were just the shenanigans the parents knew about. The mothers complained about St. Albans and the lack of supervision at the dance. But why did they allow their kids to go? They agreed that the St. Albans dance had a reputation for getting wild. Well, asked the other women, why did you let your kid go? We didn't want to complicate our kid's social life, they said. All our kid's friends were going. We want the kid to be popular.

These mothers were all affluent, well-educated, attentive parents. None were single mothers overwhelmed by everyday life or too poor to give their children nice things. None of their kids were troubled, wild, or impervious to parental control. These women had as many parenting resources as any group of mothers you could possibly assemble. But they spoke as if they were powerless victims. They did, of course, have real power. They could have simply forbidden their children to go to the dance.

This unwillingness to use available authority and the utter lack of accountability, when projected onto the big stages of American life, helps explain why there are no clear cultural standards. Standards for popular entertainment, manners, and public behavior are obviously much looser than they were even two or three generations ago. But there are still plenty of shared standards and common sense. There is a lack of willingness to use authority to enforce standards. Every once in a while there is a symbolic gesture to enforce them, as when the Federal Communication Commission issued a fine after Janet Jackson's nipple fell out of her costume during the Super Bowl show. But 99 percent of the time, it's cultural laissez-faire. And then we gripe about what offends us on television and hold ourselves blameless. We don't turn off the TV; we blame Hollywood. We blame St. Albans. We blame the DVD player. Hollywood deserves vast contempt, sure. But the "off" button was invented for a reason. We have real reasons to hate us, and our desire to let ourselves off the hook whenever possible compounds them.

The loss of social capital, virtues, and everyday competence has made navigating everyday life difficult for people like Clarissa and Paul Bascombe. They may have fat wallets but their souls are thin. How can they not hate us? Of course, these are precisely the people who are creating American culture today. We lack rules and maps for our own lives, and yet we're surprised our culture is off track.

Pollution of the water and air were justified in the name of industrial progress. That progress was real. Some of our cultural and spiritual pollution also comes from progress that is real. But we're swamped and disoriented. As I reread the books discussed in this chapter I was often reminded of a passage from *Zen and the Art of Motorcycle Maintenance:*

> There are eras of human history in which the channels of thought have been too deeply cut and no change was possible, and nothing new ever happened, and the "best" was a matter of dogma, but that is not the situation now. Now the stream of our

common consciousness seems to be obliterating its own banks, losing its central direction and purpose, flooding the lowlands, disconnecting and isolating the highlands and to no other purpose other than the wasteful fulfillment of its own internal momentum.

Three decades after this was written society is more flooded than ever with new rivers of information, media, data, and culture. They say it is a revolution.

Chapter Four

OMNIMEDIA

As our family historian, I used to interrogate my grandmother about her life. She was born in Chicago in 1903. As a little girl, she was taught that it was important to be a good conversationalist so she could make anyone feel comfortable. She could always find what someone liked to talk about and she would know enough about the subject to draw them out. That took work. It meant keeping up with news, politics, sports, books, gossip, art, and popular entertainment.

When my grandmother was young, culture, news, and commercial information came to her only from printed material (books, newspapers, magazines, catalogs) and live events (theater, sermons, or speeches). My parents were both born in 1923. In their childhood they had movies, broadcast radio, records, books, newspapers, magazines, catalogs, and live events. I was born in 1958. I had access to seven over-the-air television stations (though one was in Spanish), audiotapes, movies, broadcast radio, records, books, newspapers, magazines, catalogs, and live events. My children were born in the 1990s. They have access (in theory) to the Internet, video on demand, downloaded music and movies, home and car satellite radio services, video and computer games, e-mail, portable cells with text messaging and video and Internet, TiVo and other digital video recording devices, DVDs, videotape recordings, hundreds of television stations delivered by over-the-air transmission or satellite or cable or broadband Internet, audiotapes, movies, broadcast radio, records, books, newspapers, magazines, catalogs, and live events.

We spend a massive chunk of our day with media, every day. A dirty little secret of our times is that consuming media is a big part of what we do with our hard-earned bounty. With liberty unmatched in human events and prosperity only Scandinavians don't envy, we go forth and play with electronic devices.

Media constitutes a large part of what we experience. It puts pictures in our heads we could never see otherwise. A medieval serf couldn't imagine the life of a Masai warrior because they did not have the pictures. Vikings didn't know how much better the Mongol hordes had it. With modern media, distant images become the basic bricks and mortar of our inner lives. That changes what makes up our world.

Chris Eads, the young pastor at CrossCurrents Ministries in Virginia, feels media's images are an invisible burden on his congregants. "You build up a picture, an image, of what your life is going to look like when you grow up," he said. "And the image is all about outward things, things that really aren't the things that we're all about—cars, houses, neighborhoods. Now we're spending all this energy changing those things. We know the internal things really matter the most, but we all chase the external things. . . . I believe most human beings have a good soul and they know what matters, but it gets buried by culture, by Hollywood, by marketing and all that."

Media puts different pictures in our heads in different ways than real life does.

Size Matters

WE ARE OBLIVIOUS to the sheer mass of media we absorb day in and day out. Media is not just "the media," which we think of as the news media. Everything we experience in "mediated" forms is media, everything that we experience *only* through representation via some medium like television, radio, or the Web. "The media" is just a snack in our gluttonous daily media diet. Never have human brain diets contained so many info-calories, many of them from junk.

Here's the cognitive routine my nervous system encounters most weekday mornings. After ingesting caffeinated fluids, I read two newspapers (the old-fashioned kind) while eating breakfast. The sports section always comes first. Before I leave the house at 7:30 to carpool the kids to school, I generally check my e-mail on my BlackBerry personal digital assistant, or PDA. After the kids get out of the car, I'll listen to either some news on the radio or a book on tape. Often I'll grab the silence before the onslaught.

When I get to the office around 8:15, I look over the website where I work and then read the wires. Next it's triage on e-mail. Most mornings, assuming I've sifted through my in-box after dinner the night before, I'll have thirty or forty e-mails by 8:30. Some will be from people in Baghdad, London, Islamabad, and Moscow. I'll deal only with the important ones first thing, or the mental health e-mails—the jokes and news of the weird. Then I'll read or scan two more newspapers and plow through at least five competing news sites. (I am getting nearly instantaneous information about news events from around the world with what is now the most basic technology; there is virtually nothing I see as a "professional" journalist that isn't commonly available.) By now I am also taking and making phone calls. But the real action is on IM—instant messaging. Our newsroom communicates by IM. "Typo in graf 2, LA bomb threat story." "Take a look at 2745488." "You there? . . . No! OK, gonna call then." "OK, OK, I'm here." "Cool, u c BuzzMachine post on Yahoo?" "Yeah." "OK. Later."

I'll also check at least three media business sites or blogs. I'll have read three or four opinion pieces from various political sites that a producer has recommended we run. I'll scan ten others. I'll finish up with my e-mail, check sports news one more time, and only then be "read in" enough to really start the day. Then I turn on the cable news; it stays on all day. I will have uploaded enough real-time data into my cerebral microprocessor to interface with the world coherently.

Then I can begin to contribute to making editorial decisions about a truly absurd number of matters. Consider June 26, 2007. The Louisiana state legislature approved a ban on a late-term abortion procedure, the first state to do so since the Supreme Court upheld a federal ban earlier in the year. The CIA released documents long kept secret that showed new details about how the agency illegally spied on Americans decades ago and had hatched failed assassination plots. Two Americans were killed in Iraq, Marine Corporal Derek C. Dixon of Riverside, Ohio, and Army Sergeant 1st Class Nathan L. Winder of Blanding, Utah. Tony Blair spent his last full day as British prime minister discussing global warming with California governor Arnold Schwarzenegger. Two influential Republican senators issued some of the sharpest intraparty criticism yet of President Bush's handling of Iraq. First Lady Laura Bush began a five-day trip to Africa focusing on AIDS prevention. Pope Benedict XVI changed the rules for electing a new pope. But what was the big story of the day? Paris Hilton was released from jail in California.

I will need a complete re-upload in the afternoon. Unintentional brain deletions are already a problem at my age.

I'm an info piker compared to my colleagues, a rusty Volkswagen Beetle on the information autobahn. On conference calls, I'm the one who gets teased for having the slowest cerebral microprocessor, the feeblest multitasking skills, the least high-tech know-how, and the most antediluvian vocabulary. I don't take in any RSS feeds. I cast no pods. I was the last kid in my class to get a BlackBerry, and my thumbs are all thumbs. But I soldier on, brain fried and soul soggy.

Life, Liberty, and the Pursuit of Media

YOU MIGHT THINK my media morning is especially cyber and speedy since I work in online news. Wrong. Any financial professional runs rings around my dataflow. Most lawyers, doctors, techs, and corporate managers will have even more information, usually more specialized, to master before their midmorning re-caffeination. I have a nephew who is a government lawyer who has podcasts of his favorite columnists, radio shows, and other info-nuggets automatically fed from his computer to his iPod so he can pick and choose what to listen to driving into work.

Most high school students listen to music, download music, and IM with friends while they are doing chemistry homework. I could barely unitask when I was in high school.

This gargantuan daily data dump is simply part of the contemporary day. That is a new thing in human history.

The statistics on media consumption are interesting but not tremendously accurate. But it is almost certain they will seem alien to you. Statistically, if you are reading this sentence, you're an oddball. The average American spends three minutes a day reading a book. At this moment, you and I are engaged in an essentially antiquated interaction. Welcome, fellow Neanderthal!

The typical American spends an average of about nine and a half hours a day consuming media. Television gobbles up three hours a day per person. The Internet consumes ninety minutes a day, a figure that is growing as I write. Newspapers are down to about a half an hour and shrinking. Radio is on for more than two and a half hours a day. We consume recorded music for eighty-five minutes a day on average and read magazines for about fifteen minutes. We watch about seventy hours of recorded movies at home each year and go out to about six movies a year.

For about three hours a day, consuming media at home is all we do—no multitasking, just face time with a screen or page. We consume about 20 percent of our media at work and the rest while either multitasking or doing something with media on as background noise. So if you find yourself wondering how the day blew by or why time is flying, now you know.

The Physics of Media

Media criticism normally focuses on the quality of the content carried by media. There are film critics, theater critics, and so forth. Academic media criticism, a specialty that generates the most impenetrable jargon in all of academia, tries to get at how the "structure" of media shapes the "structure" of human thinking. How does the brain process television differently than a book? Are gender roles social constructs perpetrated by media? Do the forms of media determine the boundaries of conceptual ability? Is reality a postmodern construct with no distinct epistemological status?

But media quantity is more important than quality in society today.

Again, size matters. Or perhaps I should say the physics of media matter, the mass, velocity, acceleration, and momentum. The sheer amount of consumed media, the acceleration of new technical improvements, and the combined momentum are what most affect our brains and consume our cognitive bandwidth. Just think of how much information is put on the plain TV screen during news or sports: the main content, the crawl on the bottom of the screen, and the graphic in the upper left. Just watching television is cognitive triple-tasking. This must be reckoned with somehow before you get into the semiotics of *Seinfeld*. I am guessing this is what Marshall McLuhan meant when he said, "Media is the message."

The major reason modern media is different than its historical predecessors is not the content, but the scale, amount, and form of it. A well-off Roman could a see drama only when it was staged at the amphitheater. Today, anybody can watch performed drama twenty-four hours a day. It's available live and in several recorded forms. Some people watch more than one television show at once. You're more likely to see flame throwers than spears, and actors get naked a lot more now, but there are universal themes of content: love, hate, murder, oedipal complexes, tragedy, comedy, and betrayal. It's the delivery that has changed.

The massive delivery of content we face taxes the brain so much it has become more difficult to like the world. The soul is next. We're soaked in media. We're pickled and pruny. Our nervous systems are overstimulated, our psyches malnourished. What we face is not media as conventionally understood. It is OmniMedia.

The Biology of Media

IN BIOLOGY, A medium is a culture of a liquid or solidified nutrient material suitable for the cultivation of microorganisms. In the life cycle of our species, media is currently the primary incubator of cultural and social microorganisms, particularly harmful bacteria.

Does contemporary cultural media carry proportionally more dangerous bacteria than in prior times? It's not an absolutely crucial question because, as I said, the portions and exposure are so much greater today. It's one thing to drink dirty water once a day. It's another thing to drink bottles of it all day, every day. Still, this much seems obvious: At this point, "low" culture is squeezing out "high" culture, and tabloid or argutainment news is crowding out journalism. There's much more money in stimulating our base instincts than inspiring our higher selves. And there is an intense demand for what media capitalists call "product." It is difficult to create good cultural product under the best conditions. Today's hungry, media-consuming beast must be fed in bulk.

Much of what we hate in society today we encounter *only* through media. Most people don't have much unmediated contact with "nasty little sluts." Few people, for example, will see a political debate or a press conference in person or chat with a candidate face-to-face. We experience only mediated politics. We can only hate Britney Spears, Al Sharpton, Mark McGwire, or Jack Abramoff because of the media. They say ignorance is bliss, and that's true when it is ignorance of Anna Nicole Smith and O. J. Simpson. We suffer from media-induced anti-bliss.

Media also makes deception easier; it is harder to bullshit someone eye-to-eye than eye-to-screen. Similarly, media can make something that truly is sincere or genuine seem phony simply by carrying it. Ask any presidential candidate about that. Many politicians I have known, for example, were good people trying hard to do good jobs. The news media rarely captures that. When a positive story comes along, it's dismissed as a puff piece.

This points out an important failing of OmniMedia: It trivializes the important and inflates the trivial. The DWI arrests of starlets get far more coverage than the genocide in Darfur. It's not even a close call.

The comedian Larry David made this point in a hilarious but almost morbid way in an episode of his television series *Curb Your Enthusiasm.* Larry and his wife are celebrating their tenth wedding anniversary with a dinner and then a brief ceremony at Larry's synagogue. The rabbi asks if he could bring a friend who is a survivor and a fan of Larry's along to the dinner. Larry says that's fine and then tells his father to bring his friend Solly along because poor Solly is a survivor, too. So the rabbi's friend shows up and he's a young, WASPish, studly guy named Colby. Colby was a contestant on the reality show *Survivor*. At dinner, survivor meets survivor and they argue about their qualifications:

> *Colby: We had very little rations, no snacks.*
> *Solly: Snacks, what are you talking snacks? We didn't eat, sometimes for a week, for a month. . . .*
> *Colby: Have you even seen the show?*
> *Solly: Did you ever see our show? It was called the Holocaust!*

A show called the Holocaust. Expect the sense of moral proportionality to atrophy further in our culture.

The portability of new media is celebrated with messianic glee. You can be in a Costa Rican rain forest and get live video from CBSNews.com and send e-mail to the human resources department and check your stocks in real time. Two problems: When you do that, you are not really in the rain forest. You're halfway there. Your experience will be less intense and meaningful. Second, if you can send, you can receive: The human resources department can e-mail *you* and Aunt Edna can call *you* and your cell phone can tell *you* just how much dough your 401(k) lost that day. You aren't away from anything. The freedom that media gets you is cheap. Media is a cruel wench: What she gives she takes away.

The Epistemology of Media

HERE'S MY FAVORITE quote about the media: "As long as I assume that the world is something I discover by turning on the radio . . . I am deceived from the start." The author is Thomas Merton, the Catholic monk, philosopher, and theologian.

The proper postmodern response is that Merton is all wet, structurally speaking. The whole hip, relativistic, ironic, deconstructionist, comp-lit-department way of looking at the world is based on the idea that seeing a picture of a zebra is as real as seeing the zebra itself. This defies common sense, which ought not to be defied in this case.

This has been called the Lassie effect, after the famous dog of early television. There is a difference between watching Lassie bark and watching Lassie bark on television. Both are real perceptual experiences, obviously. But they are experiences of different things. For example, the real bark could only happen once. The recorded bark can be repeated infinitely. Seeing and hearing the live bark cannot be manipulated except in extremis, like by slipping the watcher some LSD. The representation or mediated bark is easily manipulated in ways that are impossible for the viewer to perceive. The viewer can't see the trainer holding the lamb chop just out of the frame. The viewer doesn't know the audio mix of the bark has been altered to make it sound more urgent. And, by the way, the viewer doesn't know that the dog that played the female collie Lassie was, in fact, a male.

Daniel Boorstin, trying to make sense of what he called "pseudo-events" in the early days of television in *The Image: A Guide to Pseudo-Events in America* believed Americans preferred mediated events to live, unmediated ones. "The American citizen thus lives in a world where fantasy is more real than reality, where the image has more dignity than its original." Americans would rather watch *Lassie* on TV than watch real dogs bark. I certainly would in most cases. Take it one more step and ponder these two conversations.

"I saw a car accident yesterday on 95 and it turns out a guy was killed. I saw it. I was like a hundred yards behind and I saw it."
"Wow, that's tough."

Or:

"Did you see that story on the news last night about the crash on 95?
"Yeah, a guy died, right?"
"Yeah, I saw it. I was like a hundred yards behind and I saw it."
"Are you serious? That's wild."

The fact that the crash was on the news gives it more gravitas and drama. In some ways, the pseudo-event, the television news story, has more experiential impact than the actual event. Media can shrink things, too. If you told some people the story of the crash and the grisly, scary things you saw, they would be sympathetic. If they had seen you saying the exact same things to a reporter on TV, some people would think you were a self-important, melodramatic putz.

What matters most here is that there is a difference between the mediated and the unmediated. The dramatic increase in the percentage of our experiences that is mediated is an enormous change in the daily life of us featherless bipeds.

Thomas Merton understood this and more. I think Merton was also saying that whatever it is that can be discovered over the radio is not "the world" in a spiritual sense; it is not the place to look for truth, virtue, community, connection, love, or depth. The guy was a monk and he had a radio, so he's not saying turn off the radio. Just don't think that what it plays is reality.

The Behavioral Psychology of Media

YOU SPEND A tremendous amount of time with your television. Are you nice to it? Are you kind? Do you think I have gone off the deep end?

These are the sorts of questions that intrigued Stanford University scholars Byron Reeves and Clifford Nass. So they did some experiments to get some answers. One was the "Ed Koch Experiment." Koch was a mayor of New York in the eighties who was famous for asking everyone he met, "How am I doing?" Reeves and Nash noticed that people almost always told the mayor to his face that he was doing just dandy. But pollsters got very different, more critical results on the phone when they asked, "How is the mayor doing?" People were simply being polite to the mayor.

Reeves and Nass put a test group together and had them individually go through some basic tasks on a computer. They were presented with various factual statements such as, "According to a Harris Poll, 30 percent of all Americans kiss on the first date." The participants were then asked if they knew "a great deal," "somewhat," or "very little" about that statement. After all these steps, the computer gave the participants a short test and then told them which questions they had answered correctly or incorrectly. Finally, the computer gave a positive statement about *itself* saying it had measured the test taker well.

Then the participants were asked to evaluate how the computers had performed. Half answered the evaluation on the same computer they had been working on; the computer essentially asked, "How am I doing?" The other half moved to a different machine and were asked to evaluate the computer they had been working on. "The participants who answered questions on the same computer gave significantly more positive responses than did the participants who answered on a different computer." The participants were polite to computers, just like people were polite to Mayor Koch. They treated computers exactly as they would people.

The conclusion the authors reached has been influential among technologists, Web designers, software developers, and engineers. "The media equation—*media equal real life*—applied to everyone, it applies often, and it is highly consequential," Reeves and Nass wrote in *The Media Equation: How People Treat Computers, Television, and New Media Like Real People and Places*. "People can't always overcome the powerful assumption that mediated presentations are actual people and objects. There is no switch in the brain that can be thrown to distinguish the real and mediated worlds."

Perhaps this is part of why teenage boys are reported to have actual crushes on female characters in video games. In September 2007, the AOL website had an item headlined "Virtually Sexy: Ada's there for you when the real babes aren't." Ada is Ada Wong, "the gun-toting hottie from the Resident Evil games." The story was part of the series "Babe of the Week" in the gaming section of AOL.

If you buy this media equation but you also accept Thomas Merton's warning about deception, the more honest media equation is more like "media equals deceptive life." And indeed this gets at part of why it is so exhausting to live in the media monsoon of the twenty-first century. We're stalked by deception. "Media equals real life" is a handy aphorism for website designers. For example, experiments show that users don't like to click on faces on websites because it feels aggressive or rude. However, the fact that human responses to certain media situations are irrational does not change the metaphysical status of things—media in this case. Media is not real life.

The Ed Koch Experiment does help us understand that OmniMedia engages us on several levels regardless of content: cognitive, behavioral, and emotional. OmniMedia consumes vast swaths of our mental bandwidth even in passive interactions. It is draining. And it will get worse because technologists have read *The Media Equation* and will design media that confuses and deceives us more. Good things will come with new designs and techno-leaps, too. But at a cost. There is no such thing as a free download.

The Existentialism of Media

POP QUIZ: WHO said, "Ours is the age of advertisement and publicity. Nothing ever happens but there is immediate publicity everywhere"?

Hint: Children used to taunt him when he took walks, chanting, "Either/or, Either/or!"

If you said Søren Kierkegaard, Danish philosopher, theologian, patron saint of existentialism, 1813–55, you win.

In a short essay called "The Present Age" written in 1846, Kierkegaard said what people like Andy Warhol spent careers trying to express. And he didn't get rich and famous doing it. In an age of "advertisement and publicity"—an age of media—there is a certain kind of personal validation that comes only with being represented in media, in "advertisement and publicity." Warhol didn't think everyone would be famous for fifteen minutes simply because he thought the media could make it happen practically. The point was that people were going to *need* to be famous for fifteen minutes in order to feel properly acknowledged on the planet. As Lasch said, "Success in our society has to be ratified by publicity." Being a billionaire is not enough for Donald Trump. He has to be famous as well. This is why Paris Hilton and Britney Spears go out for a night of "fire crotching"—appearing in public with no underwear so the paparazzi take naughty pictures that make them more famous.

The same effect is in play when we bestow on mediated events more value or "reality" than real events, when the story of the car crash has more weight than the crash itself. Robert Pirsig understood this when he arrived on the West Coast after the long trip through the Dakotas and Montana in *Zen and the Art of Motorcycle Maintenance:*

> There's this primary America of freeways and jet flights and TV and movie spectaculars. And people caught up in this primary America seem to go through huge portions of their lives without much consciousness of what's around them. The media have convinced them that what's right around them is unimportant. And that's why they're lonely. You can see it in their faces. First the little flicker of searching, and then when they look at you, you're just a kind of an object. You don't count. You're not what they're looking for. You're not on TV.

Today, what do you do after you meet an interesting new person? Google them. If there are absolutely no hits, there might be an issue. Does the person really exist? Younger people are more likely to scour Facebook or MySpace to seek authoritative proof of a new acquaintance's existence. I mean, sure you meet someone and talk and stuff. But you need Facebook to *really* know them.

Consider the phenomenon of reality television in this light. To a large degree, it gives you the vicarious thrill that you, too, can be famous just for being yourself, for exposing your reality. Just being on a television show can bestow the fame that justifies an existence. You don't have to have talent or commitment. You don't have to be an actress or a senator or a quarterback. Just become a *Survivor.* You get to indulge in fantasy exhibitionism come true; your everyday life is fame-worthy. And you help supply the audience with the voyeurism they need to keep the dream alive that they, too, can have their fifteen minutes.

The Oncology of Media

KIERKEGAARD THOUGHT PEOPLE were basically media sheep, as have most media critics ever since. Thomas de Zengotita figured out how wrong that is by watching TV and listening to his kids. In *Mediated:*

How the Media Shapes Your World and the Way You Live In It, he says part of what is new about media these days is simply how self-conscious we are about it.

> Hasn't culture always filtered reality in some way and addressed people through representation of some kind—ranging from the categories built into a particular language to, say, symbolic insignia of rank and affiliation?
>
> Sure. But *being aware of that* is new. This crucial point must be grasped and retained. Awareness of "culture" was once the prerogative of a very few reflective individuals. In the postmodern world it is common sense.

It's the business of having to always decode the world again. This is what our old friend Paul Bascombe is all about. Because he *sees* what bullshit everything is, the only way to be honest is to acknowledge what bullshit it all is by becoming a "comic figure" and wearing plaid Bermuda shorts and tall dark nylon socks. Not to acknowledge the phoniness of it all is to be uncool. This is why a lot of culture aimed at kids is coolly ironic, self-mocking, and explicit in calling out phoniness. In *Mediated,* de Zengotita says *The Simpsons* is the classic example of this. It is a ruthless, hilarious, and relentlessly self-conscious takeoff on everything a kid could ever encounter in life. It is irreverent and mocks everything. It has been popular for years.

The detached, ironic take on the world has become ubiquitous. I noticed a book for preteens on my daughter's shelf the other day called *One of Those Hideous Books Where the Mother Dies.* In *The Sopranos,* Tony Soprano's protégé Christopher Moltisanti constantly compares his life and adventures to *The Godfather.* Literally, everyone's a critic.

Life as a wandering deconstructionist or comic figure is tough work. You can't do it all the time; you'd die. Maintaining awareness and distance from media could be a full-time job, and it doesn't pay. In the end it is futile anyway. The workload is infinite; the payoff is lean. Consider politics. In the sixties, political coverage that went behind the scenes and tried to describe the strategy and stagecraft of campaigns was avant-garde. Now it's not only routine, it is *all* that campaign coverage does. For every story about policy there are ten about strategy. It's less filling than Chinese food.

And it is essentially impotent. In 1984, my wife helped research a famous piece that Lesley Stahl did on *The CBS Evening News*. The piece contrasted the happy pictures the Reagan campaign produced of the president in settings such as day care centers, schools, and hospitals with budget cuts the Reagan administration enacted in corresponding programs. The CBS team thought it was a very tough, well-done piece. To their immense surprise, Reagan's top aides loved the piece. Richard Darman, Reagan's top domestic adviser, called Stahl to say he was grateful that she had used all the campaign's favorite pictures. Stahl says James Baker and Michael Deaver, two more top White House aides, were in the room with Darman, laughing and shouting that they "owed her one." They couldn't care less about the facts and figures in the piece. Stahl's story about the call became more famous than the original piece, a cautionary tale about how hard it is to get a good picture of the man behind the curtain.

Even if we could instantly decode politics, TV, and media, we can't control our own emotional and cognitive responses to media, as the Ed Koch Experiment showed. I learned this in an embarrassing way. *Family Ties* was a popular TV series in the eighties starring Michael J. Fox as the money-grubbing conservative son of lefty sixties parents. I didn't watch much television at all then and saw only a few episodes of the show. But for some reason, I watched the series finale on May 13, 1989. I sobbed like a baby. My wife came into the den, and I think she may have instantly regretted her decision to marry me. I wasn't just wet eyed. I was crying. My response was entirely Pavlovian, programmed into me by years of youthful TV watching. The producers of *Family Ties* knew how to press the right buttons: The intact family broke up when Alex left home for Wall Street. I proved Thomas de Zengotita's idea that people "can feel nostalgia for times they never lived through." Can you compensate for that with detached irony, Bermuda shorts, or a Jacques Derrida decoder ring?

The bottom line about being self-conscious and critical about our media consumption is this: It is a defensive posture. It is protecting ourselves and our kin from a predator—pernicious culture. Decoding input doesn't add to our net social capital, our time with family, our happiness, our capacity to empathize or be kind to people. It doesn't nourish our souls. It is just like putting on SPF 55 sunblock. You do it to avoid cancer.

The Moral Philosophy of Media

OMNIMEDIA: GOOD OR evil? Helpful or harmful for the species?

This argument, of course, is interminable, as we know from Alasdair MacIntyre. There are two prominent camps in the debate now. Media traditionalists basically extend Newton Minow's "vast wasteland" description of television to all nonprint media, present and future. Except for isolated spasms of quality and virtue, the culture carried by media will be infected. Whether the content is drama, comedy, social networking, or text messages, more is less: more mediation, less authenticity. It is perfectly compatible to be a media conservative and a political radical. In fact, academic liberals are among society's loudest critics of mainstream media culture, along with religious conservatives, neoconservatives, and parents of girls. People really ought to talk to one another more.

Media progressives believe the Internet is truly a world-transforming technology and a clear force for good. Internet evangelists hype the power and virtues of their technology with fervor as great as any nineteenth-century industrialist's or sixteenth-century explorer's. There are Web proselytizers for every corner of the realm: Citizen journalism and blogs will transform the news business; the eBay effect will transform commercial life; social networking will reinvent political campaigns, marketing, and puberty; the Web will carry the wisdom of crowds to a tipping point where in a blink seven habits will make society highly effective and we'll live in a perpetual state of cyber-Kumbaya.

There is a third camp, media agnostics like me. To some degree my view of media is similar to the National Rifle Association's view on guns: The media doesn't kill culture, content producers kill culture. An overdose of media—any media—is dangerous, and we are overdosing. But "media" itself has no absolute or intrinsic moral status. At a time when society is so unhappy with its public culture, more media is very simply more of a bad thing.

I think we already know who the central moral agents are in determining whether media is used for good or evil: parents. To think that the media conglomerates that control Hollywood, Madison Avenue, and newsrooms, or the government agencies charged with regulating media, are going to be a force for good is to wish for the resurrection of Abraham Lincoln. Economists might make the argument that if media is as toxic now as I say, the market will respond and produce better, healthier choices. If it doesn't, that means people like what the market is delivering to them, and people like me are just elitist curmudgeons. Well, cocaine users liked the product the market once delivered, but sure, there was demand for something better. And the market developed crack.

I have been polling most everyone I meet about what they think about media for several years. Readers e-mail me on the topic constantly. The people who like mainstream media without reservation are few.

Parents are both the front line and the rearguard. They have an affirmative responsibility to decide and control what and how much media their children consume.

Broadband Babies

IF THERE IS one crucial area that will determine the broad social benefits of new media, it is this: Can new media generate social capital and social inheritance? The single greatest explanation for why we hate us is the decline of organic community. Replacing that—reinventing it, to use a term I have grown to despise—is vital. Internet evangelists deeply believe new media is somehow replacing social capital already. But the little research into the social aspects of new media that has been done to date has been inconclusive. Some studies say media is antisocial and some say it strengthens social ties. There are also studies that show, for example, early exposure to video games and television can increase cognitive functioning; there are more studies that show they increase violent impulses, social detachment, and attention issues. There are not yet empirical answers. Don't believe anything you read for at least twenty years. Here's why:

The Broadband Baby Generation will not be graduating from college until after about 2020. We think kids born in the nineties are cyber-savvy, and they are. But only children born at the turn of the century or later are truly Broadband Babies. Only then was fast Internet service widely and cheaply available at home. Only then were desktops and lap-tops cheap enough for middle-class families to have two or three at home. Google became a verb around 2000. The iPod was launched in October 2001 and the revolution in hyper-portable OmniMedia began then. The BlackBerry wasn't common until after 2004. Technology changed massively from 1995 to 2005. We won't begin to understand the developmental, neurological, psychological, and sociological effects of true OmniMedia for another twenty years, if we're still interested and haven't outsourced thinking to India.

Until then, OmniMedia will remain disorienting.

The Journalism of Media

FINALLY, THERE IS the small matter of the media in its common usage—the news media. There is no question that the news media is a substantial carrier of why-we-hate-us germs. Much of what we hate, we encounter in the news media. Partly, that is because the news represents or covers things we hate; partly, it's because of the way the news media covers "real" things and "mediated" things. I won't get into a full polemic about my chosen profession here—don't panic. But news media is a leading second-tier cause of why we hate us.

One obvious point: There is more news media than ever before. That is not to say there is more original reporting and good journalism. There isn't. But the proliferation of online news, which is very cheap to produce, and cable news, which is relatively cheap to produce, means there is much more bulk. The vast majority of that bulk comes from a few original sources—the Associated Press, the big television operations, and the major newspapers. That basic material gets sliced, diced, and run through the news Cuisinart into virtually infinite portions served on thousands of websites, local news broadcasts, and blogs. Much of the al-leged news content we see is commentary or talking about the news. That is the cheapest content to produce. This is not intrinsically bad, but it adds to the bulk. And by the way, most people hate it, especially on television.

Is today's journalism better or worse compared to earlier American history? The very short-term answer is worse. American journalism experienced a golden era roughly from World War II until the fall of the Berlin Wall. In this period, journalism became a respectable vocation for the first time. Reporters even acquired some social prestige, which they never had before. The rise of radio and then television created jobs for reporters and real competition with print. Corporations increased manufacturing products on a mass scale, for the whole nation, not just regions: cars, beer, cigarettes, toothpaste, breakfast cereal, cookies, antacids, soft drinks, blue jeans, shampoo, aftershave, and TV dinners. These nationwide businesses needed vehicles for advertising and marketing. Television, radio, magazines, and newspapers were the only games in town and the economics of news were great. Advertisers paid for quality. Moreover, most large news organizations were in the private and benevolent hands of people like William S. Paley, Henry Luce, and the Sulzberger, Graham, Chandler, Bancroft, and Knight families. Three broadcast companies divvied up an enormous national market. And eventually most small cities had just one newspaper. These were virtual monopolies that printed money and financed the glory days of American journalism.

But that was an aberration, not the norm. Journalism in the colonial period was much like blogging today. Cheap printing allowed most anyone to become a pamphleteer, and they all had blatant ideological or partisan commitments; the notion of journalistic independence was still in gestation. The pamphleteers who waged war on people like Alexander Hamilton and Thomas Jefferson make today's tabloids look like wimps. The big difference is they didn't cover sex as explicitly and there were fewer horrible, violent crimes. The scale and quantity of journalism increased in the nineteenth century, but the quality didn't very much. Yellow journalism was born. Big newspaper wars between moguls Joseph Pulitzer and William Randolph Hearst at the turn of the twentieth century made today's news business look like the Enlightenment; their manipulations helped drive the country into the Spanish-American War. The tabloid coverage of the Leopold-Loeb murder trial in Chicago in 1924 made the coverage of the O. J. Simpson trial seem responsible. So don't think that schlock journalism is new.

Journalism by its nature focuses on the atypical, not the normal or the routine: "Fire at Lincoln Chemical" is a headline and "Lincoln Chemical Operates Normally Yesterday" is not. News is mostly bad news: "Harold Klotz Arrested for Embezzling" is a story and "Harold Klotz Completes Another Day of Business as Usual" is not.

So really what is most different today is quantity and speed, the physics of news. Fresh news is available to consumers 24/7. It is instantaneous and global. Cable's argument-as-news is new, though not hugely different in spirit from the pamphleteers. But it is new in our times. It has contributed substantially to the decline of trust in the media. As Deborah Tannen wrote in *The Argument Culture,* "The spirit of attack today—aggression in a culture of critique—is disinterested, aimed at whoever is in the public eye. And a show of aggression is valued for its own sake. In other words, it's agonism: automatic, knee-jerk aggression." "Agonism" is a good word. To biologists, "agonism" involves instinctive aggressive or defensive behavior. Political philosophers use "agonism" to describe the idea that conflict is both socially useful and perpetual. Tannen's "agonism" nicely combines these two notions plus what we see on cable every day.

News consumption has also become bulimic. Readers and viewers gorge on one story at a time and then get sick of it and purge. News purveyors know this and prey on it. During the binge, audiences become mavens; they know every detail of the story and follow it with devotion and fervor, almost addiction. The stories we have binged and purged on are almost impossible to recollect a few years later: the Rhode Island nightclub fire; the D.C. snipers; the Elizabeth Smart case; the murders of Laci Peterson, Chandra Levy, and JonBenet Ramsey; Anna Nicole Smith's death. The stories aren't always trivial: space shuttle disasters, Columbine, Virginia Tech. But it is all part of the raging OmniMedia tsunami. Awash in it, it is challenging to discern the trivial from the vital. The trivial generally triumphs.

The Internet has certainly made it easier to get news and original material from multiple sources, a wonderful thing. You can read the daily papers of any country on the planet at your desk. News consumers are generally sophisticated and skeptical, also a good thing unless it turns into abject cynicism. We're nearly at that point today. Overall, the economics of the news business are disastrous. In 2007, the only sectors that were growing were online news and the ethnic press. Online news, however, provides little original reporting or news gathering. It processes news and distributes it conveniently and efficiently. But it is not yet replacing print and broadcast reporting. One of the larger news sites in the country actually has no human beings doing news work. Google News automatically finds and formats news stories from other outlets.

In a period of social stress and technological change, expect quality to decline further in journalism, providing even more reasons to hate us.

Master of Your Domain

THERE IS ONE major difference in OmniMedia's Phase Two change compared to chapter 3's Phase One social change: You can turn it off. "In a mediated world," Thomas de Zengotita wrote, "the opposite of real isn't phony or illusional—it's optional." You can say no. You can't avoid the staph infection in your leg; you can avoid reading every article on the Web about flesh-eating bacteria. But can you avoid the "pictures in your head" that shape the lives of Chris Eads's congregants?

Too many pictures, too many options, overload us, despite what modern economics preaches. After a certain level, more choices usually mean more stress, more time devoured, more buyer's remorse, and more feeling out of control. Most people know this by experience, but psychologists have shown it in the lab as well.

So worship the off button. Cherish the no-cell-service zones. Accidentally lose the BlackBerry on purpose. Instead of decoding your media life more vigilantly, just denounce it more. Diet, don't binge. Don't listen to the radio to find the world or soothe the soul.

And don't kid yourself that phoniness and artifice are packaged only by media. The real world is full of it, too. And there is no off button for that.

Chapter Five

PHONY PEOPLE, PHONY PLACES

PHONINESS IS ONE of the things we hate most. It is what I hate most in everyday life. Sure, injustice, war, famine, and racism are all more hateful than phoniness. But down a few notches on scales of seriousness, phony people, fake places, and artificial products drain our spirits.

I began this book with a story about the Tomb of the Unknowns. The fact that the Pentagon put human remains in the tomb that were not, in fact, unknown was a more profound insult to Vietnam vets and the country than not putting in any remains at all. That is the special perniciousness of fakery; it breeds distrust and cynicism. And we are bombarded with it relentlessly. Every time the phrase "managed care" is used, phoniness is being perpetrated. Like medical sheep, we are asked to believe the "managed" part of the care is getting us better doctors, treatment, compassion, and savings. I have never met a person who experienced this to be the case. But there's no choice but to swallow "managed care" because there *is* no other kind of care, as millions of uninsured people know. The fakery of "managed care" is like the daily lie we are told by companies that advertise, "We care about you."

Phoniness is not trivial. For example, much of the rage over the second Iraq War comes from the fact that the Bush administration's case for war came to be seen as phony and even fraudulent. This was true with the Vietnam War as well. Of course, we recognize the cruelty of the bloodshed and the tragedy of war. Obviously, we deplore the inept state-craft and military execution. We accept with some fatalism the role of human error, confusion, and fear in war. But to intentionally deceive a democratic country to legitimize starting a war? This infuriated the American people. Before the war, Congress and the voters were told Iraq was harboring al-Qaeda, hiding and building weapons of mass destruc-tion, poised to destabilize a region, and, finally, capable of flourishing into a beautiful democracy for all the world to be inspired by—right after it was conquered. None of that was true.

The stagnant, procrastinating debate over global warming is phony in a different way. The Bush administration and a diminishing group of propagandists simply dismissed the science of climate change until very recently. They were supported by a shrinking cadre of scientists who agreed. The press felt it had to give the two sides equal time to be fair and balanced. But in the "reality-based community" of scientists, there aren't two equal sides. There is a scientific consensus and then there are a few renegades. There's certainly deep disagreement about what to do about the problem, but not about the basic factual picture. The honest, adult debate is about policy in the face of uncertainty. But arguing with the Bush position was like arguing with Holocaust deniers: absurd. Ex-cept in this case, George Bush, the Global Warming Denier-in-Chief, was president, so he won.

This is macro-phoniness. Micro-phoniness is the twenty something indie rock music hipster who hangs out at a trendy, anti-trendy club wear-ing a vintage gas station shirt and orders Pabst Blue Ribbon because he's trying to look working-class and cool at the same time. Or the white sub-urban teen who calls his buddies "dawg" and wears baggy pants and a do-rag so he looks like a ghetto hip-hop stud. Or Emily. One fall during a week of extraordinary monsoons, our hot water tank burst and flooded the basement, and I had to call a company my insurance carrier assigned to help dry out the basement. "It's a great day at ServePro, this is Emily, how can I help you?" Emily said. How could this possibly be a great day at ServePro? Basements were flooded all over Washington. Their office was going nuts. Great day? No way. This is the phony, synthetic, corporate claptrap of the sort we're supposed to politely swallow every day.

Micro-phony is the brochure I got from a planned community in Oak Ridge, Tennessee, "Rarity Ridge: A Place Called Home." Home? I live in Washington, D.C. Still, Rarity Ridge could enhance my family's "active lifestyle" with a health club, sidewalks, a water park, a marina, and its own nature director, the brochure assured me. Sidewalks—as part of my personal lifestyle! "With so many incredible amenities to choose from, Rarity Ridge will become your haven for healthy, active living in a world set apart from any other place you could imagine." Huh? Like Hogwarts Academy or Narnia or something?

A "Ritz-Carlton managed community" outside Washington, D.C., called Creighton Farms advertised that it "is a new community rich with tradition." Oh, what rich bullshit. How can a *new* community be rich with *tradition?* How can a real community be managed by Ritz-Carlton?

During the Vietnam War, Lyndon Johnson was hamstrung by what was called the "credibility gap." We now face a chronic authenticity gap.

The opposite of phoniness is authenticity. Perceiving that someone or something is a fake stimulates a frustrated, unmet desire for the authentic, and that creates anger. Or belligerence. Or comic irony if there is a degree of self-awareness and detachment. Phoniness is easier to spot than authenticity, and it is far more available. OmniMedia promiscuously creates opportunities for fakery on a historically grand scale. The fluidity of modern lifestyles does the same. It is very hard for a shepherd in a subsistence economy to pretend to be a Hell's Angels biker or a beatnik. It is very easy for a commodities trader to pretend to be a bohemian or a housewife to be a yogi. Our friend Dana, a songwriter, went to a Christmas party in Manhattan and casually asked a man she was chatting with what he did. He said he played the violin. Being a musician, Dana was excited and curious. Was he in an orchestra? A teacher? Well, actually, he worked at a hedge fund. But he did play the violin.

The Opposite of Phony

WHAT PLEASES US, what we crave, is authenticity, in people, places, performance, and products.

So what is this thing we call authenticity? "Authenticity" is a word used by philosophers and is associated with the other Big A's of existentialism: anomie, angst, and alienation. The authentic man or woman defies convention, shuns naïveté and blinders, and wears only black. That use of authenticity became mainstream and almost commercial after the sixties. Authenticity was equated with being "healthy" in the therapeutic sense. If you were too accepting of convention, it implied you were either faking it or were simply brainwashed, hence inauthentic. The Me Decade created a whole character trait the modern American had to embrace—"being real." Gag me.

The first truly modern articulation of this view of authenticity came from Jean-Jacques Rousseau during the eighteenth-century Enlightenment. Philosophy had been primarily concerned with absolute truth, divine truth, the good, virtue—things that supposedly existed in the objective world. Rousseau was interested in Rousseau. He was interested in the idea that the new frontier for finding truth and meaning was to be found by looking in, not *out*. Rousseau believed society corrupted human nature as it existed in the original "state of nature." Like centuries of Holden Caulfields who followed, Rousseau thought the phony conventions of society deformed authentic human nature. He intended to reclaim it. Thus Rousseau began his *Confessions* with this ever-so-humble declaration:

> I have resolved on an enterprise which has no precedent, and which, once complete, will have no imitator. My purpose is to display to my kind a portrait in every way true to nature, and the man I shall portray will be myself.
>
> Simply myself. I know my own heart and understand my fellow man. But I am made unlike anyone I have ever met: I will even venture to say that I am like no one in the whole world. I may be no better, but at least I am different.

"At least I am different." I am Jean-Jacques. I am Sheila, the messiah of Sheilaism, my own religion. I am Jerry Rubin, revolutionary turned seeker. I am Paul Bascombe. "I am woman, hear me roar," as Helen

Reddy sang to the giggles of generations. This is the kind of authenticity we know and loathe. It is *not* the kind of authenticity we truly crave, but it is what we are served all too often. It is pseudo-authenticity.

A picture-perfect example of Rousseau's authenticity cheapened is in the 2004 movie *Garden State*. Andrew is an uncommunicative struggling actor in Los Angeles who comes back home to New Jersey for his mother's funeral. He falls for a bouncy girl named Sam.

> **Sam:** *You know what I do when I feel completely unoriginal?*
> **Andrew:** *What?*
> **Sam:** *[She sings nonsense sounds.] I make a noise or I do something that no one has ever done before. And then I can feel unique again even if it's only for like a second.*
> **Andrew:** *So, no one's ever done that?*
> **Sam:** *No, not in this spot. No. You just witnessed a completely original moment in history. It's refreshing. You should try it.*
> **Andrew:** *Oh, no. Thanks.*
> **Sam:** *No, come on.*
> **Andrew:** *I think that was good enough for both of us.*
> **Sam:** *Come on. What are you, shy? This is your one opportunity to do something . . . that no one has done before and that no one will copy again throughout human existence. And if nothing else, you'll be remembered as the one guy who ever did this. This one thing.*

This is typical pseudo-authenticity. It is a lazy form of Sheilaism. Now, the wonderful thing for practitioners of existentialism-lite like Sam is that creating a "completely original moment in history" poses no challenge and is just as authentic as writing fine poetry or developing a perfect golf swing. And it is a whole lot easier to produce. This is our old friend narcissism.

We want much more meat and style than the random noises of narcissism, however. We want human contact. We want a story. We especially love confessions like Rousseau's. We want a story like *A Million Little Pieces,* James Frey's memoir of his rehabilitation from being a drunk and an addict. It was the second-biggest-selling book in America in 2005,

after a Harry Potter novel. I never read *Pieces* because by the time I heard
about it, it was revealed that parts of the memoir were made up. Frey as-
serted what he did was acceptable because the "writer of a memoir is re-
tailing a subjective story." Frey is part of a tradition of phonies who
knowingly sell fake versions of themselves or of history. "And they remind us that self-dramatization (in Mr. Frey's case, making himself out
to be a more notorious fellow than he actually was, in order to make his
subsequent 'redemption' all the more impressive) is just one step removed from the willful self-absorption and shameless self-promotion
embraced by the 'Me Generation' and its culture of narcissism," wrote
Michiko Kakutani, a book critic for *The New York Times*. "This relativistic
mindset compounds the public cynicism that has hardened in recent
years, in the wake of corporate scandals, political corruption scandals
and the selling of the war against Iraq on the discredited premise of
weapons of mass destruction. And it creates a climate in which concepts
like 'credibility' and 'perception' replace the old ideas of objective
truth."

Frey got caught, so chalk one up for the reality-based community.
But it was a modest win. The kind of moral subjectivism that makes
James Frey think it's honorable to lie about your autobiography allows
George W. Bush to lie about torturing "enemy combatants" and Bill Clin-
ton to lie about that woman, Ms. Lewinsky. There is a continuum of
phoniness and truthiness from petty to tragic.

Way Beyond Sheilaism

ONE OF THE reasons we hate phoniness is because we all have little
pieces of Sheila, Sam, and James Frey in us, and it is not pleasant to be
reminded of that. For example, earlier I gave a sketch of my mother's
life that I thought was authentic. But I don't know that my sisters and
brother would think it's perceptive or even accurate. And every adolescent in the world has at some point wanted to be or do something brand-
new, something that has never been done, just like Sam. Most all of us
moderns believe, consciously or not, that being faithful to "who we really
are" is a paramount human virtue and an essential ingredient for happiness. So we should let that insight curb our impulse to condemn

phonies. We cannot give up phony-spotting, however. That would be sui-
cidal.

In the end, it is more important to get a handle on what is authentic than what is phony. It is essential in modern America to have a conception of authenticity that goes beyond pure selfism or subjectivism. A
good starting point is one of the most famous pieces of advice ever given.
It came from Polonius to his son, Laertes, in *Hamlet:*

> *This above all: to thine own self be true*
> *And it doth follow, as the night the day,*
> *Thou canst not then be false to any man.*

From this passage, we can unpack a richer idea of authenticity.

First, there is simple sincerity: "to thine own self be true." The Random House dictionary defines "sincerity" as "freedom from deceit,
hypocrisy, or duplicity; probity in *intention* or in communicating; earnest-
ness [emphasis mine]." Usually when we say someone is sincere, we are
talking about their intentions. Sincerity applies only to people. Authenticity, in contrast, also applies to things: "That is an authentic Picasso."
For something or someone to be authentic, there must be something
more than "probity in intention." The statement, person, or thing must
also actually be genuine or not false. Good intentions are not enough.

Returning to Polonius, why does it follow "as the night the day" that
being true to "thine own self" will also mean that you cannot then "be
false to any man"? What is the necessary connection? It is that you *cannot* be true to yourself and be false or insincere to others. Being fake to
another is to betray yourself as well. If you are true to yourself, you will
be true to others. Being authentic—"to thine own self be true"—*demands*
moral action: being true to another. Modern Americans hate those kinds
of demands. Still, this is a commonsense understanding of what it takes
to be authentic in a meaningful way that is neither selfish nor frivolous.

This reading of *Hamlet* is swiped from the literary critic Lionel
Trilling's book *Sincerity and Authenticity.* "If sincerity is the avoidance of
being false to any man through being true to one's own self," Trilling
wrote, "we can see that this state of personal existence is not to be at-

tained without the most arduous efforts." Authenticity takes more than making random noises like Sam. It takes discipline and tenacity, unlike gooey spiritualism like Sheila's. This also is common sense; we recognize and respect effort.

So here we have, after sincerity, the next essential elements of authenticity: a moral component and "arduous efforts."

Part of what is phony and empty about Sheila and Sam is that they don't consider the effects of how they act on others. We recognize the absence of this moral impulse in some seekers, in people who are finding themselves in ways that are obviously selfish to observers. We see it in parents who put finding themselves or professional glory before raising their children. Or careerists who put their march up the ladder of their "personal goals" before their obligations to stockholders, employees, and colleagues. These people easily recognize the virtue of "to thine own self be true," but they don't easily see the connection to not being "false to any man" and to morality.

We usually recognize the person who takes shortcuts to authenticity and avoids the "arduous efforts." There is a difference between someone who announces he is born again one day and my friend Greg, who studied at night after work for years to become a deacon in the Catholic Church. There is a difference between someone who reads a self-help book Oprah recommended and becomes a changed person ("a new me!") and someone who leaves a lucrative career to teach. There is a difference between the trivial, repetitive seeking of Jerry Rubin and the life of a sober adult.

Tony Hendra, the British comedy writer and an original editor of *National Lampoon,* wrote a beautiful memoir about his lifelong relationship with a monk called *Father Joe: The Man Who Saved My Soul.* Hendra was cynical, reckless, and a partier. When he became depressed about his job, he pondered the words Father Joe gave him to approach work in a meaningful frame of mind: "All this done joyfully, thankfully, unselfishly, conscientiously becomes . . . prayer?" Working and living for others with sincerity and effort may not become prayer, but it will become more sacred to you and others.

Faking Authenticity

WE ALSO KNOW how to make ourselves seem authentic to other people through easy intimacy, a notorious American quality. Post-sixties, hyper-*Oprah* culture celebrates confession and exposure. Sometimes this can be useful: When Betty Ford, the wife of President Gerald Ford, publicly told the story of her alcoholism, she not only was admired, she inspired alcoholics to get treatment. That is very different from having a just-met acquaintance share the story of her first orgasm or his newfound sobriety. "Sharing" culture counts such disclosure as acts of authenticity. These open secrets may be perfectly sincere and not at all manipulative. But when such disclosures come outside of a truly intimate relationship, one should be wary.

The confessional mode is also easily exploited by modern marketing. In one of those free, repulsive super-glossy urban luxury magazines called *DC: Modern Luxury,* there was an advertisement for a company called Aletheia Research and Management with a picture of its smiling chairman and CEO with his slicked-back hair, Peter J. Eichler, Jr. In a large font, the pull-quote said, "When I was young, I sometimes had trouble fitting in because I just looked at things differently." Poor puppy. The text talked about all his ancestors who had been in the investment business. The idea seemed to be that all this confiding might make some poor schnook invest with this character. Movie stars do this before they release a movie. They go on morning TV shows to reveal a new secret about their private life—a bout with bulimia, an autistic cousin, a flasher next door, a dyslexic child, or an adolescent battle with eczema. This is simply marketing through false intimacy.

A more extreme example is a television show called *Intervention,* a reality show that follows addicts around. It's "a powerful and gripping television series in which people confront their darkest demons and seek a route to redemption," according to the show's website. "Each *Intervention* episode ends with a surprise intervention that is staged by the family and friends of the alcohol or drug addict." The show is a perfect orchestration where exhibitionism serves voyeurism and alienation feeds exploitation, all supposedly in the name of intimacy, authenticity, and honesty.

Surrounded by blatant phoniness and pseudo-authenticity, and confused ourselves, we need some clarity about what is authentic. In sum, there are three elements of an authentic person that we rightly seek and admire: sincerity, moral consideration, and effort. Selfishness and sloth are warning signs of fakery.

Beyond Chop Suey

WE ALSO CRAVE and recognize authenticity in things, activities, and places, not just people. The concept of the "authentic Picasso" applies broadly. This aspect of authenticity entails sincerity, moral honesty, and effort but goes further. The authentic thing or action must be virtuous in the sense in which Alasdair MacIntyre used the word. For any craft, art, work, or practice, there are virtues. There are virtues unique to a cabinetmaker, and so we can distinguish authentic cabinetry from cheap, artless carpentry.

I grew up thinking takeout chop suey was great Chinese food. But I had never visited a Chinese restaurant until after my first year of college. When I encountered well-made, authentic Chinese food, it was unimaginably better. When we discover such virtues, we are pleased. We don't need to be experts to recognize pride in craft, individuality, and commitment. We know the difference between a McDonald's hamburger and a mom-and-pop burger. We settle for McDonald's, but that is not really what we crave. But often instead of seeking better, we seek more. Bigger portions. Bigger houses. Bigger jewelry. Bigger breasts. Bigger without better is never filling. Once you have become gluttonous, satisfaction is unattainable. There is never enough. You want bigger portions and "all you can eat" buffets. Someone always has a bigger house, a more expensive car, a more famous acquaintance. Soul gluttony is infinite.

We have become obese, physically and spiritually.

Marketers know this, and they also know what can stimulate *feelings* of authenticity or "fullness" and cravings for it. Something about the mix of salt and fat in a McDonald's Quarter Pounder is addictive. Old things usually feel more authentic than new things. An established neighborhood with wide streets, old shade trees, and modest, lived-in homes will feel different than McMansions on a razed cornfield. Many, maybe most, people prefer the big, new house, which is fine. But the places do have a different emotional feel. Unfortunately, marketers and designers can incite the feelings of authenticity with nostalgic language and graphics. "Old-fashioned root beer" and peanut butter sandwiches at a chain restaurant like Potbelly stimulate the "comfort food" glands. The pseudo-authentic is cheap in every way.

This is also true of beliefs. What religion are you? When someone simply says Catholic, Baptist, Hindu, or Jewish, 99 percent of us don't bat an eyelash: a natural answer to a natural question. When the answer is born again, pantheistic, "born Jewish Reform but now I'm Orthodox," or Buddhist from a WASP family, there is a cognitive twitch. It may be rank prejudice, but the authenticity radar picks up something nonetheless.

Phonies vs. Hypocrites

THERE ARE DEGREES of phoniness. In public life, there are blatant phonies who have been fully exposed. Former speaker of the House Newt Gingrich is a classic exposed phony. While he was leading the charge to impeach Bill Clinton for essentially philandering, Gingrich was conducting an extramarital affair of his own, he admitted long after the fact. Richard Mellon Scaife inherited the Mellon family fortune and used a chunk of it to fund the infamous "Arkansas Project" that tried to dig up dirt on Bill and Hillary Clinton; it turned out that Scaife had his own skeletons, including a long affair with a prostitute who had a rich criminal history, according to a lawsuit brought by his second ex-wife. The former congressman and boy-partisan Mark Foley is another hall of famer. Preacher-poachers like Jim Bakker, Jimmy Swaggart, and Ted Haggard are clerical examples. Rush Limbaugh's moralism and get-tough-on-crime shtick was belied by his troubles with illegal possession of prescription drugs. Jesse Jackson's preaching was fatally undermined when it was revealed the married father also had an out-of-wedlock child as an adult; his phoniness was sealed when he kept on preaching from his high horse. Until about ten years ago, Congress exempted itself from almost all the laws that applied to every other workplace in America—safety, equal opportunity, and the like.

Public hypocrites are one tier down on the phony food chain from blatant phonies. The measure of hypocrisy for a public person and a private person is different, which is proper. For example, we have a hybrid car but we also run the air-conditioning too much. That is somewhat hypocritical. On the other hand, my family doesn't publicly pose as a "green family." We don't take taxpayers' money or contributions from donors. We don't go around smashing in the windshields of Hummers. But when I write a column or a book, I've entered the public domain. So my writing is rightly held to a different scale of hypocrisy than my family's private life. And trust me, for most everything I write I will be called a hypocrite (or worse). People who know me privately and think I'm a rat also think I'm a hypocrite for even publishing my opinions. Journalism is public, and there are consequences for missteps that are tolerated in private—like hypocrisy. Worse forms of phoniness ought to carry worse punishments. When a young reporter at *The New Republic* named Stephen Glass was caught making up stories, he was fired. Good. When a movie was made about him, he was given the greatest treasure society bestows besides money—celebrity. Very bad.

So what's the difference between blatant phonies and public hypocrites? Blatant phonies set themselves up as moral exemplars in public while engaged privately in behavior they publicly condemn. Public hypocrisy can be more in the eye of the beholder. Usually hypocrisy stems from inconsistency: A senator's position on gas mileage is inconsistent with his Lincoln Town Car or his vote on global warming, for example.

The role personal history plays in judging public figures provides interesting debates now, and I am not just talking about sex scandals, immigrant nannies, and financial chicanery. In the years of Bush the Younger, there was a group of Republican government officials and outside academics or propagandists who were known as the chickenhawks. Some of the most vocal and self-certain backers of the second war in Iraq had no military experience themselves: Karen Hughes, Karl Rove, Condoleezza Rice, Richard Perle, Douglas Feith, I. Lewis "Scooter" Libby, William Kristol, Paul Wolfowitz, and Tom DeLay. Oh yes, and Vice President Dick Cheney. For some reason I don't fully understand, it wasn't considered polite or legitimate to call someone a chickenhawk. I don't know why. Some of these chickenhawks explicitly condemned John Kerry during the 2004 presidential campaign for what he did while in combat in Vietnam. These people, who were never in the service themselves, questioned Kerry's honor by attacking his later criticism of that war and challenged his bravery by giving credence to rumors that some of his medals weren't properly earned. Call it the Gall of the Chicken-hawks.

For his part, John Kerry was one of the wealthiest people in history to run for president. His way of living was extraordinary beyond imagination thanks to his marriage to the heiress to the Heinz fortune. His running mate, John Edwards, who made his own fortune as a trial lawyer, made poverty the focus of his 2004 and 2008 presidential campaigns. There are lots of megarich Democrats. The Clinton family is among them now. I don't begrudge the rich high office, but they do have a credibility problem when they attack "the rich and powerful" and call for raising taxes. The limousine liberal is a cousin of the chickenhawk. Strangers to war decide soldiers' fate and strangers to the middle and lower class decide their taxation and claim to be of the people. A CEO eliminates a corporate pension plan while maintaining a lifelong payout for himself.

The Phony Next Door

SO FAR I'VE been talking about phonies seen only through media—famous phonies. What about everyday phonies? Of course there are blatant phonies and hypocrites in almost any kind of community—Congress, a local school board, or a condo board. Generally, a phony used to be either a poseur or a blind conformist. (And for the record, I'm not being a poseur by using the word "poseur"; my grandmother used the word all the time. I swear, I inherited it. It's authentic!) Those are the kinds of phonies Holden Caulfield hated. A poseur is a dentist from New Jersey who wears a cowboy hat or a greeting card writer in Kansas City who wears a beret. Easy to spot and hard to feel sorry for, though that is the proper response.

Conformists are rarely considered phonies anymore. That is because we long for something to conform to. Say a young woman totally and thoroughly buys into the whole Harvard-MBA, investment-banking-career, hedge-fund-husband, two-kids-raised-by-nannies "picture of life." She isn't phony, and few would call her that today. You might say Our Ms. MBA is shallow, greedy, smart, or sympathetic, depending on your own life aesthetic. But unless she was hypocritical—say by always denouncing *other,* greedier young investment bankers—there appears to be nothing intrinsically phony about her life.

But there is. We are now getting into the most important and most insidious aspect of modern phoniness, and I don't think even Holden Caulfield would easily recognize it.

The Marketed Life

THE ISSUE WITH Our Ms. MBA is not quite phoniness. It is artificiality, another form of inauthenticity. She doesn't need her head examined; she needs the "picture of life" in her head examined.

The pictures in our heads are increasingly the product of an amorphous, invisible blend of media, marketing, and a deficit of social inheritance and authority of tradition. Marketers now push whole lives and lifestyles, not just shampoo and breath mints. The risk is that individuals buy into this unwittingly. When that happens, when a life is heavily and blindly influenced by marketing and commercial culture, a life is a product. This kind of life is supposed to look a certain way, have a theme and consistency, and be authentically crafted by the consumer of that life— you. When you use a ring tone to help define yourself, you're in trouble.

Allow me to take another quick example from my buddy Frank Bascombe. At the opening of *The Lay of the Land,* Frank, who is being treated for prostate cancer, reads a news story about a woman who was teaching a nursing class at a college in Texas. A male student and war veteran, Don-Houston Clevinger, "who had done poorly on the midterm," came to class with a gun in a rage. He asked the teacher, "Are you ready to meet your maker?" The teacher said, "Yes. Yes, I think I am."

This sent Frank into a tailspin. Frank wasn't at all ready to meet his maker. Remember, he hadn't even found his "character" yet. It suddenly occurred to Frank that he had not yet "fucked a movie star, adopted Viet-

namese orphans and sent them to Williams, hiked the Appalachian
Trail, brought help to a benighted, drought-ravaged African nation,
learned German . . ." Frank didn't have his obituary ready, his organ
donor card filled in, or his pallbearers selected. Frank wasn't ready to
meet his maker because he hadn't yet "gotten my message out properly."

We have imposed on ourselves a bizarre notion that a life should
have a message, just like a candidate or an advertising campaign. That's
part of why the hipster wears the gas station shirt, the New Jersey phony
wears the cowboy hat, and Paul Bascombe wears plaid Bermuda shorts.
A life needs a good theme these days. Without being known by people
in a community, we need spin and a message.

Pimp My Kid

IT'S MUCH WORSE than that, though, and I need Steven Roy Goodman to help me explain. Goodman is a college admissions consultant in
Washington, D.C. He graduated from Duke in 1985, has a law degree
from the University of Southern California, and has a master's degree in
education from the University of Pennsylvania. For about twenty years,
Steve Goodman has been helping high school students try to get into the
college of their choice. His full-service plan begins in a student's sophomore year and cost $43,000 in 2007. That buys the family virtually unlim-
ited access to Goodman, a very smart and kind man. He will help select
a child's extracurricular activities, summer plans, courses, test prepara-
tion programs, and sports regime. If the child signs up junior year, the
parents pay only $29,000.

Check your gag reflex and try to transcend how repelled you may be
by the concept of rich people paying $43,000 for admissions consulting.
Ignore totally the unfairness of it and the advantages it gives the
megarich over the rest of us, as if they need more. Ignore even the fact
that Goodman says parents often "outsource" parenting to him. He told
me one story he said was typical about parents who called him on a Friday night because they couldn't agree on whether to let their daughter
go out Saturday night. The mother thought it was a good idea to let the
girl play off some stress. The father thought preparing for some upcom-
ing tests was more important. It was up to Steve Goodman, college ad-

missions consultant, to decide. Another couple couldn't decide about letting their child go on an expensive tour and "community service" trip to Costa Rica. Many high schools now require students to prove they have spent a certain number of hours performing community service. So there are upscale programs that send rich kids to places like Costa Rica, Thailand, Senegal, or Peru to climb mountains, raft whitewater rapids, and get their needed community service hours out of the way. The father in this couple thought this was ridiculous, "purchased" community service. The mother was all for it. Steve made the call. In his opinion, such decisions matter "very much" to admissions.

"My students plan and plan and plan," Goodman told me. This is different from twenty years ago. "The kids now are much more career driven, much more." Goodman was shocked when he went to a twenty-fifth-year reunion for an Ivy League school and attended a seminar on "reinventing yourself." "I was amazed at what I saw. It was so far removed from the conversations I have with my students and families. They are so linear. My students are planners." The fortysomethings at the reunion were still using the pre-dot-com, antiauthoritarian dialect of selfism, where fuzzy feelings are paramount. Goodman's young students use the new, OmniMedia and OmniMarketing dialects of selfism that are equally Me-focused, but the Me needs to be messaged, credentialed, coherent, and marketed. Feeling is not enough. Selling oneself is the goal.

At the same reunion, Goodman was stunned by something else. "Someone at the reunion won a big award; she was very famous," he said. "In her acceptance speech, she didn't mention what she did, what her accomplishments were! My students just list off their accomplishments."

The essence of Goodman's job is to give those accomplishments and all that planning a crisp theme. "There's an expectation that the things you do in your life fit together. I'm not sure that was true twenty or thirty years ago." He's right, it wasn't. If it were, I wouldn't have gotten into college.

Goodman's challenge is to make these seventeen-year-old lives "fit together" in the admissions application. A good applicant's life needs some coherence. If a kid is not going to excel at violin or baseball and turn the activity into a credential, get rid of it and focus on what will build a better application. The fun of or passion for baseball is a luxury the modern college applicant can ill afford. It is not what you *do* that matters, it is how you *appear*.

There is a word for this: marketing.

Goodman is there to market a child to colleges. Colleges say they don't want this. "So many students, like presidential candidates, seem to work under the management of a handler," the dean of admissions at Pomona College wrote in *Newsweek*. "How do we sort out the genuine student from the image essentially manufactured for admissions purposes?" With good intentions, people like Steve Goodman make that job harder. "I always make sure there's at least one mistake so that the application doesn't appear so slick, or so packaged, I guess," he said. Perfection is now a turnoff. Pick your flaw carefully; you get only one.

The Product of Your Life

THIS IS INSTITUTIONALIZED phoniness. It has a social cost. When the admissions director of Brown University met with a group of alumni who interview applicants around Washington, D.C., he said they see a lot of credentials in today's applications but not a lot of joy. That's one price of peddling a soul.

Marketing a student for college does not require a $43,000 consulting fee. Parents, students, and high school college counselors know how to do this from knowledge passed down through the grades. They also know how by osmosis, because we all know how to mimic the marketing and advertising that envelops our lives. Some people submit to it, some don't.

There are complex and unintended reasons that kids are marketed to colleges, and there is no single villain. Colleges now compete for students nationally and internationally. They want to have many more people apply than could ever be admitted, because this makes them appear more selective, and they get higher rankings in *U.S. News & World Report* and other sources. So admission rates are now scarily daunting. This understandably stresses out parents and students even more. They also know that education boosts earning power more than it once did. For a generation or two now, kids have left home, gone to college, and never come back. Few parents have farms or businesses a child can join someday. Fewer and fewer live in communities where people spend their whole lives. "College choice is one of the few things they [parents] think they can control," Goodman said. "A lot of parents pretend the prestige of the school or the success of their child doesn't matter to them, but it does. A lot of parents have a sense that if the kid doesn't perform well, it's a reflection on them or on how they raised their children."

The admissions marketing process can be alienating for a kid, as it should be. In the final analysis, it is a sick way for our children to spend their adolescence. Kids feel a neurotic mandate not just to perform and achieve but to groom their "message."

Temptation also comes in the form of the popular social networking sites such as Facebook and MySpace, which give kids the opportunity to practice marketing themselves in the name of fun and socializing. They create virtual rooms for themselves on these sites that are open to almost anyone. They decorate the rooms to give others the picture of themselves they want to present. A teen will sort through hundreds of digital photographs to get the perfect few to post on Facebook. For girls, the spicier the picture, the more virtual "friends" will come calling. Most kids' pages are hilarious, irreverent, creative, and honest. Kids goof around at the edges of their identities and personalities on Facebook just as they do with their wardrobes, music, and bedroom walls. And teenagers are allowed to be narcissists, as long as they also have other duties like schoolwork, chores, jobs, and sports. But it is naïve to ignore the aspect of Facebook and its kin that is like marketing and objectification.

After college, a child must, of course, be marketed for the workplace, which often entails more credentialing in graduate school. Then there's mating. Couples often meet on websites where they can groom their image further, at least until the first date. One matchmaking site, eHarmony.com, ran ads hawking their "Compatibility Matching System" that "matches you with other singles based on 29 deep dimensions." Wow, twenty-nine dimensions, that is deep. I only have three deep dimensions and seven shallow ones.

The next marketing milestone, as we have seen with bridezillas, is the wedding. SamanthaandAlec.com has to be at least as cute as

Nick+Daisy.com. In a few years, SamanthaandAlec.com will have little Caleb and will fertilize him with Baby Einstein tapes beginning at six months so he can get into preschool, which requires tests and recommendations. (If you think this is just the province of rich urban brats, you're wrong. In fast-growing suburbs of many different income levels, the competition is just as intense and the prestige factor just as strong.) Pretty soon Caleb will be a sophomore in high school and Samanthaand Alec.com will have to decide whether to hire Steve Goodman. When Caleb has eventually entered the workforce it will be time for Samantha andAlec.com to pick a "retirement lifestyle." Here's where the market really is glutted. They might choose a golfing community, a tennis community, a skiing community, or a boating community. There are now several trendy working-farm-themed communities, gay and lesbian communities, and ones with ethnic architecture, restaurants, and style, though not necessarily ethnic people. Most will have a nice clubhouse, a fancy Amish barn, or a posh marina where AlexandraandCaleb.com can get married. Given the miracles of medicine and plastic surgery, the retirement lifestyle will be one where ninety-five-year-old Tiffanys, Ambers, and Britneys—fully Botoxed, augmented, liposuctioned, stretched, and dyed—will be romping around with one-hundred-year-old Ethans, Ryans, and Joshuas powered by Viagra and coiffed by Rogaine.

These lives are not led with malice. But from afar there is something askew and artificial about our "lifestyle" arrangements. Up close, it is often, not always, very different. The "pictures of life" for Our Ms. MBA, SamanthaandAlec.com, Steve Goodman's clients, and Chris Eads's congregants come from media-land, not from real communities or great literature and teaching. These pictures and lives compare favorably to the rest of the world. These are not families of terrorists, bigots, oligarchs, zealots, or ruling classes. These are tolerant, mostly gentle people. But collectively, we're not happy in proportion to our advantages, and we are not proud of the direction we're headed.

We have used our affluence and abundance to build screens and false idols that obscure what matters most, what is authentic, what is unmediated. We miss the seeds of happiness, which are simple: people and useful connections to people.

The Opposite of Gluttony

FINDING PEOPLE IN private life and public we deem authentic is difficult. We saw earlier the decline in the number of confidants Americans have. One can't go out scouting for authentic people. Wise people hold on for dear life to those they find, remaining blindly loyal and grateful. We also look for authenticity in *what* we do. This is the opposite of bigger portions and spiritual obesity, and we need to figure out how to do more of it.

When I am at loose ends I read survival stories, especially of South Pole adventures. Nothing soothes me like reading about Sir Ernest Shackleton's voyage on the *Endurance.* I've come to think it is because those life-and-death situations feel so unmediated, unmarketed, and unphony to me. That is reality. There's no image of anything, no spin. Just ice and death. I lust for it. Seriously. Read *Endurance* by Alfred Lansing and e-mail me if you disagree. (I once saw some huckster had cobbled a management theory out of Shackleton's epic story, and I was depressed for a week.)

The appeal of Jon Krakauer's book *Into the Wild,* and of the movie version by Sean Penn, is similar. It is the story of a college graduate, Chris McCandless, who gave away all his money after college and tried to live completely alone in the wilds of Alaska. The battle for survival and the return to the "state of nature" unfouled by human folly is a compelling fantasy of the search for the purest authenticity. It's the story behind Sam Gribley in *My Side of the Mountain,* the classic children's novel by Jean Craighead George. Sam was my introduction to the wilderness hermit world.

I saw a similar lust for the unphony in an exhibit of new American portrait artists that commemorated the opening of the renovated National Portrait Gallery in Washington, D.C. It was unusual for an exhibit of contemporary art because it was so square. There was very little high-concept, supercool, self-referential, idea-based art. Most of the pictures conveyed emotion, and most were representations of reality. Few of these portraits had prominent embellishments outside the human form. Most were stark and plain portraits. Some were hyperrealistic and looked like rich, sensuous photographs. Many were tight in on the face and intense. Others were of full bodies and more relaxed. Few had anything in the background. There weren't often noticeable settings. Symbols were rare, and few paintings hinted at any kind of story, narrative, or whimsy. I could viscerally feel the artists yearning to pierce the veils of artifice, phoniness, media, and appearances. I could feel the craving to portray the essence of a human being with heart and emotion.

Normally when I see hip as opposed to square contemporary art, I feel like I'm not one of the cool kids. I am emotionally unmoved and feel like a hick for preferring art that displays beauty or craftsmanship. Those qualities are mocked in contemporary art because they are naïve and lack irony. I went to this exhibit because a friend, Costa Vavagiakis, had a painting in the show. We all call him Gus. His portrait, *Arthur VI,* exemplified what I felt about the show.

"Arthur" is seated and shirtless, square to the viewer, before a blank, neutral background. He looks to be about sixty-five, bald, with a goatee, bags under his eyes, thick lips, saggy pectoral muscles in his chest, and a weary countenance. The painting has much more dimension than a photograph and so looks more real. It looks like a man's life.

Gus told me he was "getting down to the basics of a person . . . breaking a person down, stripping off veneer. My motor is emotional. To get intimate is what I need in the work." I've known Gus for a long time and until this conversation I never quite understood his "motor." While talking about "Arthur," he described how when he was a kid in Queens his parents made him go to Greek school. Gus would spend the time making pencil drawings of the ancient busts in the textbooks. His first drawings were of sculptures, and he got lost when drawing them. Gus feels like what he is really doing now is just trying to re-create that old feeling of immersion and add to it the years of craftsmanship. His ultimate goal is intimacy.

Gus thinks "people hate the art world." He means the world of academia, fancy galleries, and cool. "Art today is based on irony," Gus told me. "It is a passive-aggressive way to deal with the world. It's a filter." There is no room for craft or excellence in the ironic pose, Gus said. Intimacy is corny. It is the enemy. There is no room for authenticity.

Gus Vavagiakis's whole life is devoted to authenticity with his painting and what he calls "the honor of excellence." Most people try to find corners of authenticity in their lives, areas where they pursue excellence and don't compromise, perhaps with a hobby or passionate obsession—genealogy, gardening, bass fishing, marathons, or needlework. Food has become a popular and natural pursuit for authenticity hounds. Good cooking and dining is one area where you can seize control. There's a huge interest now in sustainable agriculture and cooking local and organic food. Authentic ethnic food is cherished and sought after in a way it wasn't in my chop-suey youth. Some people are rebelling against fast food, though on average Americans are getting more and more obese. Books on food—not cookbooks, but idea books—are big sellers: *The Omnivore's Dilemma: A Natural History of Four Meals* by Michael Pollan, *Fast Food Nation* by Eric Schlosser, *Heat: An Amateur's Adventures as Kitchen Slave, Line Cook, Pasta-Maker, and Apprentice to a Dante-Quoting Butcher in Tuscany* by Bill Buford, and *Animal, Vegetable, Miracle: A Year in Food Life* by Barbara Kingsolver. It's a whole new genre.

Finding a good meal or the freshest corn is also much simpler than finding a nice, affordable neighborhood to live in.

Rancho Mirage

NO PLACE ON the planet is more aptly named than Rancho Mirage. Rancho Mirage is the very wealthy neighbor of wealthy Palm Springs in the California desert. It is a freakish island of manicured green in a sea of pale sand. Bob Hope Drive, Ginger Rogers Road, Dinah Shore Drive, Gene Autry Trail, and Frank Sinatra Drive host gated communities, country clubs, malls, and occasional trailer parks. Baked dry from the desert sun, tan old men with spindly, veiny legs extending from madras shorts cruise immaculate compounds in custom golf carts. Plastic surgeons advertise on billboards next to the busiest roads. "Botox Buses" drive ladies to Mexico for discount enhancements. Shrubbery is spray-painted green.

They say Rancho Mirage is where rich people go to die, after eighteen holes.

When I visited Rancho Mirage, I fell several times for the same eerie optical illusion. I'd be walking around and notice a woman in the distance.

She'd have tight jeans, a skinny, hard-body figure, blond hair, and hip sunglasses. My Pavlovian brain, that untrustworthy microprocessor, would register "attractive female." After a few more paces, closer inspection would reveal the female apparition to be least eighty years old, her skin stretched tight as a snare drum, her body sculpted by silicone, liposuction, and plastic surgery. Hair dyed and coiffed, teeth capped, skin lasered and peeled, face painted, fingers and toes manicured, eyebrows plucked, these creatures have special devices to squeeze into jeans tight enough to choke a chicken. More than once, I gasped out loud when I realized one of these visions was a mirage. They scared the hell out of my son, who was about nine at the time. He held my hand when we walked on the street, or, more accurately, through the malls or cavernous, frigid grocery stores.

I wonder if anybody is born in Rancho Mirage. The lives of the town's more senior residents would seem unimaginable to their parents. Even their bodies would be unrecognizable. You just can't imagine people living through natural life cycles there. It suffocates with its phony "picture of life." That picture must appear to be youthful, groomed, luxurious, new and improved. It is a sum of all marketing: a mirage.

Seeking relief and adventure, my son and I drove to Legloland near San Diego. Wrong move if avoiding artificiality was my goal. The Lego castles and princes were the most realistic part of Legoland. There was more plastic surgery there than I'd ever seen in my life except in Las Vegas, where hotels put condoms and lubricants in the bathroom along with the shampoo and conditioner. The young mothers of Legoland were nipped and tucked to within cosmetic inches of their lives. Petite young women had gravity-defying boobs the size of Mount Lego. Bottle blondes had sirloin-red collagen lips that made Angelina Jolie's look like pencil lines. There were noses on long Mediterranean faces tiny and sharp enough to pierce Kevlar. Some men had steroid-pumped bicep guns that looked like flesh-toned grapefruits. Many more were fat. There were a lot of big tattoos. I don't understand tattoos at all. But you can imagine I don't think they are a sign of social enlightenment.

Taking Place Seriously

PEOPLE LEAVE THE towns and cities where they were born or even where their children were born. That is a demographic fact of life. It happens everywhere in America. It is worse in places with no more jobs. With that in mind, does it matter that a place like Rancho Fake-o feels artificial? Lots of places feel fake. And I suppose phoniness is purely in the eye of the beholder when it comes to places. My friend Robin, whom I have known since we were two, is a New York girl even though she wasn't born there. She visited often as a kid and moved there the day after college and never left. She is a singer and actress and quickly settled on the Upper West Side and began her reign. A year or two ago, we were having dinner and I was complaining about how ostentatious and unpleasant midtown Manhattan had become. Robin looked at me like I was a slow person. "I never go to midtown," she said. Neither did her friends. She described how in her eyes, the flood of investment bank money, hedge fund money, and foreign money had transformed the ultimate chic, stylish, sophisticated but campy American downtown into a museum of conspicuous consumption. Only very rich people live and shop there now, or people who want to look rich. The artists and middle class fled years ago. Most of the stores are "brands" or "labels" and not unique (restaurants are the exception; perhaps it's the food exemption). "It's not a place real people go," Robin said. I actually prefer Rancho Mirage to midtown.

Do these kinds of visceral responses to a place matter? If you throw out the extremes of poverty and climate, does physical place affect human well-being very much? Is there such a thing as authenticity of place? Or are these inconsequential matters of taste?

I've thought a lot about this because of two words that strike terror into the hearts of parents of kids born after about 1985: travel soccer.

Thanks to travel soccer, I am an expert on the suburbs and exurbs between Baltimore and Richmond. I've driven through the acres of anonymous tract housing. I may dislike Rancho Mirage and Manhattan, but many, many more Americans live in the homogeneous sprawl of places like Centreville, Virginia. And many of them hate it. The suburbs started as an idealistic, post–World War II vision of the perfect place to rear children, safe and roomy. They've become enemies of authenticity.

One of the nicer places I visited was Woodlake Village, in Chesterfield County, Virginia, southwest of Richmond, where we spent a tournament weekend. The population of Chesterfield County grew from 75,000 in 1970 to 300,000 in 2006, mostly in planned communities and tract housing. Woodlake is a "planned community," not an actual municipality. In Chesterfield and other counties around Virginia, there are many such communities in unincorporated areas with no town government, just county services. The lack of any local civic organization symbolizes a lack of deeper engagement, investment, and roots in these manufactured living zones.

According to Woodlake's website, or rather the website of its developer:

> With 5 miles of lake shoreline, Woodlake is a sparkling gem in Virginia's Chesterfield County. Beautiful homes and amenities and a true sense of community make Woodlake one of the best places to live in America.
>
> Woodlake's 53 distinctive neighborhoods are designed for comfort, recreation, and safety, and include special play areas for children and bike underpasses.
>
> *Amenities include:*
> - *1700-acre recreational lake with sailing, fishing & rental boats*
> - *Woodlake Swim & Racquet Club*
> - *Olympic-size indoor pool*
> - *Several unique outdoor pools & 60-foot waterslide*
> - *Volleyball courts*
> - *Soft & hard tennis courts*
> - *Fitness center*
> - *Central Park Soccer & Baseball Complex*
> - *Tom Sawyer Island Playground*
> - *Amphitheater & Pavilion*

- *Biking & jogging trails*
- *And more!*

Can "amenities"—"And more!"—compensate for mega-commutes, the pressure of debt, the transience of the population, the generational segregation? Can amenities replace community? This is what developers try to do. They do so either futilely or dishonestly.

Marketers try to trigger the Pavlovian responses we need to feel "nested" in "planned communities." The "neighborhoods" of Woodlake have country-squire names like Woods Walk, Waters Edge, Country Walk, Bent Creek, Shelter Cove, Mill Spring, Duck Cove, and Boyle's Cove. The tastefully landscaped homes are situated nicely near the woods, and the area has an organized, resortish feel. But there is nothing like the business section of a small town, only strip malls on both sides of busy four-lane roads a couple miles away.

We went out to dinner at a Ruth's Chris Steak House in nearby Midlothian, a town with local government. On its website, the chamber of commerce said, "Despite severe pressures, the Village of Midlothian had retained its sense of place, unlike too many suburban towns in the U.S. that have been 'lost' under corporate concrete, poorly planned asphalt and franchise-business plastic." Maybe.

Our waiter at Ruth's Chris was Dylan. He told us convincingly that his favorite was the "Oscar style" variation on any of the steaks; for an extra $12.95, they'd serve your steak with some crabmeat, three spears of asparagus, and béarnaise sauce, all on a five-hundred-degree plate. After the entrées came, the manager stopped by. He said, "My name is Kemp, K-E-M-P. If there is anything I can do to enhance your dining experience, please let me know." Like Dylan, Kemp was very friendly. Or should I say he was friendly enhanced? His language seemed programmed and market tested. It was like talking to robots there. The emphasis was on pounds of meat, ounces of fish, and degrees of the plate—the engineering of the dining experience. There is nothing left that feels imperfect, idiosyncratic, local, or spontaneous. Wine by the glass came in classy but precisely measured mini-carafes.

This stuff feels so painfully artificial. But again, so what? Some people may prefer to judge their meals by the ounce. Some people like amenities.

An interesting book by Andres Duany, Elizabeth Plater-Zyberk, and Jeff Speck called *Suburban Nation: The Rise of Sprawl and the Decline of the American Dream* says place matters intensely:

> For all of the household conveniences, cars, and shopping malls, life seems less satisfying to most Americans, particularly in the ubiquitous middle-class suburbs, where a sprawling, repetitive and forgettable landscape has supplanted the original promise of suburban life with a hollow imitation. In an architectural version of *Invasion of the Body Snatchers,* our main streets and neighborhoods have been replaced by alien substitutes, similar but not the same. Life once spent enjoying the richness of community has increasingly become life spent alone behind the wheel.

Suburban Nation makes the case that man-made geography can literally build social isolation into living places. The book was useful to me in pointing out the qualities real neighborhoods have that sprawl-burgs lack: business districts instead of shopping centers; short walks to necessities and shops; a network of small, kid-friendly, connected streets without frequent, busy four-lane border avenues that separate pods of cul-de-sacs, making biking to a friend's house impossible. In a society that is more and more nomadic, sprawl makes spontaneous, incidental "small" social contact even harder: You don't stop and roll down the car window to chat with a neighbor on a busy road; except in the most rural towns, you don't know clerks at big-box stores; you're less likely to bump into your daughter's best friend's parent in the mall than the town business district; you don't linger at a neon strip-mall convenience store the way you might at a corner store.

Suburban Nation is kind of lefty and eggheaded. And the whole anti-suburb routine can come off as snobby. But it is not. These views are shared by many suburbanites. At CrossCurrents Ministries in Sterling,

Virginia, Chris Eads recently ran a program he called "Death by Suburb." It was inspired by a book called *Death by Suburb: How to Keep the Suburbs from Killing Your Soul* by David L. Goetz, drawn from his life in the Chicago suburb of Wheaton. "Whether blue-collar or white, Yankee or Southern, west coast or east, North Dakota or southern Texas—the environment of the suburbs weathers one's soul peculiarly," Goetz writes. "Too much of the good life ends up being toxic, deforming us spiritually." "Toxic" is a word I have used frequently to describe the way many people feel about culture and the social environment today.

Death by Suburb is a smart, sometimes wise book, and it is aimed at practicing Christians. "I think my suburb," Goetz writes, "as safe and religiously coated as it is, keeps me from Jesus." If you secular readers can manage to get past the Jesus part, *Death by Suburb* sounds a lot like *Suburban Nation*. Snobbishness has nothing to do with why some people don't like sprawling suburbia.

What Chris Eads does see in his Virginia congregation is a lot of unreflective materialism that he believes is trying to fill a spiritual vacuum. "When society and culture teach to us that you have to have a Lexus to be happy, you get dissatisfaction with that old, rusty Chevy Citation. So you chase things," Eads told me, "You get a tension in your soul." That's because of the obesity syndrome: People chase more instead of better, amenities over authenticity. We pursue gluttony.

Eads had previously worked as a pastor in Marion, Indiana, near where he went to college. It was an old General Motors factory town and a stark contrast to fast-growing Loudoun County, especially the area where his church is, near the AOL campus and the tech corridor around Dulles Airport. Money came fast and easy during the dot-com boom there. "Here the roots are very loose," Eads said. "In Marion, most members of my congregation had been members for twenty to thirty years. Here, I've been at this church for two and a half years and when I mentioned to my board that I was thinking of moving on, they said that everyone would just quit the church. It's a 'serve-me' mentality. 'I'll belong and commit so long as there's something in it for me.'" Eads felt that Marion, Indiana, and Sterling, Virginia, had distinct "community cultures," even though media culture is homogenized and nationalized.

"There was a difference in materialism," he said. In Marion, "I didn't sense the same angst about wages. People weren't as worried about moving up. . . . The work ethic there was you get your reward after thirty years. You get your reward because of longevity and commitment. In the dot-com world out here, you get your bonus up front, before you take the job."

Things and amenities matter more in places with shallow social roots and scarce social inheritance like Rancho Mirage, midtown Manhattan, and Sterling than in places where people don't live among strangers, like Marion, Indiana.

A Resting Place

SOME PEOPLE DON'T really notice how unattached they are until it's too late, until it's time to think about funerals. Do you know where you're going to be buried? Have you thought about that yet? Apparently many aging boomers have just started to worry that they have no meaningful final resting places. On one level, this is just another sign of our mobility and rootlessness. For some people, it is a symbol of something more—that without community and family, there is no way, as Frank Bascombe worried, to get your message out. Stuff and money don't endure.

One popular new solution to the burial problem is "alumni cemeteries." Universities have found a market demand. Between leaving home for work or college, more moves during the career years, and often a flight south for retirement, many people have no permanent attachment to a place. Picking a plot is a disturbing reminder of this. For some people, college was the place that made the most indelible mark. Universities figured this out and then determined how to make a buck off it. Duke University charges $25,000 to have ashes buried in their small plot. "Notre Dame is designing custom coffins and urns for its 'Coming Home' mausoleum marketing campaign," reported the *Los Angeles Times*. A full-body crypt goes for $11,000. The Citadel is adding four hundred spaces for urns in its bell tower.

"There's something seminal here," the friend who first told me about this e-mailed. He is a Notre Dame alum. "I honestly don't have any idea where I would want to be buried. It's not with my parents. Washington isn't my home. New York isn't my home. There is nothing in my life that has tied me to *place,* totally different from my parents or [my wife's] for whom place was everything. And we aren't people who have moved around the world. Basically New York and Washington with a year in Tokyo."

Dying has been a business in America for a long time. But my guess is that the marketers have just begun to focus on the synergy between death and Web 2.0. Wily capitalists are not going to let colleges steal market share of burying rootless people for long. They will find a way to fill this ultimate authenticity gap. I see some kind of MySpace.com meets MeDead.com meets OurAfterlife.com in the not-so-distant future.

RIPSamanthaandAlec.com.

Chapter Six

A CIVIC WAR

THE EPITOME OF American phoniness is politics.

One reason why is that the same old teams have been fighting one another for generations. The current two-party system began in 1860 with the election of Abraham Lincoln. The Democratic Party and the Republican Party have been locked in continuous combat with no significant truces or new combatants ever since. It has been a kind of *Civic* War born in the era of the Civil War. The soldiers aren't the masses—the voters and citizenry—but the political elite who make civic life run.

The first shot in the most recent phase of this long Civic War was fired in the dark of night on August 17, 1992, in Houston, Texas, about 320 miles from the Alamo, by a renegade Republican soldier named Patrick Joseph Buchanan. It was an engagement the sitting Republican president, George Herbert Walker Bush, wished he could have avoided.

It was opening night at the Republican National Convention at the Houston Astrodome. A month earlier, the Democrats had nominated Bill Clinton and Al Gore at Madison Square Garden in New York at a slick, well-produced national convention that consistently broadcast "talking points" of change and unity. H. Ross Perot, an eccentric, entertaining third-party candidate, was beginning to look merely eccentric.

Perot actually led the three-man race in several national polls in June but then dropped out of the race. A month later, he made noises about getting back in. If he did, the polls showed he would likely hurt Bush more than Clinton. The reelection of President George H. W. Bush seemed like it could be in real trouble. Although Bush had vanquished Saddam Hussein's Iraqi troops from Kuwait in a quick military victory, the economy was shaky. Pat Buchanan had challenged the incumbent in the primaries, a sign of Bush's vulnerability. The Republican's best hope seemed to be the closet of the man from Hope, Bill Clinton. An overripe lounge singer named Gennifer Flowers had already emerged, and the Republicans were counting on another scandal or two.

That year, CBS News, where I was a junior producer, decided to cover the party conventions in a way that hadn't ever been done. The anchorman, Dan Rather, would report for most of the night from the crowded, chaotic convention floor instead of a controlled, distant anchor booth. We knew it was a stunt. But the political conventions had become so scripted and sanitized that we felt we could at least convey the energy and spirit of the event by anchoring from the floor. It was a logistical stomachache but exhilarating.

Rather was a major presence at the convention. Then the most famous newsman in the country, Rather had started his career in Houston and made his name in 1961 by reporting live from the Galveston Seawall when Hurricane Carla hit. Hurricane live shots are now a cartoonish staple of TV news, but it was a big deal then. Rather was popular in Houston. Sort of. In the 1988 campaign, Rather conducted a controversial interview about the Iran-Contra affair with another Houston transplant, Vice President George H. W. Bush, who was running to succeed Ronald Reagan. Relations between Rather and the Bush clan had been tense ever since. The Bush interview permanently put the label of "liberal bias" on Rather.

I was one of three producers assigned to work with Rather at the convention. Before we went on the air opening night, we thought an important part of the night would be an interview we had set up with George W. Bush, the president's son. The *Houston Chronicle* sent reporter Mike McDaniel to follow us that night. "It is Monday night, and Dan Rather appears tense as he prepares to enter the convention hall," McDaniel reported. "He will not enter alone. [Susan] Zirinsky will be at his side. So will floor producer Terry Martin, who will scribble out cue cards to hand to Rather. Another floor producer, Dick Meyer, will make sure interview subjects are at the ready." There was another person on the team, Stan Romaine, who was in charge of Rather's personal security.

McDaniel reported that Rather gave us a talk right before we hit the floor. "Stop. Listen. This is important," Rather said. "When we talk with George W. Bush, everything must be right. I mean it. I don't want anything wrong on this one."

The hyperventilating throng of people came at Rather from both sides. Some delegates shoved their way through to get Rather's autograph or ask if he remembered the time they met thirty years ago in Lubbock. Others turned vicious, giving Rather the finger and calling him a dirty liberal or even that long-lost insult, a Communist. There were signs that said "Rather Biased." I stopped being a producer and hunkered down as an offensive tackle blocking for my quarterback along with Stan Romaine. The interview with the younger George Bush went just fine. But that didn't turn out to be the story that night.

In the original Republican script, the magic moment of the prime-time coverage was to be a speech by their patron saint, former president Ronald Reagan. But they first had to deal with Pat Buchanan. Buchanan had leverage. He had nabbed 37 percent of the vote in the New Hampshire primary against a sitting president and was popular with the party's right wing. He would endorse Bush in Houston in exchange for a plum speaking slot, prime time on opening night—Reagan night.

With a snarling rendition of his right-wing populism, Buchanan sounded the bugle for a charge on a new flank in the Civic War:

> My friends, this election is about much more than who gets what. It is about who we are. It is about what we believe. It is about what we stand for as Americans. There is a religious war going on in our country for the soul of America. It is a cultural war, as critical to the kind of nation we will one day be as was the Cold War itself. And in that struggle for the soul of Amer-

ica, Clinton & Clinton are on the other side, and George Bush
is on our side.

The Bush campaign wanted the Buchanan endorsement, and they
even approved his speech. But they certainly didn't want Buchanan's
grenades to be *the* story. They blew it. In what turned out to be his last
major political speech, Reagan told his party that "whatever else history
may say about me when I'm gone, I hope it will record that I appealed
to your best hopes, not your worst fears, to your confidence rather than
your doubts." But the networks were out of prime-time air by then.
Buchanan was the headline.

The Illusion of a Story

GEORGE H. W. BUSH went on to lose reelection. The story that has
endured from those four broiling days in Texas, what made the 1992 Republican National Convention somewhat memorable if not historic, was
Pat Buchanan's declaration of a culture war. The story, like the convention, was a fake.

When I walked onto the floor of the convention at the Astrodome,
what I saw had about as much authenticity as the Astroturf. I saw the
same thing with the Democrats at Madison Square Garden. The conven-
tioneers for both parties weren't like other people I encountered on the
road or had covered, even people who were political junkies. They were
pretty odd, Democrats and Republicans alike. They were performing. Although we scrupulously reported that the delegates were party activists
and didn't represent the electorate as a whole, it still gave a stilted picture of the country. But we covered them because they were making
news and the convention was a news event.

Or was it?

Once upon a time, delegates at conventions had actual power. But by
1992, the conventions no longer did any real political work. Delegates
didn't select presidents, primary voters did that. Conventions weren't even
the backdrop for announcing the vice presidential nominees anymore;
that came in separately produced photo ops. Conventions rubber-stamped
party platforms that were bland, negotiated, ritualistic documents that

would be ignored the day after the election, if not before. Conventions had become fabricated marketing events, and by 1992 everyone knew it. Delegates were props. Through scripted, produced telecasts and controlled rhetoric, the party marketed its newest product, the nominee for the president of the United States of America. Now with 20 percent more cavity-fighting power.

Journalists searched for themes, conflicts, stories, controversies, fresh angles, and, most of all, glitches. But it was slim pickings. Political reporters had been writing stories about how conventions for the past several cycles had become charades, but we still wanted to believe conventions were important. We didn't want to give up the rare extended "airtime" American politics received during conventions. We didn't want to give up the parties and the expense-account fun.

A Phony War

ANOTHER PART OF the mirage was the glitch that got the attention: Buchanan's proclamation of culture war in America.

First of all, the event was orchestrated by the party and the networks. As Martin Plissner tells it in *The Control Room: How Television Calls the Shots in Presidential Elections,* the networks planned just one hour of coverage for opening night, and Bush's team wanted Reagan to be the star. But Bush's handlers had promised Buchanan time in the spotlight, too. CBS agreed to help out and start their coverage a half hour earlier than planned so Buchanan and Reagan could play a twin bill. As Plissner, who was in on the negotiations, said, it sounded like a "swell" show. ABC followed. But NBC didn't. So the Republicans delayed Buchanan a half hour hoping that both he and Reagan could squeeze into the one hour when all three networks were on the air. It didn't work.

History has shown that not all political theater is without consequence. This curiously programmed moment mattered. The story that Buchanan told about a culture war came to be written into that canon of half-truths known as conventional wisdom. It still is, pathetically. Reporters liked it and bought it. Many of the politicians and political consultants in the Astrodome liked Buchanan's culture war idea, as did Democrats watching on television. They saw job security in a long political feud. They still do. Culture war is good for the business of politics and news. There is a whole polarization-industrial complex to support it. The problem is there was no culture war then, just as there isn't one now.

There really had been a political war in the 1960s. The issues were serious, and lives were at stake. Civil rights and war protesters actually marched in the streets, and they were beaten up and thrown in jail. Young people, mostly children of the poor, were killed in Vietnam. Black children went to segregated schools in segregated towns in segregated states. Their parents often couldn't vote nor had any real protection from the government. Families fought one another. There was a "generation gap." This was a real battle. There was a cultural front, too: "women's lib," gay rights, premarital sex, drugs, soft racism, ethnic pride, and long hair.

But by 1992, the violent phase was over. In 1991, E. J. Dionne published *Why Americans Hate Politics,* which argued Americans hated politics precisely because politicians were stuck fighting old battles from the sixties. Their liberal and conservative ideologies weren't up to supplying "remedies" to the real problems of the day. "Above all," Dionne wrote, "we need to end the phony polarization around the issues of the 1960s that serves only to carry us further from a deliberative, democratic public life." Amen.

The Civic War

NEARLY TWENTY YEARS later, "phony polarization" has fossilized. All that has changed is that instead of portraying the nation as arguing over the 1960s, the political class portrays the country as literally two nations. The reigning picture of America is that it is polarized between blue and red, left and right, and fighting a death struggle for the moral compass of a nation. It is the Big Idea that informs much political strategy, commentary, and dining room conversation. It is, like so much that we hate about us, phony. It is a pseudo-narrative, a distorted and inaccurate representation. But it has guided the way politics has been conducted and perceived for nearly a generation.

It is a myth used to explain the second Big Idea about American politics: that government is in gridlock. The second Big Idea happens to be mostly true on the big issues. Government has been lame for a generation or even two.

The failure of American government on the local, state, and federal level to cope with the devastation wrought on the Gulf Coast by Hurricane Katrina in 2005 became a symbol of "can't do" government. The ineffectiveness of government is generally revealed by what doesn't get done, by those practical, solvable problems that government ignores except in television commercials and floor speeches. Over the past twenty years some of the unaddressed issues include providing health insurance for all citizens; funding the retirement and elder care of the baby boom generation; reducing the poverty of the rural and urban underclasses; controlling immigration and the ill will it breeds in some communities; rewriting a complex, time-wasting, unfair tax system; reducing pollution.

The sclerosis of American government is not caused by a culture war. One of the many causes is, however, that longer war, the 150-year battle between Democrats and Republicans, the endless game between the same two teams that now have few fans. It has alienated regular citizens not just from politics but from government and perhaps idealism. Voters divide power between the two evils in election after election.

The culture war myth is partly a cover story for the Civic War, a war fought not by the nation but by the political elite, a tiny slice of the country that earns its living from politics and a larger but still small cadre of Americans who are highly active and emotionally and intellectually engaged with civics. This includes the news media. Within this world, there is indeed extreme polarization and outright belligerence worthy of the "culture war" label. The language is bellicose and the tempers short. But when applied to all of society, it is bullshit, to use the technical term we explored earlier. "The simple truth is that there is no culture war in the United States—no battle for the soul of America rages, at least none that most Americans are aware of," wrote Stanford political scientist Morris Fiorina in his book *Culture War? The Myth of a Polarized America.* "Many of the activists in political parties and the various cause groups do, in fact, hate each other and regard themselves as combatants in a war. But their hatred and their battles are not shared by the great mass of the American people."

Most people, as everyday experience shows, are moderate and open-minded on most issues; they are pragmatic, generally eclectic, and inconsistent in their opinions, which is rational in a complex world. They might be stubborn on some issues, and their opinions might be knee-jerk habits more than fresh thinking. They might be loud after too many beers. But most people aren't dogmatic ideologues. Some get strongly attached to a single issue, but most do not. Regrettably, many of us do, however, mimic the cadences and obnoxiousness of politics as represented in the media. Our mediated reality is polarized. So the vocabulary of politics is now extreme and bellicose; manners are generally less civil, and our own conversations reflect that.

There is also Balkanization, as we have seen earlier, which may turn out to be more dangerous than fake polarization. Balkanization unfolds on several planes, not just political but social, ethnic, religious, racial, and cultural. It reflects what Arthur Schlesinger, Jr., called "disuniting America." Balkanization is empowered by the newly popular academic and political view that the "melting pot" model of citizenship is spent, that it is disrespectful of our differences. The Internet and technologies that allow like-minded people to find one another regardless of geography encourage it. Balkanization is reflected in the rise of "identity politics," which is less concerned about fixing economic inequities and more concerned with publicizing and addressing injuries and humiliations of race, gender, sexual orientation, and religious belief. Balkanization is finally inspired, however, by a more basic human need to belong to something—anything—in an increasingly anonymous, nomadic, and homogeneous society. Sometimes these attachments are rooted and genuine; sometimes they are forced and toxic. This is clear: Balkanization is not polarization.

Balkanization, though, is just one part of the landscape. On very basic civic and political values, there is a vast common ground hidden by a few stands of towering pines. The exceptions always get the attention; the negative often wins campaigns. Moderate, independent, and eclectic citizens may be the vast, silent majority, but there is indeed a market for extremes. A doctor in Canton, Ohio, once asked me if I thought there could ever be something called "The Moderate Channel." Instantly he caught himself and said, "No, that would never sell, would it?"

Polyester Politics

SELLING: THAT HAS been the key tactic in the Civic War since the dawn of television. The story of modern politics is the story of marketing. It is the cause of the thing we despise about American politics—that it is phony and unapologetic, impervious to shame and embarrassment. Advertising-dominated campaigning has supplanted governing. This is especially true in presidential politics. It is easy to understand why so many Americans are under the dangerous illusion that politics doesn't matter anymore. It looks like the long battle between Coke and Pepsi.

One of the more prominent political reporters of the baby boom generation is Joe Klein, the author of *Primary Colors,* the hilarious novel about Bill Clinton. In 2006, he published *Politics Lost: How American Democracy Was Trivialized by People Who Think You're Stupid.* Klein puts a large chunk of blame on political consultants for taking the spontaneity and humanity out of politics. He wraps up the book by describing what he yearns for.

> A politician who refuses to be a "performer," at least in the current sense. Who doesn't orate. Who never holds a press conference in front of an aircraft carrier or in a flag factory. Who doesn't assume the public is stupid or uncaring. Who believes in at least one idea, or program, that has less than 40 percent support in the polls. Who can tell a joke—at his or her own expense, if possible. Who gets angry, within reason; gets weepy, within reason . . . but only if those emotions are rare and real. Who is capable of a spontaneous, untrammeled belly laugh. Who indulges a guilty pleasure or two, especially ones that may not "test" well.

After covering politics since 1985, I can relate. I despise the absence of authenticity. But I also know it is almost hypocritical to wish for this. As a journalist, my profession has done as much as the marketers to wring the fun and color out of politics. When a politician makes a gaffe or shows an unscripted human twitch, we pounce. And then we promptly carp about how dull and phony politicians are. Shame on us.

Voters expect politicians to be different from us. We expect them to be more authentic and have more character simply because they have sought our votes and are paid with our tax dollars. We naïvely believe the virtues that it takes to be successful in politics coincide with the virtues of a good private person.

Telling an American what is hateful in politics is like explaining to a six-year-old boy why he hates liver and onions. It is redundant. It is worth reviewing, however, how we cobbled together a political system that produces twenty-three-month presidential campaigns, is dominated by marketing, and is rigged by a long-standing monopoly by two major parties—a political system we hate.

So, You Think Things Are Bad Now?

SINCE 1776 AMERICANS have thought that politicians were mostly buffoons and windbags and that politics was a messy, cockeyed way to get work done. The design of the Constitution, of course, reflects a suspicion of politicians. Power is to be divided, checked, and balanced. Political parties were given no special quarter. It has always been almost un-American to like politics too much. "Whenever a man has cast a longing eye on offices, a rottenness begins in his conduct," said Thomas Jefferson. The one-liners kept coming throughout our history. John F. Kennedy: "Mothers all want their sons to grow up to be president, but they don't want them to become politicians in the process." My favorite comes from Richard Nixon: "Politics would be a helluva good business if it weren't for the goddamned people."

James Bryce, the Scottish de Tocqueville, put a section in his *The American Commonwealth* called "Why Great Men Are Not Chosen Presidents." In 1888, he wrote, "The ordinary American voter does not object to mediocrity. He has a lower conception of the qualities requisite to make a statesman than those who direct public opinion in Europe have." He added that the antebellum presidents Van Buren, Polk, Buchanan, Harrison, and Taylor "were intellectual pygmies compared to the real leaders of that generation—Clay, Calhoun, and Webster."

There is nothing new about political complaining. Still, we're at a very low point now and something is different. "What we are witnessing," according to Warren Miller, the director of the Center for Political Studies at the University of Michigan, "is a massive erosion of the trust the American people have in their government." He said that in 1971, during Vietnam but before Watergate. Since then, Americans have held all branches of government, leaders in government, and office seekers in substantially lower esteem than in the preceding forty years, according to major public opinion polls. In the academic, think tank, op-ed world, there are *no* serious defenders of the basic mechanisms of politics today: a rigid two-party system with extremely high barriers for third parties and independent candidates, a private system of financing campaigns that is erratically regulated and constantly altered, and a presidential selection process that now takes more than twenty-three months and dominates the agenda for nearly half a president's term.

Yet our government suffers no crisis of legitimacy. There is no charge to toss out the Constitution and adopt a WikiConstitution. American traditions, ideals, and the Constitution have plenty of defenders. The nuts and bolts of elections and legislating do not.

Did TV Murder Politics?

IN TRYING TO apportion blame for the demise of character in American politics, the trick is to never, ever blame the citizenry or voters. They are the victims. The lineup of usual suspects in these high crimes includes television, consultants, big money, and more television. I'd sum it up by blaming OmniMarketing. Others simply blame television.

The four debates between Richard M. Nixon and John F. Kennedy are customarily treated as the dawn of the television era. It was a brand-new use of the medium, and it showed the power of the tube. On substance, the debates were probably a draw, but on style Kennedy won.

Nixon, legend says, looked menacing with his five o'clock shadow, awkward cadence, and forced smiles. What's remarkable in retrospect is that Kennedy and Nixon went head-to-head for hours with a command of issues large and small that seems dazzling and daring now. Every four years during the fall debate season, we watch the grainy clips and pundits remind the world how puny today's "joint appearances" look compared to the Great Debates of 1960. That wasn't so clear at the time:

> The application of the quiz show format to the so-called "Great Debates" between Presidential candidates in the election of 1960 is only another example [of the "pseudo-event"]. These four campaign programs, pompously and self-righteously advertised by the broadcasting networks, were remarkably successful in reducing great national issues to trivial dimensions. . . . They were a clinical example of the pseudo-event, of how it is made, why it appeals, and of its consequences.

The writer was Daniel Boorstin, the historian and later the librarian of Congress. Boorstin believed television, a newly glamorous industry called "advertising," the growing public relations business, and Hollywood had woven together a "pseudo-America." Boorstin was prescient. But whereas he thought the Kennedy-Nixon debates reflected a deep state of "national self-hypnosis," we now know they in fact mirrored only a light trance. Full hypnosis would come later.

The first live political television events that grabbed the country were Senator Estes Kefauver's hearings on organized crime in 1951 and the infamous Army-McCarthy hearings held by Joseph McCarthy's Senate Permanent Subcommittee on Investigations in 1953–54. In the first thirty years of television, only special events were covered live—important congressional moments like the Watergate hearings, political conventions, major presidential events, and campaign debates. After Watergate, spectacle hearings became one of the most important forms of live political theater. The most viewed and talked-about political events of the next thirty years were mega-hearings: the bloody confirmation battles of

Robert Bork, John Tower, and Clarence Thomas; the Iran-Contra hearings; the Clinton impeachment hearings; and a list of mini- and pseudo "gates" a mile long (Travelgate, Filegate, Plamegate, Attorneygate, and so forth).

A dark day came on March 19, 1979. That was when the House of Representatives initiated the first televised proceedings from the floor, broadcast live and free on C-SPAN. The first speaker was a young member from Tennessee, Albert Gore, Jr. A few years later, a maverick entrepreneur named Ted Turner launched CNN. From that moment on, there was always a live camera near a live politician—a dangerous combination.

The Senate inaugurated live television from the floor on June 2, 1986. Senators now talked to the cameras, not to one another and not to history. Special camera-ready rooms for press conferences were put in one floor up from both the House and Senate floors, and members have been parading in and out steadily for decades now. New technologies made it simple for local television stations to put their representatives and senators on the six o'clock news. Television ads became cheap to produce, and cable television multiplied the potential venues for them to air. By 1996, two more 24/7 cable news channels were in business, MSNBC and Fox News. There were plenty of television lights and plenty of moths.

Since the early 1960s, television has been *the* way politicians communicate to voters and *the* place where voters encounter politicians. You could say that we don't hate politics itself, but rather we hate politics on television.

Party Off

TELEVISION GAVE POLITICIANS a new, direct route to voters. This lessened the dependence of individual candidates and officeholders on party machines and local organizations. The parties still have the power to keep third parties off the field, and they do frame national debates—generally a process of oversimplification followed by exaggeration. What parties have lost is the capacity to govern and control individual politicians, who now have their own independent access to campaign funds (individual and PAC donations), free media (that's what pols call "news"), paid media (advertising), and marketing.

In 1972, David Broder, then a young reporter for *The Washington Post*, published *The Party's Over: The Failure of Politics in America.* "The reason we have suffered governmental stalemate is that we have not used the one instrument available to us for disciplining government to meet our needs," he wrote. "That instrument is the political party." Broder believed that when parties "do not function well, things go badly for America. The coming of the Civil War was marked by a failure of the reconciling function of the existing parties." Remember, this was written *before* Watergate. And before the Iraq War.

In the thirty-five years since, the party system went from injured to crippled. It happened partly in the name of good intentions called "reforms."

After Watergate, there was a natural impulse to clean up dirty politics. Some would say that's a mission impossible, but Washington and state capitals gave it a serious try. Congress was especially eager to prevent secret slush funds and huge donations from individuals and companies. So a series of campaign-finance reforms were passed beginning in 1974. Congress limited donations to candidates from individuals and political action committees (PACs), the legal entities companies and unions use to make contributions. There were new disclosure rules for all donations and spending. Congress tried to limit how much money independent groups could spend electioneering, but the Supreme Court wouldn't allow that. Inside Congress, members had to disclose their personal finances, and new limits were placed on outside income and taxpayer-funded allowances for "office expenses" and mailings.

The Free-Agent System

THE "LAW OF unintended consequences" is just that—a law. Crafty lawyers and operatives eventually found enough loopholes in campaign-finance reform laws so that more money came into politics, not less. The so-called good government reforms—a more open primary system, easy access to television, and new campaign technology such as computer-generated direct mail and automated phone calling—combined to create a new monster: the political free agent.

Party bosses could no longer snap their fingers and anoint a senator from Illinois or a representative from New York's twenty-first congressional district. Party leaders in the House and Senate couldn't easily strong-arm members by threatening to cut off their party money supply or give them lousy committee assignments. The "whip" once used to round up votes and keep the herd in line turned into a wet noodle. Members and candidates could now go around the party structure and "straight" to the voters through TV and campaign technology. They didn't need seniority and good committee jobs to get reelected. It is almost impossible to unseat an incumbent in the free-agent era, regardless of whether the majority leader likes the member.

This is not to say that parties are powerless. They recruit and fund new candidates, protect incumbents, train operatives, generate opposition research, and organize Congress. Indeed, a robust party system helped the American government create the New Deal, join and win World War II, build a national transportation infrastructure, enact civil rights legislation, launch the Great Society programs, and send a man to the moon.

But there has not been comparable landmark legislation since Watergate. Today, most of the power of the two parties comes from being the only two options. And the weakening of the two parties has had one profound effect on both campaigning and governing: It merged them.

The modern model of American government is called the "permanent campaign." Reelection is the goal of governing, not governing itself. If legislative accomplishment, committee power, or partisan allegiances help, fine. If not, fine. Look out for number one.

In December 1976, Jimmy Carter was preparing to take office. His young expert on public opinion, Patrick Caddell, perhaps the first celebrity pollster, wrote a memo for his boss that was leaked to the media. It was titled "Initial Working Paper on Political Strategy." He wrote, "Essentially, it is my thesis that governing with public approval requires a continuing political campaign." He was right except for one thing. Campaigning grew more effective, but governing became less effective.

Caddell thus articulated a new model of governing. Sidney Blumenthal gave it a name in *The Permanent Campaign*, published in 1980.

About thirty years after Caddell wrote his memo, John Breaux, a Democrat from Louisiana known for his ability to cut a good deal, retired from the Senate in the prime of his career. He wrote in an op-ed piece, "Today, unfortunately, outside groups, public relations firms, and the political consultants who are dedicated to one thing—a perpetual campaign to make one party a winner and the other party a loser—have snatched the political process."

Members of government, elected and appointed, needed people to manage these permanent campaigns. Amateurs and part-timers weren't good enough anymore.

The Agents

IN SPORTS AND show business, the people who handle the talent are called agents. In politics, they are called consultants.

Political consultants filled the vacuum left by weak parties. Candidates used experts and specialists to navigate television and capitalize on modern marketing techniques. This was the new political equation: Marketing equals campaigning equals governing.

In August 2002, the Bush administration was pressing its case to go to war against Iraq. The specific legislative and diplomatic strategy the administration would use was not yet known. When the White House chief of staff Andrew Card was asked about this, he said, "You don't announce new products until after Labor Day."

War as product.

In 2007, as Republican presidential candidates were trying to raise money, Christine Todd Whitman, a former governor of New Jersey and President George W. Bush's first Environmental Protection Agency administrator, said, "The Republican brand is not selling very well." Once again, there is little need to explain *why* Americans hate politics. Quips like this say it all. We political consumers don't like the products we have to choose from, but an unbreakable partisan duopoly controls the market. There is no place else to shop.

Consultants put fresh wrapping on old products. After Richard Nixon's five o'clock shadow cost him the 1960 election, no candidate would ever campaign again without proper grooming and marketing. When Nixon ran in 1968, he hired a young producer from *The Mike Douglas Show* named Roger Ailes. Ailes cleaned up Nixon well enough to defeat an incumbent vice president. The big political book of that election was called, aptly, *The Selling of the President, 1968* by Joe McGinnis. Every candidate since has had a Roger Ailes, though most aren't as good at what they do. Ailes went on to start Fox News Channel for Rupert Murdoch.

In 1981, a political scientist from the University of Virginia, Larry Sabato, took one of the earliest scholarly looks at the boom in hired guns. *The Rise of Political Consultants: New Ways of Winning Elections* went through most of the new specialties: daily tracking polls, focus groups, television ad production, time buying, negative advertising, direct mail, and general strategy. At the time, it seemed almost glamorous.

Sabato's list of specialties looks quaint by today's standards. He didn't know about front groups, e-mail, websites, robo-calling, blogs, fake blogs, chat rooms, viral seeding, virtual community, citizen journalism, search optimization, heuristic analysis, push polling, clandestine independent expenditures, or the latest neuroscience research about how the brain processes political information, images, and emotions. He couldn't have foreseen Howard Dean's success with online fund-raising.

Much of what political reporters do now is report on the tricks and tradecraft of consultants and their campaigns. They (we) claim this is a public service, that reporters are supposed to uncover the smoke and mirrors and expose the man behind the curtain. What else can you do when campaigns last twenty-three months? There are problems with this defense, though. For one, most people now consume more political advertising than political reporting, at least on television. A University of Wisconsin study found that, in the weeks preceding the 2006 midterm election, in seven Midwest states, local stations aired four minutes and thirty seconds of political advertising in a thirty-minute broadcast, while airing just one minute and forty-three seconds of political reporting. And most of the reporting was about the horse race.

Voters have become just like the pundits on television, who, in turn, are more like consultants. Everybody can talk strategy these days and everybody can deconstruct a political event. The reverse is also true: Nobody takes a political act or speech at face value. Daniel Boorstin pegged this a year after the Kennedy-Nixon debates. "We are frustrated by our very efforts publicly to unmask the pseudo-event," he wrote. "Whenever we describe the lighting, the make-up, the studio setting, the rehearsals, etc., we simply arouse more interest."

All this makes politicians and officeholders more like pygmies, to return to James Bryce's phrase. Despite the magic of consultants, politicians have never gained back the levels of trust they had before Watergate. Quite the contrary. Democratic pollster Harrison Hickman argues that promiscuous use of negative ads has made all politicians less popular, even those who win. Hickman calculated the final, preelection favorability ratings in all of the statewide races he has worked on since 1986, in nonpresidential years. The *winners* averaged an approval rating of 56 percent in 1986, but only 50 percent in 2002; their average unfavorable rating rose from 25 percent to 34 percent. "We have become so skilled at making people unpopular that it's hard for anyone to get very involved or invested with candidates," Hickman said. Once they get elected, they fare no better. As a general rule, we hate them.

Pseudo-Government

SO FAR, THE response of officeholders to the giant turnoff inspired by the triumph of stagecraft is more stagecraft.

The tricks of campaigning, as Caddell advised in 1976, are now the tools of governing, or rather pseudo-governing. That is why George W. Bush brought his top paid political consultant, Karl Rove, to the White House and put him to work in the policy shop. That is why a White House chief of staff talks about "products." That is why Bill Clinton's pollster, the infamous toe-sucking Dick Morris, polled voters on where the president should vacation. That's why Clinton went to Jackson Hole, Wyoming, in 1995 and 1996.

The insatiable desire to pierce the veils of make-believe is why so many books about politics now have titles like *The Greatest Story Ever Sold: The Decline and Fall of Truth in Bush's America; Weapons of Mass Deception: The Uses of Propaganda in Bush's War on Iraq; Governing by Campaigning: The Politics of the Bush Presidency; Whitewash: What the Media Won't Tell You About Hillary Clinton, but Conservatives Will; President Reagan: The Role of a Lifetime;* and *The Acting President.* Revealing the "pseudo" is not just what journalists and scholars do, it is what pols *try* to do to one another.

Most, not all, of these titles come from the right or the left. One side thinks they are honest, the other side is deceitful, and the media is biased; the other side thinks the exact same. As polarized as the political elite is, the vast majority of nonpolarized voters hate the farce of government as much as the left hates the right and right hates the left. The disgust with pseudo-government and its evil twin, the permanent campaign, are completely nonpartisan.

A tremendous amount of the human ingenuity that goes into pseudo-government now is directed to the creation and nurturing of pseudo-events. Daniel Boorstin saw televised debates, stupid press conferences, and "anonymous" White House leaks as pseudo-events. We still have all that. And there are more cameras. Most congressional hearings where there is a TV camera are pseudo-events. If there is a scandal in baseball about steroids, there will be a big hearing and there will never be relevant legislation: a pseudo-event. If there is a shooting in a high school or university, there will be a hearing, even though there is nothing in the world Congress can do about it: a pseudo-event. If there is a controversy about taking some poor soul like Terry Schiavo off life support that gets to be a big deal in the news, Washington will create pseudo-events to get into the act. The appearance of governing is what counts.

Unfortunately, we now have something worse: pseudo-*issues*. These are essentially Potemkin village problems: issues that generate expedient, campaign-style rhetoric but not action; issues that sometimes are not even under the jurisdiction of the federal government; issues that are dominant "single issues" to a small but vocal, politically engaged slice of the electorate, but third- or fourth-tier issues for most voters; hot-button issues that are emotionally charged, polarizing, and intractable. Some classic examples are proposed constitutional amendments to ban flag burning or allow prayer in school; government funding for contro-versial artists; late-term or partial-birth abortion; illegal immigration; stem-cell research; and gay marriage. This list contains mostly so-called wedge issues, cultural issues that one party (most successfully the GOP) focuses on to divide voting blocs with similar economic interests.

But there are other, fully bipartisan pseudo-issues. They are gener-ally trivial. They dominate the news for one or two weeks and then are forgotten.

In the spring of 2006, members of Congress from both parties be-came giddy with camera lust when a multinational corporation called Dubai Ports World, a holding company owned by the government of Dubai in the United Arab Emirates, announced plans to buy a giant British company, P&O Ports, which leased six port facilities in the United States. Instantly, fearmongers proclaimed that a nefarious multi-national corporation secretly controlled by a hostile Arab government was engineering a covert takeover of six major U.S. ports. America was at risk of losing control of its borders and compromising national secu-rity in an entirely preventable way. We might as well have turned over our nuclear arsenal to Osama bin Laden, since two of the 9/11 terrorists were UAE nationals. How could the president let this happen? Schedule the hearings! Line up the press conferences! Team One, handle out-rage; Team Two, take fearmongering; Team Three, assign false blame; and Team Four, handle misinformation. Go!

Virtually nothing in the short one-sided propaganda war was true. Dubai Ports would not have actually owned the ports, just leased some port terminals. At most ports, there are several leaseholders. In fact, 30 percent of all American maritime facilities were owned by foreign enti-ties when this deal was pending. Internationally, twenty-four of the twenty-five largest companies that operate port terminals aren't Ameri-can. That means just about every container that enters a U.S. port has come from a foreign-controlled facility.

The deal had already been reviewed and cleared by the relevant U.S.

agencies. Indeed, another Dubai company already handled port calls for U.S. Navy ships from the Fifth Fleet in the Middle East—a pretty high measure of trustworthiness. Further, the Homeland Security Department was in charge of security at all U.S. ports, not the leaseholders or private companies. The United Arab Emirates are fully and greedily capitalist and had not sponsored al-Qaeda or other terrorist groups.

There was never a real security issue. After a blaze of pseudo-legislation, Dubai Ports World sold the leases to a U.S. entity. There have been no substantial changes to security at U.S. ports since. The story was on the front pages for about one month. It was an exercise in Arab bashing and phony-baloney national security preening. It was a giant campaign stunt underwritten by tax dollars.

It was political theater.

Fake Special Interests

THERE IS ONE area of politics where we absolutely don't doubt the sincerity of the players: the lobby. We believe special interests are sincerely greedy and selfish.

Alas, even that is too simple. The conventional view of lobbying and pressure-group politics is that business interests get their way by buying votes and influence while nonbusiness interests accumulate persuasive heft by representing their membership. This rotten system can be sterilized by reform.

This is wrong on just about every count.

In reality, the bacteria that infect politics have proven to be reform resistant. The notion that lobbyists have power *primarily* through semi-legal bribery—through travel junkets, no-show jobs, kickbacks, Porterhouse steaks, and dry martinis—is misguided. There is, in fact, less of this type of bald corruption now than in most of American history. As columnist Michael Kinsley says, today's biggest scandals are perfectly legal ones. Influence is garnered in different ways. And nonbusiness special interests—ideological, environmental, elder, religious, education, poverty groups—have changed drastically in the past fifty years. They are now parts of the permanent campaign and the entrenched fakery of American civic life.

It is easy to get preoccupied with "cleaning up" dirty politics. We obsess about money in politics. All special interests make campaign contributions to the greatest extent possible. That is what funds the American campaign system. But less than seven-tenths of 1 percent of American adults made political contributions in the 2003–04 cycle. Business has the obvious advantage, but business is not a monolithic monster. Good-government types consistently overestimate the clout of the buck, just as they underestimate the degree to which all the different donations cancel one another out. Interests find other sources of influence. Office-holders still respond first to the big donors and employers in their districts. Then they read the polls. They consider the party line. And most, though it's hard to believe, consider their convictions and practical assessments.

The power of the lobby is baked into Congress in a more boring way than bribery. Many special interests provide Congress and the executive branch with specialized expertise they simply do not have. Tax legislation is often drafted by private tax lawyers. Environmental legislation is drafted by experts at conservation groups or oil companies. Health legislation is drafted by scholars at think tanks and lawyers at trade associations. Occasionally this legal scandal makes the news. For a spell, the ancient art of earmarking became the high-profile legislative abuse. This is the pork barrel practice of sneaking narrow tax breaks, government contracts, or funding for a specific company or local project into a giant bill. Many of these are drafted by lobbyists, not just for business, but for universities, local transportation projects, and research grants.

In this process, pressure groups feed Congress and the executive branch personnel coming in and supply government personnel with new jobs as they come out. Outrage is generally focused on the exit side of the revolving door—the big salaries staffers sometimes get when they leave government. The bigger scandal is on the incoming side. Again, business has more money, thus more power. There is no symmetry. But you could eliminate all campaign donations, travel junkets, and fine dining and the lobby would still have this power.

All established special interests engage in the tricks of political consultancy. Lobbying and special interests don't just scratch backs; they try to shape public opinion using all the tools of modern campaigning. In many instances this goes one step further: It invents public opinion.

I learned this firsthand from a man named Jack Bonner, known as the king of grassroots lobbying. In campaign vernacular, a grassroots organization is one that sprouts from the seeds at the bottom with volunteers, door-to-door canvassers, and do-gooders licking envelopes. What Bonner invented was a way to provide the appearance of grassroots support on demand and en masse. He could deliver thousands of phone calls to any given member of Congress on any given day. If the client wanted letters, he could do that, too. Bonner's other innovation was what he called "grass-tops" lobbying. For clients with deep pockets, he could deliver— overnight—groups of opinion leaders and "influentials" from a member's home district or state to Washington for in-person lobbying. His detractors called this "Astroturf lobbying," because it is so phony.

In the middle of a congressional debate over an energy issue about ten years ago, my colleague Eric Engberg and I did a story on Bonner for *The CBS Evening News*. He allowed us to see his operation up close, provided we didn't reveal certain details. The day we visited his high-tech phone bank on K Street in Washington, Bonner & Associates was targeting two Midwestern senators who were swing votes on their client's issue. The goal was to generate phone calls from voters in the senators' home states straight to their Washington offices. Using sophisticated call lists that targeted people likely to agree with the client, well-coached telemarketers called home state voters and tried to persuade them with scripted pitches. If a voter agreed, Bonner's system would instantly transfer the call to a senator's office. It was slick.

"We move votes," Bonner said. "We are paid to move votes." Perhaps. Congressman John Dingell told us Astroturf lobbyists were "manufacturing public opinion where none exists." That, of course, is the essence of marketing.

Bonner replied, "The more people like Jack Bonner there are taking their message to the people, the healthier it is for democracy, whether it's the environmentalists, whether it's General Motors, whether it's the AFL-CIO."

One thing politicians are constantly accused of is watching where the wind blows and paying too much attention to public opinion. Well, some of that public opinion is now genuine fake public opinion. The Internet has given Astroturf lobbying new forms and has allowed more groups to play the game by lowering costs. Some believe this will democratize lobbying and the art of political petition. That's theoretically possible, but it hasn't happened yet. Meanwhile, the sheer amount of lobbying has increased. Government is bigger and spends more money, and that means there are more spoils to fight over.

Raccoons at Risk

INTEREST GROUPS, HOWEVER, are not what they used to be. The romantic image of American civic life is the New England town meeting, the Mayberry Town Council, and the Hooterville Volunteer Fire Department. That isn't so far off, according to political scientist Theda Skocpol in *Diminished Democracy: From Membership to Management in American Civic Life*. In the twentieth century, a typical civic group was the National Congress of Parents and Teachers (PTA). In 1955, the PTA had 9.5 million members, which was then *9 percent of the adult U.S. population.* There were 40,396 local chapters. PTA members not only volunteered in their local schools, they met together in local chapters and at state and national conventions. Membership peaked in the 1960s. The national PTA had shrunk to fewer than six million members by 2004. There are just as many local school groups and parent-teacher organizations around the country now, maybe more. That isn't the issue. What's missing now are the gatherings that brought people from different places and classes together.

In 1955, the PTA wasn't even the biggest membership organization; the AFL-CIO was, with over twelve million members. Ten other chapter-based groups had membership of greater than 2 percent of the adult population: the American Automobile Association (AAA), Freemasons, the American Legion, the Order of the Eastern Star, YMCA, United Methodist Women, the American Bowling Congress, the Women's Missionary Union, the Benevolent and Protective Order of Elks, and the

Veterans of Foreign Wars. Most of these chapter-based national federations have shrunk or disappeared. Educated people, in particular, quit
participating. A few groups morphed into something more modern, like
AAA.

Most fraternal and volunteer do-good groups are gone. Instead,
there are professionally managed advocacy groups run from central loca-
tions that want money—not time—from members: the National Education Association (teachers' union), Mothers Against Drunk Driving, the
National Rifle Association, NARAL Pro-Choice America, the Christian
Coalition, the Sierra Club, and the mother of them all, the American Association of Retired People. Today, the only contacts most people have
with such national groups are giving money on a credit card and fighting
off solicitation phone calls. "Where once cross-class voluntary federation
held sway, national public life is now dominated by professionally managed advocacy groups without chapters or members," Skocpol wrote.

This has been called the "advocacy explosion." The *Encyclopedia of Associations* listed 5,843 groups in 1959; in 2007, that number was up to
22,200. The Internet has reduced the need and desire for face-to-face
meetings and conventions. In Skocpol's view, the basic shift has been
"doing-for instead of doing-with." "Doing-for" does not generate social
capital in the same way as "doing-with."

Some will greet the demise of the Elks, Freemasons, and the like with
cries of "Good riddance. These were white, exclusively male, and dumb."
If they're old enough, they think of Ralph Kramden's Raccoon Lodge or
Fred Flintstone and the Loyal Order of Water Buffaloes.

But that's a cartoon criticism. Skocpol argues that the old chapter
groups were, in fact, more democratic and inclusive than today's advocacy groups. In 1960, PTAs from every community, rich and poor and
black and white, would gather at conventions and work together as allies. Today, "Solidarity across class lines has dwindled, even as racial and
gender integration has increased," Skocpol argued. "The professionally
managed organizations that dominate American civic life today are, in
important respects, less democratic and participatory than the pre-1960s
membership federations they displaced."

How does this make us hate politics even more? Two big ways.

First, without local chapter organizations there are fewer opportunities for people to engage politically. These organizations brought people into a process in which volunteers dealt with school boards, county officials, lieutenant governors, and congressional staffers, creating the kind of personal investment that makes it harder to just write off all politics as a waste of time. Politicians were more likely to meet people as citizens, not single-issue activists. New forms of pseudo-activism like sending angry e-mails to politicians, posting essays on blogs, and joining an anti-Bush or anti-Clinton Listserv do not provide the same kind of "civic capital."

Second, the "advocacy explosion" has created another civic producer of phoniness. Professionally managed interest groups of every variety now operate under the same permanent campaign ethos as politicians and officeholders. Their membership is targeted by professional staffers to be dealt with by the likes of Jack Bonner and his Astroturf or grass-tops techniques. Modern advocacy groups, Skocpol says, produce the same kind of "crafted talk" as politicians ("crafted talk" is a crafted way to say "bullshit"). Advocacy groups hold press conferences ad nauseam just like politicians. They distort issues just like politicians. They hire consultants, pollsters, and advertising agencies just like politicians. Like politicians, they use phony "real" people like our old pal, Sal Risalvato, the gas station owner and small business serial testifier. They have an interest in creating emotional hot-button issues and vitriol just like politicians. We hate them just like politicians—unless they're one of *our* pet special interests.

The people at the top of the advocacy groups differ from elected or appointed officials mostly in that they get paid much more. By all the measures of what we dislike in politics and public life in general—phoniness, bullshit, belligerence, and boorishness—interest groups join the news media, the candidates, and all branches of government in the ranks of the disrespected.

The Truth About Polarization

ALL THE COMBATANTS in the Civic War are wounded. The candidates, the officeholders, the bureaucracy, the institutions, and the special interests are disliked and dysfunctional. The paid spectators—the press—are discredited. Looking back, we can see how Pat Buchanan's 1992 speech emblemizes so much that is rotten. Buchanan was a speechwriter turned pundit, a pseudo-candidate backed by pseudo–special interests at a pseudo-event telling a pseudo-story.

Unfortunately, that pseudo-story, the culture war, is still the basic story told about American politics. The operatives believe it, and the press believes it. Heading into the 2004 election, George Bush's pollster, Matthew Dowd, declared, "You've got 80 percent to 90 percent of the country that look at each other like they are on separate planets."

"The polarization is exceptional," Democratic pollster Peter Hart said. Bill Clinton's pollster Stanley Greenberg wrote a book called *The Two Americas: Our Current Political Deadlock and How to Break It.* In *One Nation, Two Cultures,* conservative historian Gertrude Himmelfarb wrote, "The cultural divide helps explain the peculiar, almost schizoid nature of our present condition: the evidence of moral disarray on the one hand and of a religious-cum-moral revival on the other." The 2000 and 2004 presidential elections confirmed the culture war story, according to the conventional narrative. So did the 2006 midterm election that gave Democrats control of Congress. Close elections and frequent shifts in the balance of partisan power prove the nation is polarized. Two sizes fit all.

That is a pseudo-story. There *are* culture warriors out there. But they are the political elite and a small slice of the whole. The rest of us are quite peaceful, thank you. In fact, the rest of us don't even agree with ourselves all the time. Sociologist Alan Wolfe has said that America's polarization "is not a division between red state and blue state America; it's a division inside every person." We might have so-called conservative views on national security and so-called liberal views on social issues. We might be libertarian at home and interventionist abroad. We are environmental hunters and born-again environmentalists. We might be prudish about entertainment and progressive about gay issues. We might want balanced budgets and expanded health programs for children. We might have opposed the war in Iraq and supported a strong military and aggressive antiterrorism policy. We might oppose abortion and favor the death penalty. Our actions may speak louder than our words: The Republican red states of Texas and Oklahoma have had far higher divorce rates than the permissive blue states of Massachusetts and Connecticut.

Most voters don't blog, call radio talk shows, or otherwise publicly spew vitriol. Though they might not sound like it in the middle of an argument, most voters see a complex world in shades of gray. Culture warriors and campaign consultants see in black and white. Perhaps in red and blue.

The phrase "culture war" came from sociologist James Davison Hunter's *Culture Wars: The Struggle to Define America,* published in 1991. Hunter's basic argument was that America's tradition of religious pluralism had devolved into a schism between orthodox and progressive groups, and that social conflict had become largely organized around those cultural impulses. But even he added that most voters aren't extremists. "In truth, most Americans occupy a vast middle ground between the polarizing impulses of American culture. . . . Most Americans, despite their predispositions, would not embrace a particular moral vision wholly or uncritically," he wrote. However, organizations, spokespeople, and activists take on "an existence, power and agenda independent of the people for whom they supposedly speak."

Hunter's nuance was overlooked in favor of his catchy title. Soon every conflict and controversy was seen through the prism of culture war. Political consumers began to simply assume the country was just as divided as the people yelling at one another on television. The political class, of course, really is polarized. It is divided into two teams, Democratic and Republican. And the most reliable campaign strategy is based on polarization. First, destroy the opponent with negative ads. Second, split the enemy camp with divisive "wedge" issues. This style of campaigning existed long before Buchanan's mighty oration. Richard Nixon, Pat Caddell, and Ronald Reagan knew all about it. But just because a divisive tactic works does not mean Americans themselves are divided.

Stanford political scientist Morris Fiorina added some gray to the black-and-white picture with *Culture War? The Myth of a Polarized America*. He agreed that American voters did become somewhat more engaged about cultural issues—religion and morality—than economic issues, but Fiorina saw no evidence of *deep* polarization or disagreement on most issues. For example, Fiorina took the results of a large national survey conducted by the Pew Research Center for the People and the Press two months before the 2000 election and then divided them into red-state results (Republican) and blue-state results (Democratic). Instead of finding great divisions in the "issue preferences" of these two enemy camps, he found great similarities:

	Blue	Red
Immigration should decrease	41 percent	43 percent
Environment over jobs	43	42
Favor school vouchers	51	54
Favor death penalty	70	77
Blacks should get hiring preference	13	14
Stricter gun control	64	52
Equal women's role	83	82
Moral climate: much worse	26	30
Moral climate: somewhat worse	25	25
Tolerate others' views	62	62
Abortion, always legal	48	37
No gay job discrimination	73	62

Figures combine "strongly" and "somewhat agree" responses.

This does not look like a portrait of a nation at war. Fiorina wrote that "voters are not deeply or bitterly divided" and they "see themselves as positioned between both parties."

This is key to the illusion of culture war. If the electorate is not so deeply divided on the issues, why are elections so close and why is the electoral map so divided? "The explanation is that the political figures Americans evaluate are more polarized," Fiorina wrote. "A polarized political class makes the citizenry appear polarized, but it is only that—an appearance."

Congress has clearly become more polarized. There are fewer large, bipartisan majorities. There has been virtually no bipartisan legislation that has held the label "landmark" in a generation. *Congressional Quarterly* found more unanimous party-line votes in the House in 2003 than in the previous forty years. This is less because of the power of the party whip than the ideological calcification of the political class.

The Senate has hovered around fifty-fifty for several cycles. And there are fewer moderates in Congress. When Lowell Weicker, a moderate to liberal Republican senator and governor from Connecticut, quit the party in 1990, he said the moderate wing of the party had become just a feather. Other moderate Republicans fled the Senate. Conservative Southern Democrats, long a moderating element in the party and sometimes a retrograde force, are now virtually extinct.

It boils down to this: When a moderate, independent-minded electorate must select between two—and only two—partisan choices, elections will be close. Voters must choose, but because both choices are equally unrepresentative and unpopular, roughly equal numbers vote for each. So the winning team changes frequently. Neither side has earned sustained, decisive popular support. In their invisible collective wisdom, voters would rather see power divided than given outright to one of the two creepy teams.

A close election can result from a *deeply* divided electorate, where equal numbers of voters are on opposite extremes. But a close election can also come from an electorate that is *closely* divided, where voters huddle around the center. "Americans are closely divided, but we are not deeply divided, and we are closely divided because many of us are ambivalent and uncertain, and consequently reluctant to make firm commitments to parties, politicians, or policies," according to Fiorina.

We seek the middle, yes, but we also come in lots of flavors. Think about voting the way a marketer might. An infinitely diverse and finicky market of political consumers is given only two buying options. And the options *always* come from the same two companies. Media critic James Poniewozik wrote in *Time:*

The problem is, American politics are un-American. At least, they no longer fit the a la carte ethos of iPod America. You and I can't each have our own president. We can't have our own Supreme Court or our own assault-weapons law. If you don't like the USA Patriot Act, you can't delete it from your digital playlist.

In life, we ask TiVo or the Web or the Cheesecake Factory to indulge our slightest whims. Asking this is not selfish; in fact, it is a duty. ("Have it your way!"—was that an invitation or a command?) But under a political system devised before the dawn of the fixin's bar, we are suddenly asked to settle for those options that can please half the voters or, at least, five out of nine Supreme Court Justices. That rankles our American souls. We should be satisfied! We should be catered to! We specifically asked for the vinaigrette on the side! And so the losers grow more aggrieved in defeat and the winners less generous in victory.

This makes for a cranky electorate, not a polarized one. It also makes voters act like passive consumers, not participants and not Citizens with a capital C.

The mainstream media hangs out in polarized extremes as well. That's where the politicians are and therefore where the heat and fire are. The fury over whether Terry Schiavo could be taken off a feeding tube in 2005 was a classic example. This became a full, breathless media-political circus for about a week. There were bills introduced, presidential interventions, and last-ditch appeals to the courts; there were endless live shots and interviews with experts on plug pulling. Taking a black-and-white position got a politician on television and in the papers.

The Internet painted a different picture of the Schiavo story. Every conceivable human opinion was expressed online through blogs, columns, comments, online videos, and social networking posts. Most of this commentary came with the same vehemence politicians muster, though hopefully more sincere. Some of it was bloodcurdling in its meanness. But many people also expressed the gray, the tragedy and the conflicts that red/blue America often misses. The beat of new media politics may be loud and angry, but at least there are more than two notes. This may be Balkanization, but it isn't polarization.

Still, Balkanized behavior can be just as belligerent and boorish as partisan argument. It is the closed mind-set that "the other side just doesn't get it" that we hate, the outrage that everyone isn't in your own echo chamber. The prevalence of so much animosity is not evidence of a polarized nation, just an obnoxious nation.

United?

"EVEN IF AMERICANS are losing their social bonds," Wayne Baker wrote in *America's Crisis of Values: Reality and Perception*, "the loss cannot be attributed to differences in the moral visions of Americans." Americans share abstract values and ideals more than they share concrete communities and the skills of community living. Support for the American Way and our political system is supple even when our manners and tolerance are brittle.

Argutainment focuses on the interminable squabbles, such as the Terry Schiavo case, gay marriage, stem-cell research, abortion, flag burning, school prayer, and heretical artwork, that are not what voters care about most. This is precisely what is so frustrating about the Civic War today: It is not fighting over what matters yet it is fighting at the maximum decibel level, all the time. This is why the doctor in Canton wants a "moderate channel."

In *One Nation, After All*, an exhaustive study of middle-class views of moral and social life, Alan Wolfe wrote:

> Despite their reasonableness and their optimism, there are things about this country that bother those Americans and make them wonder about their country's future. Convinced that the middle way is the best way, they believe that the modest virtues by which they want to lead their lives are not shared by those who have the power to determine how they will lead their lives. This is especially true of those in the media and

government, who, in their opinion, have lost touch with the moral truths important to them.

The irony is that most everyone in political life tries desperately to be "in touch." But those efforts are insincere and/or cynical. Voters are better advised to look for "modest virtues" in their own lives and their neighbors' than in politics, for now.

Our worst instincts are well represented. The best are not. We hate in our politics some of what we hate in ourselves. Politics pumps up those qualities into grotesque red and blue cartoons.

"The modern liberal state was premised on the notion that in the interests of peace, government would not take sides among the differing moral claims made by religion and traditional culture," Francis Fukuyama wrote in *The Great Disruption: Human Nature and the Reconstitution of Social Order.* "There would be pluralism in opinions about the most important moral and ethical questions concerning ultimate ends or the nature of the good. Tolerance would become the cardinal virtue." But the modern liberal state has waged an assault on the virtues, including the civic virtue of tolerance. Tolerance is a temperament that can't be commissioned. It can die.

Politics as a Vacation

ONE OF MY closest friends is an algebraic topologist. I don't know what an algebraic topologist actually is beyond a fancy kind of mathematician. For many years, my friend, in turn, didn't know who the vice president was. I would duly scold him for not living in the real world. I wouldn't do that now. I wouldn't argue that politics is the real world anymore. We've made it an unpleasant, third-class daily vacation from the real world. Political theater—politics through the media—largely distracts from the real worlds, public and private. But, of course, the issues and problems politics ought to address are real and dangerous.

I do not expect this to change in the foreseeable future unless a force emerges outside of the two-party system, which is far too invested in the dynamic of polarization and the apparatus of the permanent campaign to alter the status quo. The crisis of 9/11 did nothing to alter politics. The early phase of the 2008 presidential election has been encouraging. But bad habits have become entrenched and voter cynicism deeper and more understandable. Without some sort of third party or major realignment similar to the one that created Abraham Lincoln's Republican Party, it will be a long time before any party is entrusted with the power to break the gridlock in addressing enduring, fixable problems. When the voters distrust all the players, they see gridlock as a virtue.

Who would go into politics today? For all the dirty, rotten, scoundrel things I've said about politicians and their enablers, I still admire them. Most enter politics with good intentions. The same is true even of consultants and political journalists, but less so. We hold candidates and elected officials to impossible standards and unsustainable scrutiny.

Most politicians I have come across felt at some point in their lives they had a calling. There is no more difficult calling today than politics. There is no place where the potential for and reality of doing good are so distant. There is no profession where the demands of the job are so likely to collide with the demands of private morals and tastes. There is no place where failure and foibles are so public. Sadly, our politics seem irreparable and fit only for egomaniacs or masochists. The longer this is true, the deeper our civic hole will become.

The most famous piece of writing about the moral choices and inner conflicts facing a serious, thoughtful politician is an essay written after World War I by Max Weber called "Politics as a Vocation." He ends the essay with this:

> Even those who are neither leaders nor heroes must arm themselves with that steadfastness of heart which can brave even the crumbling of all hopes. . . . Only he has the calling for politics who is sure that he shall not crumble when the world from his point of view is too stupid or too base for what he wants to offer. Only he who in the face of all this can say "In spite of all!" has the calling for politics.

Citizens will have to become braver, too, if those who are called are to be heard.

Chapter Seven

OMNIMARKETING

IN EVERYDAY LIFE, we confront the world as consumers more than as citizens. You can turn off the news and ignore politics. You cannot avoid the poisonous tentacles of the peddlers and the admen: Resistance is futile, earthlings.

But resist we must if we want to save our souls.

Melodramatic? I don't think so. A reality show starring billionaire Donald Trump, a line of cosmetics called "S.L.U.T.," an ad in *The New York Times Magazine* for a $47.5 million apartment, slick ads for $100 Nike sneakers for kids, and a McDonald's on every corner can poison the soul as well as the body. OmniMarketing is probably the biggest single purveyor of what we hate about our society. The problem is, we also love it.

In reflective moments, most of us can conjure up what is most important in our lives, how we want and ought to live. We know what we value and what we aspire to value. We know our souls, albeit imperfectly. In our lives, there are forces that lead us toward authenticity and there are pressures that lead us away. We do our best. OmniMarketing almost always leads us away. It subtly coaxes us to covet things we don't need, envy people we don't know, waste time on the trivial, and ignore what is important. If you want to save your soul, you must resist it.

What Is OmniMarketing?

"MARKETING" HAS SEVERAL specific meanings and uses in the business world. I use the term in the very broad, generic sense to mean communication and media meant to sell something or promote some kind of commercial behavior. Marketing is a form of bullshit—of socially sanctioned deception. The capacity to market is now a symbol of status and power: Mikhail Gorbachev, the former president of the Soviet Union, once appeared in an ad for Louis Vuitton luggage.

The new technologies of OmniMedia have provided unimaginably more opportunities for OmniMarketing to be committed upon us. We spend eight hours a day bonding with assorted media outlets, all of which now deliver marketing: phones, computers, radio, television, books, newspapers, magazines, and movies. We are bombarded. Our cognitive bandwidth is overloaded. We are faced every day not just with scads of consumer choices, but mounds of lobbying intended to steer those choices. The Web has made it dirt cheap for anyone to market anything anytime to anyone anywhere. Many of the objects we touch and use every day are branded with marketing: clothes, food, pens, pans, shoes, cars, toothpaste, soap, and so forth. What isn't branded? This isn't eggheaded, academic deconstructionist gibberish. We *want* this stuff. We work for it. We walk away from our souls to get it.

Marketing has infected the most popular product of OmniMedia—entertainment. Entertainment is even more infiltrated than politics and news (though some argue news is a subset of entertainment now). In fact, much of what we call entertainment is marketing in disguise. It is either a vehicle for delivering advertising and marketing or it is itself a commodity to be bought and sold, constantly promoting itself, nudging you to come back after the commercial or for the sequel in the spring. It isn't art meant to stand on intellectual or creative merit; its primary purpose is to sell. For example, we have a large industry dedicated to celebrity news. Is that news, entertainment, or marketing? The audience may treat it as entertainment, but the celebrities and producers treat it as marketing. Companies pay celebrities to wear their clothes out for a night of clubbing or a trip to the Lakers game so their pictures show up in magazines and tabloids. Celebrities hire consultants to dress them and publicists to market them.

I was struck by a passing comment by the rapper Kanye West: "It's like . . . pop-luxe. Everything about me is pop and luxury." I take this as a twenty-first-century confession: I am OmniMarketing. Ralph Lauren, Paris Hilton, Martha Stewart, Oprah Winfrey, Sean Combs/P. Diddy, Donald Trump: These aren't just famous people; they are commercial brands with product lines and marketed lifestyles. In this technologically amplified era we are so saturated by "pop and luxury"—by OmniMarketing—that we are all at risk of being branded and scarred. We won't have the fame and riches, but we might have the same emptiness.

OmniMarketing Matters

SOME MARKETING AND a great deal of entertainment are harmless, even helpful. Some of it is immensely creative, socially challenging, up-lifting, and inspiring. Some of it reflects the worst in us, preying on our coarsest appetites and bypassing our consciences.

Think of the harmful OmniMarketing as a type of bacteria. Different bacteria can be necessary, harmless, or poisonous. OmniMarketing is poisonous. Different bacteria grow in different cultures. The culture of news and politics is distinct from that of commerce and entertainment. The culture of news and politics has more impact on our external lives; commerce and entertainment have more impact on our internal lives. What's scary is this: Society has no antibiotics left that kill the bacteria of OmniMarketing. The effects of the infection are that we make choices that don't reflect the values we hold dear.

For example, pop culture and pop marketing promote and exploit a vacuous, hypersexualized image of females that virtually no sane parent, teacher, aunt, or uncle would wittingly bestow on a girl. Yet we let girls romp unprotected in such a culture. And then we are aghast at "hookups," "friends with benefits," and the ways girls dress. We are un-settled by the levels of divorce and unwed parenthood. On the flip side, as we'll see, we accept an OmniMarketing portrait of boys as beer-swilling, semen-spewing, video-game obsessed meatballs. Lo and behold, we are surprised that men make up only about 43 percent of the college undergraduate population.

We are shocked that much rap music routinely refers to women as "bitches" and "hos" and men as "pimps" and "gangstas." But without a fight, this language has trickled into common usage, especially among kids, even in the suburbs and the country. MTV ran a dating reality show called *A Shot at Love with Tila Tequila*. Ms. Tequila's claim to fame was that she had a claim to fame. She had two million friends on her MySpace page, which—surprise, surprise—has lots of racy pictures on it. But the great innovation of this sexploitation show was that both boys and girls got a shot at Ms. Tequila's loving heart. It's bisexual exploitation. What a wonderful social breakthrough.

OmniMarketing has much to do with the idea of the "pictures in our heads" that Chris Eads, the minister in suburban Virginia, discussed. Eads sees his congregants going into debt because the pictures in their heads of a good father or a successful husband include *things*. "They're chasing something that really isn't at the core of human experience, but they think it is. And they complain about it while they do it," Eads told me. "We're a church immersed in suburbia. It's pace, pace, pace, and mortgages bigger than you can handle. . . . They get material lust." And they get credit card debt and foreclosure notices. But it usually begins with good intentions.

There is virtually no corner of our lives that is immune from Omni-Marketing. It is depressing to ponder the list of what is cunningly branded and marketed today: politics, religion, health care, coffee, garden tools, and nose-hair trimmers, not to mention über-products like cars, beer, soft drinks, coffee, fast food, hair care, and sneakers. From breast size to belief system, every choice we make is now susceptible to OmniMarketing. And clever OmniMarketing can get us to do dumb things, like paying for water in labeled bottles and buying SUVs that are less safe and more expensive to run than almost all the alternatives.

The ultimate consumer durable is the human body. The vast array of options runs from thick lips to thin thighs to high cheekbones. The latest product innovation is vaginal cosmetic surgery, made famous (in certain circles) by reports that porn queen Jenna Jameson's operation was botched. Whether the female seeks to replicate some image of beauty or sexiness or wants, um, a better grip, money can buy her that kind of love. Supposedly.

The ultimate consumer nondurable is religion. Few people today choose the religion of their parents. Markets abhor a vacuum, and so fundamentalist offshoots, niche denominations, and new spiritual flavors have multiplied and are often marketed like shampoo: Megachurches run ads, and preachers vie for airtime. The self-help movement offers a vast selection of secular religions, and they are marketed aggressively: Pick from chicken soup for your soul, seven habits of effective people, or "the secret." Our bodies and souls are sophisticated games of Colorforms. Marketing has become so powerful, we believe its offers help to create a New You—lifestyle, body, personality, and spirituality. There just may not be any Old You left over.

OmniMarketing is predatory.

Marketing Unbound

COMPLAINTS ABOUT MARKETING are related to complaints about materialism, an old message at the center of almost every religion. Complaining about the commercialization and coarseness of popular culture is probably as old as the first critic, who I assume was Eve. But instead of dismissing them as sophomoric, we should pursue these ancient gripes more vigorously than ever. Society has lost the capacity to impose even modest moral and aesthetic standards and expectations on our for-profit storytellers and mythmakers. According to the historian Gertrude Himmelfarb, "As people get desensitized to repeated and aggravated forms of vulgarity, violence and promiscuity, their capacity for outrage gets dulled."

Marketing and pop now prey on our most ignoble impulses without restraints of taste and morality. It is open season on consumers. Anything goes. Chris Eads thinks of it in terms of lust, not just sexual but lust for things, luxury, power, status, and other symbols of success. Traditional constraints on public expressions of "lusts" have evaporated over the years. There is nothing dishonorable now about embracing greed, violence, sex, and ambition in television ads, shows, and the prevailing culture. The puppeteers of OmniMarketing are experts on this. "Society is constantly urging us to give in to our impulses," Eads said. "It slowly erodes the maturity of us all."

It is intellectually fashionable to denounce the idea that societies could or should have standards. That is thought to be an intellectually immature idea. Standards are either tools of the ruling class or make-believe absolutes in a post-truth world, say critics. Their absence is progress. A more honest assessment would conclude that in the worlds of commerce and popular entertainment, the weakening of various old taboos that came with the liberations of the sixties has merely presented a marketing opportunity. Simply put, it is permissible to use explicit sex, naked flesh, unbridled greed, extreme violence, and extreme voyeurism to sell goods and services or to capture eyeballs. That is why it makes perfect sense for ABC to have tried out a prime-time series called *Dirty Sexy Money*.

Dirty Is the New Clean

THIS ISN'T SOMETHING completely different. The phenomenon is commonly called "decadence." Many historians have suggested that decadence is cyclical. It's common at the moment to compare America in what appears to be its middle age to Rome in its dotage (see Cullen Murphy's 2007 book, *Are We Rome? The Fall of an Empire and the Fate of America*). This seems a tad overheated. Despite the popularity of the television show *American Gladiators,* we are not quite at the stage of watching real gladiators kill one another. My hunch is that America is so decentralized, adaptive, diverse, and so often refreshed by immigration that our story will be very different.

Still, for now OmniMarketing is unleashing an out-of-control, id-gone-wild American culture. It is available on demand 24/7 to children and envelops the unwitting. With all due understatement, the prevailing culture is rotting our conscience and uprooting our common sense. We hate it—when we bother to notice. It makes us feel like culture is the enemy.

Our natural inclination is to avoid and renounce what we find distasteful and to believe we have control over what we consume. We resist, politically and personally, the kind of criticism I am spewing for two good reasons. We believe in free markets and think we must also believe in free marketing. Further, we like to believe in free will and self-determination. The idea that contemporary market culture shapes our desires and choices without our consent is insulting.

The Creation of Desire

I CAN WRITE this in the most hallowed and cherished voice we heed in modern times: the victim. Yes, I, too, am a victim of OmniMarketing, and I'd like to share.

It happened at Bray and Scarff, an appliance dealer on Wisconsin Avenue in Bethesda, Maryland. My wife and I needed to replace the old washer and dryer that came with our house when we bought it some years back. To me this was a classic nuisance errand. I checked out *Consumer Reports* and some prices online, but my due diligence wasn't very diligent. I went with my wife only to score husband points.

At Bray and Scarff, we quickly went through the usual American brands, picked the cheapest one *Consumer Reports* recommended, and my wife went to poke around the cooktops while I paid. Man to man, I asked the sales guy if this was a good deal. He shrugged, "Yeah, short-term. It's fine."

My paranoia radar went off. "What? What is it? These are lousy machines, aren't they?"

"Lousy? Absolutely not," the salesman said. "It's just if you care about your clothes lasting and want them to hold up to a lot of washings, this isn't the way to go."

"Really?" Of course I care about my clothes lasting.

"Really. When you factor in repairs, quality, longevity, and energy costs, well, like I said, short-term, you're fine, I suppose."

"Yeah, but what about long-term?"

"Long-term there's really only one product out there that's going to put you where you need to be." And then he showed me the front-loading washer and dryer in clean, glistening stainless steel from Bosch of Germany. These were properly engineered machines. Stainless steel drums. Sensotronic load temperature monitoring plus Xxtrasanitary cleaning. No other company made machines with Aquaguard so water-proof fabrics could be enhanced in home washings. Think of the savings on dry cleaning bills alone! The brochure showed me how these machines were going to maximize the longevity of my family's wardrobe, something I inexcusably hadn't given enough thought to. At less than $5,000 for the washer and dryer, it would really be throwing money away *not* to buy the BMW of soap suds. I had been a reckless fool with our family's apparel, but I was going to put a stop to that—pronto.

I called my wife over, showed her the Bosch babies, and explained to her that we needed to fly first class this time.

She looked at me incredulously. "When was the last time you did laundry?"

"Well, I mean, that's not the point," I stuttered.

"Oh, I see. Okay, well, have you ever gotten any actual pleasure from doing laundry?" my wife asked. "Do you think this washing machine would make you want to do laundry? Do you honestly believe you could tell the difference between a pair of kid's soccer shorts washed by a fancy washer instead of a regular one? Can you imagine that our happiness could possibly increase by one iota because we have a better-engineered washing machine?"

We got the basic General Electric models. I felt cheap, dirty, and used.

Crafty marketing created a desire that I simply did not have before. Never in my life had I actually wanted a washer and dryer. Certainly I had never coveted a front-loading Bavarian über-washer. It never occurred to me that our personal well-being could be even marginally enhanced by the quality of large appliances in the basement.

I was struck by thing-lust, and that is a sin.

Marketing You, Marketing at You

THE NIGHTMARE EXTENSION of OmniMarketing comes when individuals unconsciously market themselves. This happens mostly in the social processes of applying to college, joining the workforce, marrying, and then displaying their status, wealth, brainpower, or ecological virtue. Young people now get special practice advertising themselves on My-Space and Facebook. This is "marketing you."

The less-extreme consequence is simply having to endure being a constant target of marketing and peddling. Most of us end up with a lot of time and energy gobbled up by buying and wanting stuff and earning the money to get it. This is "marketing at you."

In "marketing at you," you become part of a cohort, pod, or cluster based on your purchasing history and demographics. That's the bull's-eye on your consumer forehead. Yuppies—young urban professionals—were invented by marketers, who are always coming up with new labels. Now we have "parentocrats," upper-class parents who treat their kids as objects of their life-careers and obsess over their care and feeding. "Karma queens" are middle-aged women who buy organic food and gourmet tea. "E-litists" are environmentally correct luxury hounds. The question is, which comes first—the marketing profile or the real-life stereotype?

Subsistence societies did not have marketing and advertising. In *No Logo: Taking Aim at the Brand Bullies,* Naomi Klein wrote that the first advertising simply announced the availability of a good for purchase or barter: "Eggs." In more complicated economies, advertising announced improvements: "Fresh Eggs."

"The first task of branding was to bestow proper names on generic goods such as sugar, flour, soup, and cereal, which had previously been scooped out of barrels by local shopkeepers," Klein wrote. "Melody Farms Fresh Eggs." Then came trivial or even phony product changes. "Melody Farms Fresh Large Brown Eggs."

One person who understood this was Edward Bernays, the father of American public relations. (Interestingly, Bernays was Sigmund Freud's nephew.) In 1928 he published *Propaganda.* Reading it is like reading Richard Nixon's manual of dirty tricks. Bernays wrote:

> In theory, everybody buys the best and the cheapest commodities offered to him on the market. In practice, if everyone went around pricing, and chemically tasting before purchasing, the dozens of soaps or fabrics or brands of bread which are for

sale, economic life would be hopelessly jammed. To avoid such confusion, society consents to have its choice narrowed to ideas and objects brought to it[s] attention through propaganda of all kinds. There is consequently a vast and continuous effort going on to capture our minds in the interest of some policy or commodity or idea.

Bernays describes a brutal truth but also anticipates why modern American conservatives and even many liberals cannot bear any criticism of the sanctity of the market. Market democracy is partly based on the belief that more choice is always better. This moral judgment reigns in economics and government. Humans have free will and reason. The optimal arrangement of human society maximizes the range of choices for a free will and the information available to form reasonable choices. This is the foundation of liberal utilitarianism and economics. It has provided the most stable and humane form of government yet discovered. But there is a problem when it comes to economics, consumer choice, and everyday decision making. More choice is not, in fact, a source of happiness. It is just more.

The Case Against More

TOO MUCH CHOICE generates anxiety and frustration: choice overload. Swarthmore College sociologist Barry Schwartz, in his 2004 book, *The Paradox of Choice: Why More Is Less,* argued that we suffer a "tyranny" of choice. American consumers are constantly overloaded by the sheer volume of options we must select from every day and frustrated by an unspoken pressure to maximize our choices and purchases. This is contrary to everything economic rationalists believe, but it is a fact that shouldn't frighten the heartiest capitalist. Schwartz sensibly notes that "there is no denying that choice improves the quality of our lives." But "the fact that *some* choice is good doesn't necessarily mean that *more* choice is better."

When I started drinking coffee in college, there was instant, leaded, and unleaded. Then there was espresso. Now there is coffee hell. In the movie *Moscow on the Hudson,* Robin Williams played a defector from the

Soviet Union named Vladimir. In his first trip to an American store to go shopping, Vladimir wanted to buy coffee. He stood before shelves plump with dozens of brands and styles of coffee—and he fainted, overwhelmed by the choices.

And this was in 1984, well before the Starbucks era brought radical choice to the brown, caffeinated fluid business. Today, there are important foam issues (no foam, light foam, heavy foam), milk issues (whole, 2 percent, 1 percent, or soy), and crucial issues of bean politics and taste (organic, fair trade, and country of origin). And by the way, the guy who founded Starbucks says the coffee culture has nothing to do with the actual taste. "It's the romance of the coffee experience, the feeling of warmth and community people get in Starbucks stores," Howard Schultz wrote in his autobiography. Gag me with a can of Folger's.

The Jam Experiment is typical of the type of research Schwartz draws from in *The Paradox of Choice:*

> When researchers set up a display featuring a line of exotic, high-quality jams, customers who came by could taste samples, and they were given a coupon for a dollar off if they bought a jar. In one condition of the study, 6 varieties of the jam were available for tasting. In another, 24 varieties were available. In either case, the entire set of 24 varieties was available for purchase. The large array of jams attracted more people to the table, though in both cases people tasted about the same number of jams on average. When it came to buying, however, a huge difference became evident. Thirty percent of the people exposed to the small array of jams actually bought a jar; only 3 percent of those exposed to the large array of jams did so.

More is not always better.

Everyone has experienced option fatigue. Everyone has a story where they cracked. I don't care whether the salad has French, ranch, Green Goddess, Italian, creamy Italian, Thousand Island, vinaigrette, balsamic vinaigrette, raspberry vinaigrette, blue cheese, Russian, Asian sesame, or oil and vinegar. Just bring the goddamn salad! I ordered half a dozen oysters in a new seafood place one time. Did I want Prince Edward Island, Pigeon Point, Hama Hama, Belon, Hog Island, Malpeque, Sinku, Totten Inlet, or Kumamoto? What's the difference, I asked. Well. The vocabulary the waiter used to describe oysters made a fancy wine steward seem like a garbage man. One kind had a plump, firm meat with a sweet flavor and a mild, fruity finish, another was deep cupped, plump, and sweet, and a third had a strong salt character with a dry and metallic aftertaste. I felt a pain deep in my oysters.

Bad choices lead to buyer's regret. I ordered unremarkable oysters at remarkable prices. I felt like an idiot. But making smart choices can be time devouring. With the Internet, there is no good economic reason *not* to procure the maximum amount of information before the purchase of a car, a grill, or a saxophone. But there is so much information available that being a good consumer could become an obsession. Common sense and emotion ought to rein in pure economic rationality. Normally they do, but we're still susceptible to suckeritis.

So the actual human costs of too many choices are overload, buyer's regret, time loss, and an ironic feeling of not being in control. "As ever more material things become available and fail to make us happy, material abundance may even have the perverse effect of instilling unhappiness—because it will never be possible to have everything that economics can create," Gregg Easterbrook wrote in *The Progress Paradox*. Since this is counterintuitive, most people continue to want more choices in theory and in their coveting hearts, but in practice recoil from excessive options.

We conflate freedom to choose the big things—religion, a vote, where to live—with freedom to choose among seventy-two styles of brass drawer pulls. In sum, choice is overrated. "When people are free to do as they please, they usually imitate each other," said Eric Hoffer, author of *The True Believer: Thoughts on the Nature of Mass Movements*.

The Treadmills of Thing Lust

THE MARKETER'S JOB in the face of choice overload is twofold: manufacturing desire and creating more choices where there once weren't any. These similar functions are vital to the consumer treadmill.

The lust in my heart for the Bosch stainless steel washer and dryer was manufactured. The desire a woman has for a chemical called collagen to be injected into her lips is manufactured. The desire for a high thread count in bed linens is manufactured. The desire for Nike sneakers is manufactured.

The technique used to ease me into wanting the Bosch appliances was the notorious trick of "the best." Most people want the best when they can afford it. This is true even if they actually don't know what the best is. "I bought this Rolex for the engineering," say people who wouldn't know a tourbillon from a tour bus. This reached new heights in the 1980s with the explosion of stores like the Sharper Image, where you could purchase the world's finest nose hair trimmer. In *Seinfeld,* the show that existed to make fun of stuff like this, Elaine Benes worked for the J. Peterman Company writing catalog copy for exotic paraphernalia like the finest Bengalese galoshes. Despite being subjected to some of the most sophisticated mocking ever, J. Peterman peddles on. A recent catalog (the real one) described the "4-Wale" this way:

> Out of the corner of your eye, you notice that the man climbing the ladder to thatch the roof of that sensational thick-walled cottage in Dorset isn't merely wearing corduroy pants, but extra-wide-wale corduroy pants.
>
> Aha! The Broadway director driving to work from Snedens Landing in his Aston Martin is wearing, naturally, very-wide-wale pants.
>
> The abstract-expressionist artist roughing it in his $2 million loft in Soho is wearing, what else, enormously-wide-wale pants.
>
> What is at work here is evidence of a worldwide, but unspoken, preference: wider is better.

Presto: Someone somewhere who never before cared about wales may develop a burning need for the softest, most velvety wale ever woven.

Going forward, you might be a finicky wale wearer. Thus you will start making choices about things it never occurred to you to consider as choice-worthy before. Lands' End and the Gap corduroy may not suffice. This is the pattern by which we start feeling the need to make choices about things that never before entered our consciousness.

An especially despicable style of option multiplication comes from *Real Simple* magazine, which my wife used to get. *Real Simple's* motto is "life made easier," and its promise, obviously, is to make your life more real and more simple. The magazine does the exact opposite of that by offering a mind-boggling array of ways to complicate your life. It suckers the reader into considering chores and body parts that never before occupied more than a nanosecond of attention. Time Warner, the publisher, and its advertisers want you to make aesthetic and consumer choices about, well, everything. This generates revenue, but the cover story they sell is that *Real Simple* helps readers weave a "lifestyle"—that coveted modern word.

The big lie of *Real Simple* is that it exacerbates the problem it promises to help solve.

Women with children, the demographic targets of *Real Simple,* are the country's busiest people. They juggle work, family, home, and often parents—perhaps with some social life and fun. Time Warner and its advertisers pinpoint their anxieties with precision; market research was invented to find these things out. They want to prey on that anxiety and profit from it. Radical Martha Stewartism is no path to the Zen of a simple life.

No magazine that contains 129 separate ads, as one recent edition does, can simplify anything. And this is not counting the ads disguised as articles that recommend specific products under the pretense of how-to journalism. One issue's cover story was "34 Delicious Grilling Ideas." Please; 34! The article is so chock-full of tips and pretty pictures, you will despair to ever grill again. That edition also offers a three-step program to dress up gifts by making "the biggest bow on the block in minutes." Or how about the "Aha Use" for that cute microbrewery six-pack container: "Transporting condiments, silverware, napkins, and picnic supplies from kitchen to patio." It would be wrong to transport utensils in a way that wasn't so cute. And it would be wrong not to maximize that cute microbrewery six-pack. Also, many people don't spend enough time on sponge selection and maintenance. Unsettling, I know, but true. Never fear: *Real Simple* offers "Super soakers: tried-and-true sponges for every job (and how to keep them at their germ-free best)." The tips are vital: "Know when to reach for the paper towel" and "Learn when to let go." The best sponges for large surfaces are Williams-Sonoma Pop-Up Sponges, six for $10.50. This is diseased thinking.

In marketing vernacular, *Real Simple* is an "aspirational" magazine: people don't actually do the things in the magazine; they just aspire to them. But readers might actually buy some of the products advertised. "Martha Stewart" is an aspirational brand. *GQ* and *Vogue* are as much about the ads as the articles. Few readers can afford the clothes the articles feature, but they may buy some of the products in the ads. In aspirational marketing, the content of the media is supposed to line up with the advertised products. The idea is to peddle a complete "lifestyle image."

We have been brainwashed (and dried) into believing or acting as if the most minute consumer decisions should express our individuality and taste. We've come to feel as if such choices actually make a difference to our identities, our aesthetics, even our happiness. There is a *Real Simple* for almost every corner of life you can imagine: computers, tools, home-entertainment technology, fishing, hunting, clothes, shoes, poker, reading, exercise, diet, cooking, gardening, sports equipment, travel, and, absurdly, even storage. In fact, part of how we create our individuality is with our style of consumer purchases, Balkanization by brand.

We have allowed ourselves to believe this nonsense matters.

Of course, we know in reflective moments that it doesn't. But we still want stuff and work hard to get it.

Inner Treadmills

DESIRE IS SPURRED on not just by marketing but by human nature. Marketing is an aphrodisiac for ancient material lust. People do, in fact, need to keep up with the Joneses. When the guy at work gets a new minivan with a DVD player, you want one, too. The psychologist Daniel Kahneman, who won a Nobel Prize in Economics, has called this the "hedonistic treadmill." A person focuses on something they believe will provide happiness and when they get it, it doesn't. So they instantly and voraciously want something else. In some personality types, the treadmill is infinite. The mogul with a private jet sees a bigger jet and wants it. The tech billionaire who has a 400-foot yacht spots an oil sheik's 550-foot yacht and is one-upped and frustrated.

We see this behavior in others, and we are disgusted. When we see this behavior in ourselves—well, we don't very often. It is human nature to think you have just a little less than you need and deserve and that anyone with much more has way too much.

The same is true with a mental habit Thomas de Zengotita, the author of *Mediated*, labeled "Justin's Helmet Principle." As a kid, de Zengotita rode his bike anywhere he wanted, without supervision, knee pads, or bike helmet. But, he says, "Now that I know about bike helmets, now that they are an option, it would be downright irresponsible not to strap one on to little Justin's head before he takes off along the (very uneven, quite treacherous, actually, I never noticed before) sidewalk on his razor scooter, wouldn't it?"

Of course it makes sense to get a bike helmet. I guess. All my friends got through childhood without them. The point is marketing knows how to create fears as well as desires—fears that can be calmed by the proper product. Pretty soon, Justin will need the world's safest bike helmet.

The end result is clutter—thing clutter and decision clutter. We need the right bacteria-killing hand goo in every bathroom, even though we had never heard of bacteria-killing hand goo five years ago.

The Impotence of Criticism

I ONCE READ a summary of a conference in which leading technology investors and executives talked about their strategies. A number of them said they would invest *only* in businesses that targeted one of the "seven deadly sins" (lust, greed, gluttony, anger, sloth, pride, and envy). I imagine that these people thought they were being cute. Some of them said they were specifically looking for opportunities to invest in voyeurism.

There should be no illusions about how deliberately and ruthlessly businesspeople can prey on consumers. Every cynical thought you have about cynicism in politics should be multiplied at least fivefold when it comes to commercial marketing. There are some taboos left in political marketing; there are far fewer in commercial marketing.

This is true despite the fact that society produces a tremendous amount of media criticism. Most newspapers have critics (actually, many are getting fired now), every university has a media criticism department, and even some high schools have "media awareness" programs. The evils of consumerism, materialism, bad media, and sexploitation are frequent topics of sermons. Now, much of the newspaper and television "criticism" is mere boosterism. Academic media criticism is one of the most jargon-filled, pretentious, and inaccessible scholarly specialties now in fashion. It is shocking to me how impervious pop culture is to society's superego.

This is especially true of the superego's archenemy—sex. I have been hearing about exploitation of women in media since I was a teen. Feminists have been vigilant in spotting it and outing it for years. Women have gained immense power in media, businesses, and academia. Yet advertising gets racier and racier every year. Fashions get skankier and skankier. The S.L.U.T. line of cosmetics endures. The popularity of breast implants grows.

This has stumped me. I complained out loud that I couldn't figure out this puzzle one day and my sixteen-year-old daughter was incredulous at my thickness. She explained to me that an unintended consequence of the "whole sexual liberation thing" was to liberate the use and exploitation of sex all over the place, including in pop culture and advertising. There were still strong social mores and Puritan remnants that wouldn't tolerate this before the sixties, so sex had to be snuck into ads and movies. Then liberation came—not just to free spirits but to free markets. The power of any form of intellectual criticism—from old moralities or new "isms" like feminism—against the emotive power of thick red lips, airbrushed nipples, and six-pack abs is puny. Money and sex win, Dad.

So *Cosmopolitan* magazine, once a sassy if superficial advocate of liberation for the single woman, is now a grotesque mixture of soft-core female pornography and tips for sex slaves. Consider this lead story: "The Blended Orgasm: So Deep, So Strong. How You Can Have One Tonight." The very next article was "What Makes Men Fall in Love," a story filled with manipulative "little things [to] tip a man over that edge. For example, since men have a natural desire to protect, a woman should ask their target's opinion about things like a 401(k) or travel sites, wear soft materials like fur, and have him do easy jobs around the house to build him up." Since men need to "shine," the *Cosmo* predator should never laugh at his mistakes. Show him you're smart at board games so he knows that "you're a desirable choice for carrying on his genes." Of course, 99 percent of the ads in *Cosmo* are for body products.

MarketTainment

COSMO IS ALSO an example of how mainstream entertainment is all about providing the lubricants of lust and greed to market materialism. Pure advertising would have half its allure without a story and picture behind it. That is why God invented not just Madison Avenue but Hollywood, too.

Selling and brand pornography have fully infiltrated entertainment. Jennifer Lopez reportedly signed a deal worth roughly six million dollars to let a celebrity magazine photograph her newborn twins—products at birth. Marketing is stitched into pop entertainment without irony or apology. It's all a variation of product placement. The Black Eyed Peas recorded a hideous, much-mocked but enormously popular ode to trading sex for luxury called "My Humps":

> *They treat me really nicely,*
> *They buy me all these ices.*
> *Dolce & Gabbana,*
> *Fendi and NaDonna*

The intention of vast expanses of pop culture in all its creative glory can be boiled down to a simple, humpy line from its chorus: "She's got me spending."

Extratainment

HISTORICALLY, HIGH AND low culture have been expressions of individual creativity but also of a group's feelings, aspirations, and moral teachings. Part of a group's identity and bond was its art. Indeed, the word "entertainment" comes from a French word meaning "hold together, support." It was first used in the 1400s to mean "have a guest," as in "we entertained neighbors last night." The use of "entertain" as "amuse" came later. The word "entertainer" as a public actor came after that.

The kind of "holding together" our popular culture does now is peculiar. Entertainment now erodes the social values we aspire to instead of supporting them. Of all the institutions in American life now, Hollywood is the one Americans are most ambivalent about. We spend, as a nation, an immense amount of time with its products. Yet our mistrust and disrespect of Hollywood is equally immense. In 2005, a Fox News/ Opinion Dynamics poll asked, "In general, do you think Hollywood moviemakers share your values or not?" Seventy percent said no. Only 13 percent said yes. Yet this same population will park itself and its offspring in front of the television for three hours a day to act as voyeurs and partake in programming designed to exploit interest in the seven deadly sins.

Winner-Take-All Culture

FROM AN ECONOMIC perspective, there are several categories of art and entertainment. One kind is produced for its own sake with only modest intentions of profit; we think of this as "art" or "high culture." Entertainment, by contrast, is created primarily for profit. Some forms of entertainment make money as vehicles for advertising or marketing: television, most websites, newspapers, and magazines. The other form is fee-based: movies, premium cable, computer games, and books.

For-profit entertainment is a huge business in America. This is unusual historically and a questionable benefit of prosperity. Daniel Bell has noted that in most societies, economic life has been about subsistence, survival, and security but "now on a mass scale, economics had become geared to the demands of culture." Commercial culture is just as important in how Americans make their way through life today as religion, tradition, and local mores once were. That's why the economy is geared around it. It orients our choices and shapes our imagination.

Economics have crowded "art" and unprofitable entertainment out of the mass culture market. Too much money is at stake to waste it on opera, artsy miniseries, and literary novels. In entertainment, capital flows not just to top performers but to the top genres or styles, reducing the money and "airtime" available to other forms of entertainment. The popular forms take a disproportionate share of available resources, so demand for high culture wanes.

This creates a vicious circle. High culture is less accessible than low. It takes education in the relevant traditions as well as leisure time to appreciate it, which are both in short supply. Interest ebbs so investment ebbs. Newspapers cut the classical music, book, and art critics but try to keep the television and movie critics. Radio stations that play jazz or classical music are nearly extinct. The sales of literary novels are minuscule. Independent films are not widely distributed and are difficult to finance, as are documentaries. PBS imports its dramas.

The media explosion was supposed to change this. Cable television, the Internet, and satellite radio were supposed to reverse the conglomeration of media. And they have to some degree. They do supply special content to niche audiences. And people formerly known as "the audience" supply content to one another. But the production of high culture is expensive and time consuming. It costs money to stage an opera, support an orchestra, or make a fine movie. There is also the little problem that the very idea of high culture is ridiculed as politically incorrect, snobbish, and perpetrated only by dead white men who happen to be alive, like me.

The bottom line is that there is shrinking bandwidth for art, the most authentic, rebellious, mischievous, inspiring, and independent form of entertainment.

OmniEntertainment: Boys

MUCH, THOUGH CERTAINLY not all, for-profit entertainment mirrors or supports marketing. The effects of this can be insidious. A fine example is a phenomenon I call the Oaf Boy, a cousin to the Slacker. Sensitive and knowing people have been indoctrinated about the evils perpetrated on young women by craven mass media for decades. The sociological victims of female-stalking marketing are famous—fashion victims, anorexics, shopaholics, Botox addicts, Lolitas, and—of course— low-self-esteem sufferers. The curriculum at my kids' school teaches how to recognize and criticize unworthy stereotypes, imagery, and messages in marketing and pop culture, which I applaud.

But boys have been ignored.

As rampant as the sexualization of girls is, so is the new moronization of boys. One example of the genre was the Bud Light ad campaign star- ring "Ted Ferguson—Bud Light Daredevil." In the ads, Ted strapped on a crash helmet and attempted drunk-defying stunts, like seeing how long he could stand going without a Bud Light after work on a Friday. He made it about fifteen minutes before collapsing. In another witty adven- ture, he dared himself to go shopping with his girlfriend on a football day. Separated from beer and ball, he soon fainted and his buddies re- vived him with Bud Light, a La-Z-Boy, and a television set. The striking thing is that Ted is a pudgy, baby-faced kid who doesn't look to be even close to the legal drinking age. This is a commercial image of a man today that apparently is effective.

I have some sympathy for ad makers. They're trying to be funny, and I'll excuse most things if they're really funny. But as author and ad exec- utive Marian Salzman once told *The Washington Post,* "The only people they [advertisers] are still allowed to offend these days are straight white men with a full head of hair."

In the modern guy ad, the guy must be portrayed as misogynistic, ad- dicted, stupid, slobbish, and mean—an oaf who should be repulsive to girls and all humans. This is a variant of the modern Peter Pan, an infan- tilized boy who won't grow up—guys like George Costanza and Cosmo Kramer, Jerry's best friends in *Seinfeld.* The Oaf Boy is witless and charm- less. You can find the stereotype all over television comedy, movies, and pop music. There is a whole film genre, "gross-out movies" like *American Pie, Jackass: The Movie,* and *Dumb and Dumber,* dedicated to the beer- swilling half-witted Oaf Boy. The director Judd Apatow made two inter- esting movies that sort of take the Oaf Boy genre to task, *The Forty- Year-Old Virgin* (2005) and *Knocked Up* (2007). Both movies are about men who are boys who simply cannot or will not grow up. The forty-year- old virgin is not just a virgin, he is a little boy; he collects figurines of action heroes. In both movies, the hero is surrounded by even worse examples of infantilized Oaf Boy buddies. Eventually he escapes their grip and begins growing up.

Deborah Roffman is a Baltimore educator who wrote *Sex and Sensibility: The Thinking Parent's Guide to Talking Sense About Sex.* In an op-ed piece in *The Washington Post,* she argued that the portrait of boys and young men as slackers/swillers/sloths/slimeballs/slobs that popular culture peddles is every bit as toxic as its more scrutinized female counterpart:

> No matter how demeaning today's culture may seem toward girls and women, I've always understood it to be fundamentally more disrespectful of boys and men—a point that escapes many of us because we typically think of men as always having the upper hand.
>
> Consider, though, what "boys will be boys" thinking implies about the true nature of boys. I often ask groups of adults or students what inherent traits or characteristics the expression implies. The answers typically are astonishingly negative: Boys are messy, immature and selfish; hormone-driven and insensitive; irresponsible and trouble-making; rebellious, rude, aggressive and disrespectful—even violent, predatory and animal-like. Is this a window into what we truly think, at least unconsciously, of the male of the species? Is it possible that deep inside we really think they simply can't be expected to do any better than this?

Roffman actually is too generous. The syndrome is not one of "boys will be boys" but "boys will be pimps." Marketing and entertainment both play on this "psychographic" profile of boy-men. It is hard to imagine this being permissible twenty or even fifteen years ago. It is hard to imagine how this is progress.

Any employer who has to interview people in their twenties knows that the Oaf Boy and the Slacker are not just fictional stereotypes. Apparently, college admissions offices know this, too. In 2005, 57 percent of all undergraduates were women, even though there were slightly more men than women in the 18–24 population as a whole. That year, 10.8 percent of males in high school dropped out while 8 percent of females did.

OmniEntertainment: Girls

THOUGH IT IS true we are more clued in to the sexploitation of girls, it is worth noting that it is getting worse, not better, despite feminism and the fact that young women are performing better than young men academically and, in some select areas, financially. The escalation of sluttiness seems unstoppable, and it is mixed with approving messages about greed, manipulation, and materialism. One new aspect is the unfettered, unapologetic debauchery—sluttish clothes, unchecked greed, and calculated "partying"—of the female celebrities who are marketed to young girls. Entertainment news in 2007 was dominated by four women: Anna Nicole Smith, Paris Hilton, Lindsay Lohan, and Britney Spears. Smith was in the news because she died of a drug overdose. The others got attention for various crimes and misdemeanors—drunk driving, public drunkenness, and brief spells in prison and rehab.

Socially approved skankiness is now seeping through society, as anyone who has strolled on a city sidewalk on a sunny day knows. Something new is the more or less explicit sanctioning of the imagery and language of prostitution. This goes beyond the "ho" word. Salon.com for several years ran a column by a New York prostitute named Tracy Quan, who went on to write fairly successful novels, *Diary of a Manhattan Call Girl* and *Diary of a Married Call Girl.* Expect a movie. Washington produced a new kind of hooker scandal in 2004. Jessica Cutler, a twenty-something assistant to a Republican senator, became famous for blogging under the pen name "Washingtonienne." She published her Web diary, which was little more than a cheeky, cynical chronicle of her sex life that included sex for money. Surprise, surprise—she was "exposed" and got her fifteen minutes of fame. Her postings featured so many different partners and accomplices that she had to publish this "key" to keep them straight:

J=The intern in my office whom I want to fuck.

F=Married man who pays me for sex. Chief of Staff at one of the gov agencies, appointed by Bush.

J=Lost my virginity to him and fell in love. Dude who has been driving me crazy since 1999. Lives in Springfield, IL. Flies halfway across the country to fuck me, then I don't hear from him for weeks.

MD=Dude from the Senate office I interned in Jan. thru Feb. Hired me as an intern. Broke up my relationship w/ MK (see below).

MK=Serious, long-term boyfriend whom I lived with since 2001. Disastrous breakup in March, but still seeing each other.

R=AKA "Threesome Dude." Somebody I would rather forget about.

RS=My new office bf with whom I am embroiled in an office sex scandal. The current favorite.

W=A sugar daddy who wants nothing but anal. Keep trying to end it with him, but the money is too good.

Shit. I'm fucking six guys. Ewww.

Of course Jessica Cutler was fired from her Senate job, but Washingtonienne became a celeb with the requisite *Playboy* spread and the inevitable book deal for a reported $300,000. The fact that she was essentially a prostitute only added to her market value.

Washingtonienne's story got lots of play in the news because the connection to a Senate office gave it a hint of newsworthiness. The news media is eager to cover this sort of thing whenever there is a whiff of "news" about it: Anna Nicole Smith's death, Paris Hilton's prison time, or Washingtonienne's government connections. Even the highbrow media is guilty. A subtle example of this came when *The New York Times Book Review* reviewed a book about plastic surgery by a beautiful female reporter at the *Times*, Alex Kuczynski. The reviewer was Toni Bentley, a former ballet dancer who had recently published a memoir of her newly discovered passion—I'm not kidding—for anal sex and the profound spiritual enlightenment it brought to her life. Bentley's book, an unparalleled display of boomer exhibitionism and narcissism mixed with sexual merchandising, was also lavishly and voyeuristically reviewed in the *Times*.

So the culture of this weird sexualization reaches into places that would seem the most vigilant. In Cleveland Park, an upscale but lefty neighborhood in D.C., the local gym occasionally offers exercise classes with a stripper theme. Apparently women with fanny packs and Birkenstocks come in to learn how to do splits on a pole.

Women willing to flaunt their greed and sexuality are also the staples of reality television, the most popular form of mass voyeurism feeding on exhibitionism. In the *Survivor* series, thonged and Botoxed hotties battle buffed and waxed Oaf Boys for the million-dollar prize. Most game-based reality shows are variants on that formula.

Reality shows that purport to show people in normal environments are worse than the concocted ones. There was a show on the cable network Bravo called *The Real Housewives of Orange County* that was a "reality" show based on the "pretend" ABC series *Desperate Housewives*. *Real Housewives* was all about wealthy women in Orange County, California, who, with staggering exhibitionism, allowed cameras to see their most venal, vain, greedy, shallow, and embarrassing moments. One mother, Lauri Waring, desperately wanted an invitation to a negligee party at Hugh Hefner's Playboy mansion. "I'm competing against girls younger than my daughter," she said. Another one, Jo De La Rosa, candidly said, "I'm happy to be engaged to a man who has the potential to make a kabillion dollars. But if he doesn't make kabillions, if he just makes millions, I'll be happy."

That is a bizarre but apparently infectious image of happiness. More than staged, traditional television, reality television lets passive viewers come one step closer to believing they can be just like the people on television. This is also part of why audiences are so drawn to the "real personal lives" of the Paris Hiltons of the world (even her name is a brand). This isn't harmless. Women want to buy the clothes, jewelry, and makeup gossip girls use. Girls permanently alter their bodies to achieve this "brand" of happiness. Breast implants are a common prize in radio call-in contests. And of course there is a reality show about just that, *Extreme Makeover*. In each episode of the show, two self-described ugly ducklings trade their dignity and privacy for free plastic surgery. After confessing their insecurities to the show's hostess, they are whisked off to Hollywood for massive structural rehabilitation, including face-lifts, eye jobs, nose jobs, breast augmentation, liposuction, microdermabrasion, and ear pin-backs. When the scars and swelling are sufficiently reduced, it's time for cosmetic dentistry, new hair colors and styles, expert makeup jobs, and, finally, chic clothes. Then the Cinderellas are brought back home to Arkansas or Nebraska or wherever and unveiled to their friends and families. They are instructed to live happily and beautifully ever after. We're shown only a few graphic and grisly pictures of the surgeries and recovery. One writer called it "mutilation as entertainment."

Celebrity culture explicitly promotes and rewards this. A cover story in *Us Weekly* magazine was headlined "Revenge Plastic Surgery." It was about an aspiring starlet-singer named Heidi Montag who got a nose job and a boob job to exact revenge on boys who teased her in high school. Giving *Us Weekly* an exclusive interview was an important step for Heidi to get comfortable with her bold actions. She looked through *Playboy* to pick the pair she wanted and studied four hundred pictures of noses. *Us,* being such a responsible journal, reported in a sidebar story that "an August study found that women with implants have triple the suicide rate of women without."

Once upon a time, feminists could pretend that heightened, "honest" sexuality in entertainment was somehow "empowering" for women. The only people who say that now are people who profit from it. In an article in *The New York Times* about the unfettered use of the word "slut," a former editor of *Seventeen* magazine named Atoosa Rubenstein said, "Today, 'slut,' even 'ho'—girls use it in a fun way, a positive way." When the editor of *Seventeen* is defending the "fun, positive" ways girls can be called sluts and whores, there is a problem. Rubenstein has since left *Seventeen* to "gather her tribe" (her words), set up a production company to promote the brand that is Atoosa Rubenstein, and try to become the "alpha kitty" (her words) to the thirteen-to-thirty beta girls set.

Tolerating Taboos

THE EXAMPLES OF uncultured culture I've cited are mainstream and prime-time. Just as I could find counterexamples with redeeming social value, I could also find much worse. The most discussed examples of taboo-shattering culture come from popular music, especially rap, hip-hop, and heavy metal. It is actually quite difficult to imagine something that might *not* be acceptable in music today. It's a contest to be the most offensive. Violence, murder, robbery, guns, and drugs are all praised and glorified. Women aren't objectified, they're just hated and insulted, routinely called hos, bitches, and a bunch of other words I'd rather not use. Consider the lyrics of just one, almost randomly selected song, "P.I.M.P." by 50 Cent:

> *I'm bout my money you see, girl you can holla at me*
> *If you fucking with me, I'm a P-I-M-P . . .*

> *That other nigga you be with ain't bout shit*
> *I'm your friend, your father, and confidant, BITCH*

Or this from Eminem's "Drips":

> *All these bitches on my dick*
> *That's how dudes be getting sick*
> *That's how dicks be getting drips . . .*
> *From these bitches on our dicks*

Can you imagine what could be a forbidden lyric?

There are many other infected strains of pop culture now, and in some ways the more extreme music has more virtues; it is at least angry and rebellious. The synthetic teen sex-kitten dreck of Britney Spears is pure marketing with no talent, edge, or anything to say. There's kinky, twisted stuff all over. The most popular shows on prime-time television from 2005 through 2007 were the *C.S.I.* shows, which are essentially about autopsies and the details of crime scenes. Slasher movies with outrageously sick violence target teenagers. Adventure movies are filled with gory violence and body counts in the hundreds or thousands. Strip clubs are newly popular and people no longer sneak into them; they go with dates, coed groups, and colleagues. Pick your poison.

Why do we as a society tolerate such cultural toxins? Why are they entertaining? This is at the very heart of why we hate us.

Society at large has lost its confidence and capacity to impose standards on culture such as music and film, but why would parents let their children listen to Eminem? Actually, why would a child want to? What is the appeal? Why would girls listen to 50 Cent? Why would suburban kids want to imitate ghetto culture? Why would a guy like me be entertained by novels and movies about Hannibal Lecter, a serial-killing cannibal?

There are many theories. A common one is that OmniMedia has desensitized us. We have seen so much sex, violence, and suffering—both real and imaginary—that it takes larger and larger doses to make us feel something, even something upsetting or painful. To get a rise out of an audience, the sex must be more explicit, the violence bloodier, the lyrics nastier, and the jokes raunchier. To feel entertained, we seek out increasingly decadent delights. We need to be shocked. But the bar for what shocks us is raised after each new, taboo-shattering thrill. In this environment, young people need to shock themselves and their worlds with grotesque tattoos and piercings. They feel like they're being creative, just like rappers do, but in reality they are just embodying and reflecting the deformities around them.

Others think sexual and violent entertainment is soothing because we see our nightmares enacted, and we survive. Or it allows us to indulge fantasies or unconscious urges. I suppose that's all true, but it doesn't explain why we have become so permissive and indulgent.

Defining Deviancy Way Down

THIS IS SIMILAR to what the scholar and Democratic senator from New York Daniel Patrick Moynihan called "defining deviancy down," a social dynamic where the definitions of normal or acceptable are changed to include behavior once considered impermissible or unhealthy. Moynihan suggested that there is only a certain amount of deviant behavior than we can "afford to recognize" at any given time. For example, as crime increased in the 1960s and 1970s, definitions of crime changed both legally and culturally. Some crimes were relabeled as misdemeanors. High levels of crime eventually came to be perceived as normal. Moynihan notes that in 1929, the St. Valentine's Day Massacre, in which four mobsters killed seven other mobsters in Chicago, was considered an appalling national atrocity. Today, it would be a one-day story but only on the local news. It takes much more violence than that to appear deviant, to get our attention. So we are not shocked by songs about pimps, TV shows called *Dirty Sexy Money*, or movies filled with close-up pictures of heads shot by bullets. "We are getting used to a lot of behavior that is not good for us," Moynihan wrote in 1993.

That is an understatement.

While Moynihan helps explain how society can come to permit or passively tolerate more "deviancy," he doesn't explain why "deviant" culture—sexually exploitive and violent "entertainment"—has such a powerful draw. Charles Murray, the always controversial conservative writer, has an interesting theory taken from the British historian Arnold Toynbee. In a 2001 essay in *The Wall Street Journal*, Murray put forth a variation of the "America Is Rome" idea:

> One of the consistent symptoms of disintegration is that the elites . . . begin to imitate those at the bottom of society. His [Toynbee's] argument goes like this:
> The growth phase of a civilization is led by a creative minority with a strong, self-confident sense of style, virtue and purpose. The uncreative majority follows along through mimesis, "a mechanical and superficial imitation of the great and inspired originals." In a disintegrating civilization, the creative minority has degenerated into elites that are no longer confident, no longer setting the example. Among other reactions are a "lapse into truancy" (a rejection, in effect, of the obligations of citizenship), and a "surrender to a sense of promiscuity" (vulgarizations of manners, the arts, and language). . . .

That sounds very much like what has been happening in the U.S. Truancy and promiscuity, in Toynbee's sense, are not new in America. But until a few decades ago they were publicly despised and largely confined to the bottom layer of Toynbee's proletariat—the group we used to call low-class or "trash," and which we now call the underclass. Today, those behaviors have been transmuted into a code that the elites sometimes imitate, sometimes placate, and fear to challenge. Meanwhile, they no longer have a code of their own in which they have confidence.

Whatever the dynamic, no class today has the confidence to fight the prevailing culture. Only the elite profits from it though.

Chris Eads has a simpler theory. He thinks life is just hard and busy despite our prosperity, or perhaps because of it. With long commutes, lots of errands, too much debt, demanding bosses, little job security, and little support from family and neighbors, people are hurting at the end of the day. They long for relief and escape. "It's a lust for just feeling good for a while," Eads said with sympathy, not judgment. "Marketers have figured out what will push those emotional pleasure buttons in different kinds of people. We're rich enough so we have more time and space to push those lust buttons."

Real Culture Warriors

THE PICTURE I drew of commercial and entertainment culture focused on the negative because I am trying to understand why we hate so much of it. There is plenty of positive, creative material out there as well. Society is not just rolling over and taking culture abuse entirely passively.

Resistance to the capacities of marketing and branding to infiltrate lives and souls is now a common form of political activism among young people, who tend to understand the power of the brand to interfere with individuality and enforce conformity far more than their parents do. It is obnoxious to be marketed to—to be a constant target of advertising and branding. People hate it, again, when they notice. My kids understand this. When they were fifteen and twelve, they became excited when they spotted a piece of graffiti that said "Converse = Nike. Fuck Cool." They understood exactly what it meant: that cool is just another marketed thing. They took a picture of the graffiti. Perhaps resistance is not completely futile.

If there is one track where multicultural America and pseudo-polarized America may be coming closer together, it is in the frustrated distaste for the prevailing spirit of OmniMarketing. When Tipper Gore joined up with conservative Christians to lobby for labels on raunchy records back in the 1980s, she was ridiculed. She might have more respect today. In 2007, for example, the Reverend Delman Coates of the Mount Ennon Baptist Church in Clinton, Maryland, a primarily African-American congregation, led a protest at the home of Debra Lee, the chief executive officer at Black Entertainment Television (BET). They protested the demeaning portrayal of black people, playing to the "pimp" and "gangster" images of black men and "bitches and hos" images of black women. They objected to shows like *Hot Ghetto Mess.* The church protesters were joined by members of the National Organization for Women and the Feminist Majority Foundation.

There are many thoughtful liberal people—perhaps even most liberal people—who are unhappy with the commercialization of culture, the materialism of society, and the vulgarity of pop culture. Their views aren't reflected in the Democratic Party at all. Similarly, there are many cultural conservatives who are critical not just of permissive culture but of permissive, unfettered, greedy market commerce. Sometimes conservative politicians express their views on entertainment but never their views on the power of markets and marketing. Opposition to Omni-Marketing is a potentially de-Balkanizing issue, which is why it is not on any political agendas.

OmniMarketing is an unpleasant, chafing part of the change in America over the past forty years. Living fast-paced lives, immersed in media and separated from community, has made us squirrelly, to put it bluntly. The pathologies—the dark sides—are reflected and then exaggerated in public culture, especially in politics, advertising, and popular entertainment. That culture inevitably shapes our identities and values. Most important, it shapes our conduct and how we treat others.

Chapter Eight

THE CHARACTER GAP

IF HOLDEN CAULFIELD, the consummate American phony spotter from *The Catcher in the Rye,* had managed to get through college, he might have ended up like Benjamin Braddock, the alienated but earnest and awkward antihero of the 1967 movie *The Graduate.* Played by Dustin Hoffman, Benjamin was fresh out of college "back east" and camped at his parents' home in California's sterile suburbs. He was lonely, directionless, and disillusioned. There was no community for him to rejoin, no vocation calling him, and nobody who had a life that inspired him. His options were personified by two people, perhaps his potential role models. There was a pompous fool who ceremoniously took Ben aside at his poolside graduation party and offered him a famous one-word piece of advice: "Plastics." And there was Mrs. Robinson, the older, dissolute sophisticate who seduced Benjamin. His world's lack of anything to admire was captured in the refrain of Paul Simon's musical tribute to Mrs. Robinson:

> *Where have you gone, Joe DiMaggio?*
> *A nation turns its lonely eyes to you.*

The following year, 1968, came to be seen as the official start of a new era in American history. Hippies and yippies battled Mayor Richard J. Daley's police force at the Democratic National Convention in Chicago; Lyndon Johnson, who had signed the most important civil rights legislation in a century, withdrew from the presidential campaign because of the Vietnam War; Richard Nixon was elected president. But most significantly, Martin Luther King, Jr., and Robert Kennedy were killed. They were not just "gone" like Joe DiMaggio. They were murdered.

We have been wondering "where have you gone" about leaders, heroes, and even simple role models ever since. There has been no one to compare to King in the decades since he died. The idea that politicians like John F. Kennedy or Bobby Kennedy could even fleetingly reach hero status seems quaint today. Our contemporary Joe DiMaggios are either pumped full of steroids or so obscenely rich that they are somehow off our radars. Fictional mob boss Tony Soprano goes to therapy to control his anxiety attacks and wonders where all the Gary Coopers have gone.

Our culture has proven much more adept at tearing down public figures and building up worthless celebrities than at producing genuine leadership. Perhaps only children need heroes. But we have few public figures who don't become embarrassments, much less steady moral exemplars. We generate celebrity but not leadership, fame but not honor.

There is no shortage of impostors. There is a shortage of good and sane people willing to endure the 24/7 gaze of OmniMedia that leadership and public service now require. So there is a vacuum of character in the public realm. We hate it, perhaps because we see the same deficit in ourselves. We should consider that soberly. In the end, we control only ourselves. Building in ourselves the character we wish leaders had, and then practicing the habits of behavior—the manners—that express character, is the best way to hate us less and to contribute less that is hateful to our communities.

Etched and Polished

"CHARACTER" IS THE name of the amorphous quality we seek in public figures. It is akin to the authenticity we seek in our own lives. It is what transforms the merely powerful into leaders. Warren Buffett has character; Donald Trump does not. Tiger Woods has character; Barry Bonds does not.

"Morality is character, character is that which is engraved," wrote Søren Kierkegaard in *The Present Age*. The word comes from the Greek *charactēr*, "to sharpen, cut into furrows, engrave." We say a trait is etched in one's character. Character guides our choices, but importantly, it is also visible to the world, if the world chooses to look closely.

Character's first cousin is politeness. "Polite" is an interesting word. It doesn't have the same root as "politics" but comes from the Latin *politus*, "to polish, to make smooth." Politeness is the polished surface we present to the world; character is engraved more deeply.

We think of character as innate and manners as learned, which is a mistake. Certainly aspects of personality are determined by nature, not nurture, by genes, evolution, and hardwiring. But only the most radical determinist would argue that the environment, family, and will are trivial. Character is also taught and learned, as manners are, but it is etched in, not just polished on. The task of building character is deeper and more difficult than learning manners. But the goal of teaching both character and manners is to habituate a person to acting on higher impulses, to being respectful toward other people automatically. (Omni-Marketing is the reverse, targeted at base instincts, like desire.) The challenge comes from spontaneous situations, when snap decisions and a quick tongue are required. That's when instinct takes over. Character and manners ought to guide instinct, not in a way that makes us phony but in a way that makes us authentic (sincere, moral, effortful) and respectful. Manners are always needed when dealing with others; character can be displayed or perceived more or less permanently in a person, but it is most necessary in important or stressful situations, which is why they are often called "tests of character."

I Swear

CHARACTER AND MANNERS are mostly conveyed by talking, though actions are obviously the ultimate measure. Like many people, I am not articulate unless I am completely relaxed, a rare occurrence. Most of the time, like many people, I hope manners and learned character take over where my wits are slow. Consider swearing.

When I was about eight or nine I was playing with my cousin Tommy in the upstairs hall of our grandmother's house. All of a sudden, my mother appeared and in a glance I knew I was in serious trouble. And I knew exactly why. I had been swearing to impress Tommy, who was one year older, a better athlete, and way cooler. I was from a suburb. He was from a city, Fargo. Mom dragged me into a bathroom, the one Tommy's parents were using, and washed my mouth out with soap. I'm quite sure it was yellow Dial.

Despite the application of this traditional remedy, I still swear a lot. My dad swore. I was the class clown who would do most anything to get a laugh, and body functions were a pretty reliable source of yucks for boys (and men). It became a habit. The soap didn't work, but my mother tried.

Eventually the time came when I swore inappropriately at work. It happened more than once. I offended people and in some cases I hurt people's feelings. I now try to swear less, not just because it is good manners, but because I finally figured out it was a disrespectful way of treating people. We might say it was a sign of weak character, which is true. Character, we too often forget, *can* be taught, improved, and cultivated. It isn't genetic and immutable. To think so is a slothful cop-out. I was a slow learner.

So I am the swearing police with my kids. And they think I am a hypocrite because I still swear. I have not broken the habit entirely by a long shot. But I would rather be a hypocrite than allow my children to develop a habit of swearing. So I keep at it. But public culture is my enemy.

Habits of the Heart

THE ENVIRONMENT FOR character education today is rotten. The times are not exactly ripe for etiquette, either. The screaming lack of both virtues contributes enormously to the "why we hate us" saga. We hate weasels and we hate rude people. We should. But—big but—when it comes to character and manners we are obliged to again consider not just what we think of the world, but what we contribute to it. Do we, in public, exhibit good character? Do we have good manners?

These sound like goofy, ancient questions today. The motto of New College at the University of Oxford is "Manners Maketh Man," attributed to William of Wykeham, 1324–1404. In today's world that motto makes about as much sense as "The world is flat." If manners maketh man, man today is unmade. Even in England.

But character and manners do, substantially, maketh man—and woman. This is exactly why we used to spend so much time and love instilling character virtues and good manners into our children and why some people still do. After loving them, this is perhaps the primary challenge of parenting.

But parenting isn't enough. Character and manners make up what Alexis de Tocqueville called "habits of the heart." Robert Bellah chose that phrase for the title of his 1985 book to express his worries that sociable, unselfish habits of the heart were atrophying because fewer and fewer Americans belonged to the robust communities necessary to inculcate them. Cultivated habits of the heart, he argued, were a lubricant for politics and for happiness.

The Queen

ONCE UPON A time, common people looked at kings and queens for models of character and manners. The Brits still do apparently. But there has been a shift. The difficulties public figures face in trying to display good character and manners in these times of changing traditions, and in the OmniMedia world, are beautifully captured in the movie *The Queen*. The movie is about Queen Elizabeth II's struggle to find her proper role during the mourning for Diana, Princess of Wales. The queen had never before had to invent or discover a "role" for herself as all her life her duties had been prescribed by explicit tradition. But Diana changed that. The difficulties of protocol brought about by the fact that Diana was the prince's ex-wife were the least of it. The British people felt they knew Diana intimately, not formally as they had past royals. They came to crave this intimacy. Diana knew this and had the charisma, beauty, and exhibitionism to play to it through the media. She shared her feelings and confessed her weaknesses. Her upper lip was not always stiff, though always glossed.

This was a new kind of regime for the Windsors. Queen Elizabeth slowly and painfully came to realize that the British people, indeed the world, desperately wanted to witness her grief—her private feelings! But Elizabeth had been taught for her whole life that a monarch was to be private, dignified, stoic, and wholly unemotional in the face of all hardship. The times seemed to demand different character and different manners. In a touching scene, Helen Mirren's Elizabeth struggled to figure out what to do in a stroll through the gardens of Balmoral Castle with her ancient mother, the Queen Mum. "Something's happened," the queen said sadly. "There's been a change . . . a shift of values."

Indeed, there has been. It has come to America as well, changing our character and manners. And our kings and queens—our leaders— are struggling to cope as well.

Hustlers and Character

MANY FORCES OF darkness conspire to threaten public displays of character. In 2007, Larry Flynt and *Hustler,* his porn magazine and empire, ran a full-page advertisement in *The Washington Post* with a million-dollar offer. "Have you had a sexual encounter with a current member of the United States Congress or a high-ranking government official?" the ad asked. "Can you provide documented evidence of illicit sexual or intimate relations with a Congressperson, Senator or other prominent officeholder? Larry Flynt and HUSTLER magazine will pay you up to $1 million if we choose to publish your verified story and use your material."

What's not to hate about this?

Think about just a few of the questions related to public character that immediately crop up. Why would *The Washington Post* run such an ad? Did people actually respond? How many people's private lives can withstand this kind of scrutiny—not just from the media, but from blackmailers, campaign dirty tricksters, and quick-buck grifters of various stripes? Why are sex scandals worth one million dollars on the open market? Why do the players in sex scandals gain fame and riches so often? Public life is stacked to destroy, not create, exemplars of character.

There is another famous hustler named Henry Blodget. A Yale graduate who tried to become a writer, Blodget ended up at a Wall Street investment bank. He became the most famous "analyst" of the dot-com boom in 1998 when he predicted that the stock of the online bookseller Amazon.com would hit the buck-o-spheric level of $400 a share—and it did. Blodget jumped over to Merrill Lynch for a reported $3 million salary, which seemed like a lot of money in those days but which is now chump change in the hedge fund world. He became an omnipresent media oracle, the rock star of dot-com analysts.

Investment banks and brokerage houses are legally supposed to have an iron curtain between the analysts and the salesmen. Analysts are meant to be objective, while the salesmen sell securities to the public or financial services to institutions. At Merrill, this was a joke. Analysts and their so-called reports were tools of the salesmen and pushed stocks they didn't believe in. Blodget, the most celebrated analyst, wrote internal e-mails trashing stocks Merrill Lynch was publicly plugging. One was a company called InfoSpace that Blodget in an e-mail called "a piece of junk."

The New York attorney general got wind of this and accused Merrill Lynch of securities fraud. Merrill eventually agreed to pay a $100 million settlement. Many other Wall Street firms paid similar settlements. Blodget accepted a buyout from Merrill for a reported $5 million in 2001, a fraction of what he had already earned there. In 2003, he settled with the New York attorney general and paid a $4 million penalty but admitted no wrongdoing.

Like many good-looking famous criminals, Blodget got a book deal. Rather more incredibly, Slate.com hired Blodget to write about white-collar crime. *Slate* was one of the first professionally edited, high-quality Web-only magazines. It is smart, sarcastic, hyper-ironic, and morally high-toned. *Slate*'s stunt struck me as more disappointing than anything Blodget ever pulled off. I guess giving legitimacy and a platform to a proven rat is worth it if it provides a couple of good sassy stories, a little PR buzz, and maybe some new readers.

What happened to the impulses of sound character that ought to have prevented the *Hustler* advertisement from ever appearing in *The Washington Post* or Merrill Lynch from allowing Henry Blodget to pimp stocks or *Slate* from hiring and marketing a crook? Slow atrophy appears to be the murky answer. Two consequences are clear. In OmniMedia and OmniMarketing culture, bad character is frequently rewarded with fame and fortune; this is a truly perverted incentive mechanism and we hate it. There is also a severe deficit of that form of character known as leadership. And there is an egregious oversupply of leadership's evil twin: celebrity. We hate this, too, rightfully.

The Character Gap

PLEASE TAKE OUT a piece of paper and pencil for an experiment. Write down five names of living American public figures who you believe have true character. They don't have to be people you agree with or people you'd like to have dinner with. Show this list to five random people. I predict every name on the list will be wildly and hideously condemned by at least two people, probably more. No one on the list will get more than three approvals. Chances are high that four of the five people will think you are a complete jerk because they hate one of the names on your list so much.

I inadvertently tried a version of this once several years ago. In a column, to make a tangential point, I ran a list of some people I thought were widely seen as *not* being total bullshit artists or phonies: "John McCain, pre-Bush Colin Powell, Don Imus [pre-fall], Jon Stewart, and Oprah Winfrey." Well, I shouldn't have bothered with the rest of the column because this little list was all people noticed. I might as well have listed Hitler, Stalin, and James Earl Ray. I was flooded with vitriolic and vicious e-mail. How could I include that warmongering phony hypocrite John McCain? Oprah was nothing but a raging egomaniac hyping false dreams of self-improvement to make her second or third billion dollars. Powell betrayed the nation and all those who trusted and admired him by lying to the world in his United Nations speech justifying the invasion of Iraq. Jon Stewart was just a liberal comic hack whose cynicism was stunting any hope of political idealism among his young viewers. Don

Imus was a racist, homophobic loudmouth. He could dish it out but couldn't take it, which became apparent when he was fired later for racist comments.

I'm not sure that any list of well-known names would fare much better. When that changes, the times will have changed. Obviously, there is no famous person everyone respects. But are there really so few public figures that at least most people don't detest? Actually, there aren't. Annual surveys of the most respected people by Americans always put the sitting president, some ex-presidents, the pope, and the First Lady at the top of the list with less than awe-inspiring ratings. Writers and intellectuals aren't widely known and don't register. Few politicians below president and vice president register for long. Admiration is fleeting and shallow today.

The question is, why? Why so much celebrity and so little character?

Character and Community

JUST AS AMERICANS consistently mistrust public institutions such as government and the media, they mistrust the people who represent those institutions—the people at the top. To the degree that we dislike public culture, we dislike the people who populate it. To the degree that we think the public environment is a polluted health risk, we think of public figures as polluters. It is next to impossible to be an admired leader of a corrupt institution, a noble player in a decadent system, or a clean pool in a toxic stream.

As we saw with politics, this creates a vicious circle. The sleazier politics gets, the less inclined people of high character are to enter politics, and so politics becomes even sleazier. The vicious circle is probably irrelevant in fields where financial incentives are growing most rapidly: law, technology, real estate, high-end corporate management, and especially financial services. But it does apply to recruitment in many professions that are not extremely high paying but that have become less respected, socially valued, quality oriented, and thus less rewarding: politics, journalism, medicine, teaching, publishing, and even the clergy. Good people are discouraged, and that further hurts those professions.

Character is taught by community, not just a parent or a pair of

parents. A child who grows up away from a network of relatives simply
has fewer naturally accredited teachers of character. Children who grow
up in neighborhoods where the grown-ups who live on the block or the
cul-de-sac aren't around or don't know one another have fewer potential
teachers. Kids who don't get to be around old people miss out. Omni-
Media and OmniMarketing fill the void. They provide character education whether we like it or not. The programming, of course, is designed
to be addictive and profitable, not redeeming. Real people do, in fact,
act like characters on *The Simpsons, Family Guy,* and *South Park.* Controlling children's media consumption is now an essential part of parenting.
Or at least it should be.

The Character of Leaders

AS WE ARE short of community and confidants, and spend so much
time with OmniMedia, it isn't surprising that we now want to see public
figures exemplify good, sound private character. Where else are we supposed to go for models? But we do love it when the famous misbehave,
and we can gloat. It is as if they are real people in our lives. Our expectations are unrealistic and even childish, of course. Private and public
virtues are different and often in conflict. Ignoring that is part of the immature culture of narcissism. As with Diana, Princess of Wales and *The
Queen,* we seek personal candor and emotional availability (even vulnerability) from public figures today. We want famous people to feel what
we feel, but we won't tolerate their foibles. We want much more than
competence and public virtue, which are hard enough to find.

Showing emotion used to be a sign of weakness. The American version
of a stiff upper lip is machismo in men and a kind of nurturing stoicism in
women. Americans were not always obsessed with the private feelings of
our American royals. Franklin D. Roosevelt didn't want to be seen in his
wheelchair, and reporters obliged. The dashing John F. Kennedy and his
beautiful wife were allowed to keep their lives private during his lifetime.
There was a sense that public and private were distinct. Indeed, there was
a sober recognition that a good public person was not necessarily a good
private person. Now we expect both. And we expect public figures to display mutually exclusive qualities: openness and certainty, sensitivity and

toughness, independence and empathy. We expect the impossible. We get roughly what we deserve.

In a country that is Balkanized culturally, ideologically, and ethnically, there are some leaders and maybe even heroes within smaller communities. What is missing is leadership or inspiration *across* groups. By definition, there cannot be a leader without a functioning group of followers. There is no functioning national group in America today.

Character Cannibalism

"THE FEAR OF missing out means today's media, more than ever before, hunts in a pack," said former British prime minister Tony Blair. "In these modes, it is like a feral beast, just tearing people and reputations to bits." Well, the American feral pack is bigger than the British feral pack, though maybe not quite as rabid.

It is not the press's job to create heroes. It is also not the press's job to devour those who dare to speak in public. But nothing animates the press corps—and the ratings—more than the scent of blood in the water. The frenzies over Monica Lewinsky and O. J. Simpson showed us that. Sometimes it feels like the press pines for those glory days of tabloid fun. They—we—get our juices flowing when Congressman Mark Foley gets caught sending lewd e-mails to teenage male pages, when Anna Nicole Smith overdoses a few months after having a baby, or when I. Lewis "Scooter" Libby lies to a grand jury about a leak from the Bush White House. There are so many seemingly legitimate targets.

Leaders intentionally seek and retain public power or influence. Much of the time, when they fall, there is good reason and proportionate coverage. An apt example is William J. Bennett, a high-profile neoconservative academic who served as Ronald Reagan's secretary of education. After leaving office, he went on to write a series of moral guidebooks: *The Book of Virtues: A Treasury of Great Moral Stories*, *The Children's Book of Virtues*, *The Book of Virtues for Young People: A Treasury of Great Moral Stories*, and *The Moral Compass: Stories for a Life's Journey*. As America's most famous moral tutor, Bennett made millions from his books, lectures, and television appearances. He was a top-flight pundit with stern opinions on the likes of Bill Clinton.

Then in 2003, a small political magazine called *The Washington Monthly* broke the news that Bennett was a heavy-duty gambler, not an activity sanctioned by his books on virtue. Gambling may not be as high on the sin list as adultery and embezzling, but Bennett rode a very high horse. His fall inspired a great deal of schadenfreude. Bennett's credibility was certainly harmed, but not as much as his detractors wished.

Talk-show host Don Imus fell by crossing the invisible barrier of appropriateness. Imus was an openly recovering addict who seemed to be a guy with no bullshit left in him. He said what he thought, acknowledged he was half nuts, and didn't take himself enormously seriously, though he was intense. He raised a tremendous amount of money to build a camp for children with cancer in New Mexico. But Imus was also funny as hell. He had an on-air posse of straight men, mimics, and gonzo cretins who would do anything for a laugh. The stream of puerile, insensitive, crude, and politically incorrect humor was constant. No one was spared: gays, Jews, African-Americans, Irish, Bill Clinton, George W. Bush, rednecks, holy rollers, business moguls, and alcoholics. On any given day, there was plenty to offend.

Unlike Bennett, Imus didn't present himself as a role model of virtue or hold high office. He constantly referred to himself as a drunk and an addict. But people listened to him. In the spring of 2007, he and his posse went on a riff making fun of the Rutgers women's basketball team, which was in the NCAA finals, calling them "nappy-headed hos." Imus and company obviously thought they were being funny, but it crossed the line. It wasn't just politically incorrect, it was racist, sexist, and mean. And he picked on kids. Full media frenzy ensued. Imus apologized. Not enough. He made a pilgrimage to kiss the ring of Al Sharpton, the publicity-addicted self-appointed civil-rights leader. Not enough. MSNBC cancelled him on television. Not enough. CBS Radio pulled his show. Enough.

Imus and his crew, however, produced equally or more offensive comments and cracks routinely. There was something random in the nature of his final fall. For some reason, the feral pack gathered on this one. His fall became inevitable. The video of his comments took off on the Web. Few survive this sort of media garroting, though Imus was back on smaller stations eight months later.

One more example: In late 2003, an unknown former governor of Vermont named Howard Dean unexpectedly became the front runner in the Democratic presidential primaries. He was seen as a gutsy, passionate maverick and was the first presidential candidate who figured out how to use the Internet. As a neighbor of the mighty primary state of New Hampshire, he had a built-in advantage. Iowa, where the first nominating event is held, was where Howard Dean needed to win if he were really to go from fringe candidate to nominee.

He did poorly in Iowa, finishing third. Late at night he went to a rally of his troops and committed what became known as "the Dean scream." He tried to inspire the troops at the top of his lungs; they roared back and so did he. The punditocracy instantly declared this display too much. It was a sign of bad character, a sign that he might be unstable, a nut job.

I have watched this event many times. It was a bit zany, but not very different than many other election-night rallies. Dean was pumped up, sure. His behavior displayed absolutely nothing more than that. At the very most, it was a minor gaffe.

The press feasts on gaffes in a way that parades its own hypocrisy. Journalists complain that politicians are phony, programmed, and polished, yet the minute they depart from their script, we squash them. One misspoken word, one raised voice, one off-color joke, and the gaffe "gotcha" machine kicks into high gear. That's what happened to Dean.

There is no benefit of the doubt for anyone. We love to watch them squirm. We are hooked on serial character assassination. "We" includes the audience and press pack. Both are feral beasts.

We hate our leaders for being too much like us.

And then we wonder why good people won't go into politics.

Celebrity Cannibalism

THE LIFE CYCLE of entertainment celebrities is different. In some ways, celebrities are just as important as political leaders because children pay attention to them. Generally, so-called mainstream media lets the entertainment press handle celebs, at least until they stumble. Then OmniMedia turns actors, actresses, "scandalistas," and the simply famous into figures of obsessive, repetitive pathological attention. You could chart the patterns in the stories of names like O. J. Simpson (charged with murder), Anna Nicole Smith (inheritance, overdose), Michael Jackson (charged with child molestation), Hugh Grant (lewd conduct), Winona Ryder (shoplifting), Martha Stewart (insider trading), Robert Blake (charged with murder), Lindsay Lohan (driving under the influence and cocaine possession), Britney Spears (general insanity), and Paris Hilton (driving under the influence and jail for violating parole).

This is not necessarily new in America. There have been trivial scandals for a long time. There have been people who are famous for being famous for a long time. But the scale is different. And so is the fact that society perversely grants fame to celebrity reprobates who deserve incarceration or condemnation instead of magazine spreads and book deals. Sydney Biddle Barrows was a high-society woman who made an unconventional career choice: She became a madam, a female pimp. When she got caught, she became famous. Perhaps she would have preferred to avoid the fame but that didn't stop her from writing a bestseller, *The Mayflower Madam,* and two other books, one called *Just Between Us Girls: Secrets About Men from the Madam Who Knows.* Heidi Fleiss was a Los Angeles madam, a doctor's daughter, who had a similar story. Paris Hilton was just another heiress until a video of her having sex hit the Internet. Pamela Anderson was the well-endowed starlet of a cheesy T&A television show called *Baywatch.* But when home videos of her having sex with rocker Tommy Lee on their honeymoon surfaced, she became an icon.

We love to hate celebrities. We love to watch them fall, even if they get rich doing it. Maybe this is a way we collectively reassure ourselves that our lives really don't suck compared to the rich and famous.

The Cheating Character

THE MOST CONSEQUENTIAL social character flaw displayed in America lately is cheating. More specifically, it is cheating by trained, successful, highly compensated individuals who work in prestigious organizations. These are not frontier robber barons, independent scam artists, and crooked entrepreneurs. They are men and women with poor character operating in corrupt institutional cultures. When a huge embezzling scandal broke in Washington, D.C.'s tax office, an employee was quoted in *The Washington Post* saying, "This is such a shock. A lot of folks have worked together for a long time. It's always a shock when you find someone you work with is a crook." It always is, isn't it?

In sports, cheating by hormone is widespread, going beyond the big names like Barry Bonds, Mark McGwire, and Jose Canseco. One admitted steroid user, a third baseman named Ken Caminiti, told *Sports Illustrated*, "At first I felt like a cheater. But I looked around, and everybody was doing it." Caminiti died of a heart attack at the age of forty-one. Still, in high school and college football, "everybody" is using steroids, too. Floyd Landis won the Tour de France in 2006 but had to return the crown because of blood doping. Marion Jones, once considered the greatest female runner in history, had to return the five gold medals she won in 2000 because she used steroids. There are recruiting scandals in college basketball and football. Bill Belichick, the lionized coach of the New England Patriots, cheated by videotaping his opponents' sideline signals in 2007. So much for the ideal of sports as an even playing field.

In journalism, there have been famous recent cases of serial fabricators, the most famous of which were Jayson Blair of *The New York Times* (who got a book deal out of his malfeasance) and Stephen Glass of *The New Republic* (who had a Hollywood movie made about him). But there are others. These guys didn't plagiarize; they just made things up. At CBS News, a piece by Dan Rather on the show *60 Minutes II* used documents that had not been authenticated in a piece about George W. Bush's National Guard service; four people were ousted and Rather soon left the company.

Academic scandals appear to be more common as well, and several popular historians faced accusations of plagiarism, including Michael Bellesiles, Doris Kearns Goodwin, and the late Stephen Ambrose. The Internet has made cheating by college students easier, and it is a growing problem on campuses.

The Business of Cheating

LOW CHARACTER IN colleges and ballparks doesn't affect many lives. Cheating in business does. The most important examples of "elite deviance" come from the corporate world. The turn of this century saw a corporate crime wave unlike anything the country has seen since the Roaring Twenties, which was also the last time the gap between the rich and poor was so wide, and the last time the superrich—the top 1 percent—controlled so much of the country's combined personal wealth. The outrages of gargantuan CEO pay, investment banker bonuses, and billion-dollar annual incomes for top hedge fund managers are accompanied by plenty of good old-fashioned cheating.

The names of the companies include Enron, Tyco, Computer Associates, Rite Aid, Global Crossing, Lucent, HealthSouth, WorldCom, Qwest, Merrill Lynch, Comverse, Adelphia Communications, Hewlett-Packard, Xerox, AIG, and KPMG. Some of the cheating names in the news (and some in the prisons) include Kenneth Lay, Jeffrey Skilling, Dennis Kozlowski, Martha Stewart, Leona Helmsley, Bernard Ebbers, Maurice Greenberg, David Stockman, and Jack Grubman. In many cases, the headline makers were aided and abetted by lawyers, accountants, and MBAs, highly trained and credentialed professionals.

William Lerach was famous as the king of class-action lawsuits brought by investors against corporations. He positioned himself as a crusader for the little guy getting screwed by unscrupulous multinationals. Lerach became fabulously wealthy in the process. Still, in September 2007 he pled guilty to conspiracy charges. He had essentially paid investors to become named plaintiffs in his cases. The good guys are bad guys, too.

Such well-known celebrity cases are just a patch of the pond scum. For example, on the same day in September 2007 that Freddie Mac, the government-sponsored mortgage finance company, agreed to pay $50 million to settle federal fraud charges, four large manufacturers of artificial hips and knees paid combined fines of $310 million to settle charges that they had paid kickbacks to doctors. There was little news coverage. But there is no corner of commerce too upstanding or prosaic for the cheating culture.

I talked about the white-collar cheating phenomenon with two lawyers I know who happen to be general counsels at corporations. One is a Democrat and the other a Republican. Both saw an increase in unethical business conduct in the relatively short span of their careers. The Republican, however, felt the problem had been blown way out of proportion by the media, which pays attention to only bad news and bad guys. The Democrat blamed a free-market, "greed is good" mentality that has sanctioned all kinds of selfish and unfair practices in the name of wealth creation and the sacred bottom line.

The Predator Class

THERE'S SOMETHING TO both theories, but they are only partial explanations. The best exploration of the recent lapses of practical ethics is *The Cheating Culture: Why More Americans Are Doing Wrong to Get Ahead* by David Callahan. Callahan describes cheating in everyday life, not just among the rich and powerful. "Cheating is everywhere," Callahan wrote. "Most of it is by people who, on the whole, view themselves as upstanding members of society. Again and again, Americans who wouldn't so much as shoplift a pack of chewing gum are committing felonies at tax time, betraying the trust of their patients, misleading investors, ripping off their insurance companies, or lying to their clients."

Callahan cites several factors: "New pressures" in an economy that has more international competition and more ruthless performance expectations; rewards for winners in pay and bonuses that are proportionately greater than historic levels, increasing the relative payoff for cheating; and "trickle-down corruption" and envy that come from the constant media attention, in both news and entertainment, on the rich and glamorous.

All this makes sense, but there is still more going on. There is a "cheating of narcissism." It is no coincidence that the baby boom generation, with its abundance of college degrees and Patagonia fleece, is also the cheating generation. Moral relativism and truthiness declare, "Whatever I want is okay as long as it doesn't directly and openly hurt anyone." This is our old friend selfism, "me" worship. It has been so broadly legitimized in the "feeling" arenas—psychology, education, relationships, self-help—that it is easy to use as a rationalization applied to work, business, and money. If a CEO appoints cronies to the board and they approve a $50 million salary, who is really hurt? And damn it, I deserve it. It is a grandiose form of ego entitlement.

In the early 1980s, someone I knew did "est," one of the most famous of the "human potential" fads then popular. In college, this man had been brilliant, idealistic, and political. A few years out of college, he also wanted to get rich, but he felt conflicted and guilty. Est, he reported, got him over the hump and made him realize it was okay to just go out and "get it." Whatever he wanted was okay, by definition. The est business didn't last long; it wasn't mature. My friend's idealism won out in the end, but it doesn't for many people. The conversation I had with him about his epiphany, however, was simply one of the more explicit variants I have had with people of my generation hundreds and hundreds of times. "I deserve it" can be liberating and corrupting.

In the fall of 2007, *The Washington Post* profiled a baby boom baron named J. Christopher Flowers who had $2 billion to his name and a $53 million home. The piece quoted a friend about their time at Harvard: "I would make the case for social democracy, and he would be making arguments for Darwinian capitalism. I would say, 'What would you do with all that money that is our responsibility to go out and earn?' He would say, 'It doesn't matter. He who has the most at the end wins.' " That has become a bumper sticker of boomerism: He who has the most at the end wins. It is self-congratulatory greed.

The powers of rationalization are indeed strong. But when we see others cheat, we hate it. We all have cheated, and on some levels we hate ourselves for it. Most people have brought home office supplies from work or haven't returned the extra newspaper grabbed by mistake or didn't mention that the bartender forgot to put the third beer on the tab. But we feel guilty.

Well, most people feel guilty. The higher the rewards, the less guilt there is. There is today a "predator class" of Willy Suttons with MBAs, Turnbull & Asser shirts, and Franck Muller watches who are raiding pension funds, conducting bogus audits, turning a blind legal eye to malfeasance, and trading on inside information for financial rewards as great or greater than those received by the titans of the Gilded Age and Roaring Twenties. These people are mostly not risk-taking entrepreneurs, brilliant technologists, visionary inventors, or charismatic leaders. They are lucky and ambitious employees in bureaucratic organizations such as hedge funds, investment banks, and corporations. Of course, cheating and stealing is extreme behavior. But there is no shortage of simple cynicism and unfettered money lust. In Dallas, Charles Norton runs a mutual fund called the Vice Fund that invests only in "sin stocks" like gambling, tobacco, alcohol, and military contractors. The goal, he told *The New York Times,* is "to just make money."

Poker Man and Pig Man

MANY OF THE richest of the rich have bad manners, not just bad character.

I have a friend who is a serious poker player. He plays in tournaments with pros and in the World Series of Poker every year. He is a passionate student of the game. He reads about poker and writes about poker. He takes notes while he plays and studies his notes later. He loves it. My kids refer to him as "Poker Man."

Poker Man is also an enormously successful attorney. He has won some very large cases and has even been on the good guys' side. Financially, he has done well. Every year Poker Man organizes a syndicate of "investors" to back him. He raises money from them to pay tournament entry fees. If he wins, they win. If he loses, they lose. Over the course of a full year, they have always won. Poker Man keeps scrupulous records and writes his investors detailed dispatches from the tables.

At lunch one day, I asked my friend why he bothered with the investors. The tournament fees were chump change for Poker Man. In his worst year imaginable, he wouldn't lose enough to make a dent in his finances.

Poker Man had an easy answer. "In my family, we have too much respect for what others don't have to do that with our money," he said. His demeanor and cadence were totally devoid of sanctimony and preaching, two qualities I too often exude. It was a simple statement of fact.

It took a while for me to really understand what he meant—and what

it meant to me. One thing hit me right away. Poker Man didn't say, "*I
have too much respect for what others don't have to do that with *my*
money." He said, "my family." Good character is not a solo act.

More important, Poker Man felt like risking a large sum of his
money on poker would be an act of disrespect toward those with less. In
his view, and others might disagree, gathering up small sums from a
group is different—less indulgent or reckless. No one would spend so
much it would cut into their charitable giving. Even though no one
would be likely to notice, Poker Man did not want to act disrespectfully.
He wasn't looking to make a self-righteous statement or express himself.
He just had a habit of considering the "ethical footprint" of his choices.

Now consider a man my family calls "Pig Man." I don't know his real
name. Pig Man sat directly behind my wife on a U.S. Airways flight from
Boston to Washington, D.C., on a Sunday afternoon in August. I was in
the aisle seat across from my wife and two children, diagonally across
from Pig Man. Pig Man was Caucasian, roughly six feet three inches tall,
between thirty-five and forty-five years old, and "buff," with a stylish hair-
cut, a designer shirt, and a very expensive watch. He carried himself like
a rich guy. Even the boxer shorts that extended rudely below his gym
shorts exuded "I own the world and I don't have to dress up for you
slobs."

Pig Man boarded with a heavy black roller bag. While stowing it in
the overhead compartment, he smashed my soft carry-on without hesita-
tion or apology. Pig Man sat down and immediately got out his cell
phone and began shouting into it. Using a cell phone on a plane before
takeoff is, sadly, common and apparently acceptable. Many, but perhaps
not most, airplane cell talkers will try to talk softly, cover the phone, or
hunch over as gestures toward the surrounding humanity. Not Pig Man.
He sat up straight and barked. I learned that Pig Man barely had time to
shower before the flight, that he had had an athletic morning at the
club, that some buddies were having fun at a picnic, that he expected
whomever he was talking with to stock up on liquor before he got to his
destination, and a few spicier things I will not repeat. Pig Man ignored
polite but dirty looks from at least three neighbors besides me.

On takeoff, Pig Man immediately removed his shower slippers and crossed his legs so that that his bare foot and its five heinous toes grazed my left arm. One doesn't have to be Emily Post to know that one does not touch a stranger with bare feet. He responded to my instant swivel and heartfelt scowl with a dismissive wave that said, "Sorry, pal, don't be so uptight." My evil eye also spotted one of his testicles that had squirted loose from his gym shorts. Pig Man kept his grotesque foot in the aisle but moved the offending appendage closer to my wife and her considerable olfactory gifts. She reported the foot to be stinky.

Every signal this man sent, from his physical carriage to his dress to his yelling, communicated a blanket "Screw you." This would be an example, one might say, of bad manners. We all hate Pig Men.

Aggressive Ostentation

PIG MAN EXHIBITED a complete lack of the thoughtful respect that was a habit of the heart for Poker Man. The socially aggressive way he honked into the phone is typical of how people act in public when engaged with their portable gadgets. Pig Man's body language also expressed anger similar to road rage. The combination of thoughtless aggression and social obliviousness expressed what Pig Man felt toward others: disrespect.

Disrespect expressed through material display is one of the most blatant and consequential forms of contemporary bad manners: aggressive ostentation.

Today it seems odd to think of showiness or materialism as having anything to do with manners. In a world where people wear obscene T-shirts and pornographic tattoos and don't say thank you to waitresses, public displays of wealth don't seem especially rude. That hasn't always been so. In many societies, showiness has been considered rude and even immoral. Material restraint was a prominent virtue in American Puritanism, a pillar of the Protestant work ethic and Yankee thrift. Obviously there has been plenty of greed and excess in American history, but some of the social restraints on it have been tossed out in the "we hate us" epoch. People desperately want to show the disrespect they have for what others don't have. They see their own self-expression as trumping any moral or even mannerly claim.

In 1899, a scholar named Thorstein Veblen published a book he thought was a serious work of economic and social theory. Somewhat to his chagrin, reviewers read *The Theory of the Leisure Class* as satire. Still, it was popular. And Veblen would surely be delighted that his misunderstood theories spawned a phrase that is instantly recognizable—and meaningful—over one hundred years later: "conspicuous consumption."

Veblen wanted to use anthropology to understand economic behavior. Unlike traditional economists, he didn't believe consumers and individuals acted rationally in pursuit of their self-interest. He thought much economic (and social) behavior had primitive roots, relics of the customs and survival mechanisms of subsistence societies. But his turn-of-the-century audience thought it hilarious when he compared the fine silver and grand mansions of Midwest burghers to tribal chieftains who had more goats than their families could possibly eat and more beer than they could possibly drink.

Veblen, however, was dead serious and saw conspicuous consumption as an important way for people to signal their wealth and status to others, especially strangers. A key to this kind of social display was being able to afford to waste things. A wealthy chief displayed waste by having more food, drink, shelter, and weaponry than he could possibly consume. This made him appear more powerful. A wealthy industrialist of the Gilded Age had more homes, staff, cars, yachts, and railroad cars than he and his family could possibly take advantage of. So it is with today's hedge fund manager, real estate developer, or dot-com entrepreneur.

A chieftain had fat wives, huge feasts, fine feathers, and thick furs; a railroad baron had private trains, silk clothes, gold watches, and Rembrandts. In old European and Asian cultures, dress and ornament signaled precise caste and status. And that is why even now a Rolex watch or a Chanel bag is important: They may not be prettier or longer lasting than less costly alternatives, but they are instantly recognizable to strangers as expensive and wasteful. The branding is what is important.

As societies grew larger and more dispersed, Veblen said, conspicuous consumption needed to become more complex. It's one thing to show a village of one hundred that you're rich; it's another to signify this to a city of one million. It wasn't enough for the chief of a big tribe to adorn himself; he had to outfit his wives, children, and servants to reach the larger group.

Today, driving a Bentley, sporting huge diamonds, and wearing designer clothes can signal wealth only to someone who actually sees you. But in a nomadic country of three hundred million, signifying wealth to the larger group takes far more sophistication. In the OmniMedia era, status competition is cosmopolitan and instantaneous. There is a global battle between the haves and have-mores. A Las Vegas casino magnate competes with an Indian manufacturing mogul and a Hong Kong financier. To signal wealth and power on a proper scale, today's American chieftains and their kin need more than mansions, they need multiple resort-like compounds that can accommodate scores of guests; they need private planes as large as commercial aircraft, art collections, four-hundred-foot yachts, and staff and family members fully outfitted to maximize their signaling and make the message "go viral." A large staff generates publicity and celebrity, so the megarich hire their own curators, family concierges, household managers, celebrity decorators, pet handlers, butlers, chauffeurs, famous money managers, personal physicians, acclaimed chefs, and in-house landscape architects.

A staff also adds to the insulation the megarich want—or need. It is important for the megarich never to do what regular people do unless it is done consciously to be campy or down-to-earth; it is important not to go to normal airports or golf courses that aren't on your property or museums during regular hours. A modern chief must now signal wealth and power by creating and living in a separate world.

So chiefs now abandon the tribe. That is more antisocial and corrosive than wasting food. A 2007 book by Robert Frank is titled *Richistan* for just this reason, because the author argues that the post-dot-com megarich essentially live in their own borderless country. Robert Bellah's *Habits of the Heart* saw this coming. "What is even more disturbing about this . . . elite than its secession from society is its predatory attitude toward the rest of society, its willingness to pursue its own interests without regard to anyone else." Robert Reich called this the "secession of the successful." This ability to withdraw from the common world further enables the predator class since they really don't have to see much of the preyed-on world (except through OmniMedia).

Though we can't know their hearts, the public behavior of the megarich is more flamboyant than it has been in several generations and is seemingly free of any remnants of guilt, Puritan, Catholic, Jewish, secular, or hippie—you name it. "My ladies are rich, and they make no apologies," a socialite designer named Douglas Hannant told *The New York Times*. "They want to look rich and they even like to use the word rich."

The most well-off are aggressively ostentatious. This is socially sanctioned and admired and one of the standards for society that are reflected, multiplied, and celebrated by OmniMedia. It is hard to imagine nastier and more unprovoked manners than today's aggressive ostentation.

Some of the richest people I know are wonderful, generous people. Some aren't. But many have become oblivious. They have lost a sense of humility and their own luck. They don't respect what others don't have. This is partly because our society and our manners have become conducive to withdrawal and anonymity. We live among strangers. We don't live in small tribes. Chiefs really don't know their subjects and the people they disrespect. And they haven't been taught and trained to behave as if they do.

This inconsiderateness of the megarich reinforces a gap between the very rich and the rest that is among the widest in U.S. history, if not the widest. The megarich of today are as wealthy as any Americans have been at any time in our history, arguably richer. In 2004, a household in the top 1 percent of incomes pulled in an annual average of $940,000. That's just the rich. If you wanted to be among the megarich (the top tenth of that 1 percent) in 2004, you had to earn an average of $4.5 million. To be filthy rich, a true Midas in the top one-hundredth of the top 1 percent, you needed $20 million a year. That's $385,000 a week.

From 1990 to 2004, real income increased just 2 percent for Americans below the top 10 percent of earners. But in that same time, real income increased 57 percent for the top 1 percent and 112 percent for the top 0.01 percent. To put it in wider perspective, economists Thomas

Piketty and Emmanuel Saez found that the top 10 percent of earners in 2004 made 42.9 percent of everything that Americans earned. The top 1 percent alone gobbled up 16.2 percent of total income. The distribution of wealth and income has not been so out of whack since the 1920s, if then.

There is a sense that 99 percent of the population is having its face rubbed in the unparalleled wealth of the top 1 percent. It is a sign of broken community. It is a hateful aspect of the culture today, despite conservative claims that the "mega-ness" of the megarich is really good for us all.

I don't mean to trivialize the income gap by looking at it from the angle of considerateness. I am simply offering a different perspective from the usual ones of economics and political philosophy. Manners are moral habits that affect income distribution as well as sales of Bentleys. Manners die in a vacuum of community, and that is what America faces today. Manners may have a Darwinian purpose (preventing bloody chaos) but they can die out.

Manners Aren't Phony

GOOD MANNERS INDICATE a sincere, open, and honest exchange of respect between people and therefore have no place in the Land of the Fake. The lack of manners is probably the most constant and unavoidable source of why we hate us.

But we don't think explicitly about manners and etiquette anymore. It's square and somehow not even politically correct. In the wonderful essay "Who Killed Modern Manners?" Judith Martin, better known to newspaper readers as the columnist and writer Miss Manners, answered the question this way: "It was idealism that killed modern manners." She means selfism, the me-first, sixties adolescent version of "to thine own self be true." Bad manners are a perversion of a legitimate sixties ideal.

For example, the liberated and liberal modern person believes, "Good surface behavior is not a truth-in-packaging guarantee of a virtuous heart inside." This is undeniably true. But, says Martin, "It is not therefore true that a virtuous heart excuses surface behavior if it inadvertently inconveniences, antagonizes, or disgusts others. And an evil heart that is constrained by the demands of politeness is less of a public menace than one freer to follow its evil impulses."

Manners in a culture of narcissism are practically an oxymoron. What matters is your honesty and commitment to the true you. If others can't see the true you, hey, that's their problem. You are obligated to be true to yourself even if that means letting the door slam on old ladies, talking about genital warts on a cell phone in Starbucks, sporting tattoos with barbed wire and swastikas, or wearing a polo shirt to a funeral. After all, etiquette is random, dude. Martin nails this stunted, teenage outlook: "Oddly enough, the greatest scoffers at the traditions of American etiquette, who scorn the rituals of their own society as stupid and stultifying, voice respect for the custom and folklore of Native Americans, less industrialized peoples, and other societies they find more 'authentic' than their own."

There is one bright spot in the story of modern manners. Many groups in America are treated more respectfully than they were a generation or two ago. A nonprofit called Public Agenda studied public attitudes toward rudeness and found majorities felt there have been improvements in "being kind and considerate" toward African-Americans, people with physical handicaps, and gay people. And 41 percent did admit they had been rude and disrespectful themselves. I presume Pig Man was one of them.

After Manners

MANNERS ARE NOTHING more than a language for respectful statements, a system of symbolic behaviors humans use to signal respect and consideration for other people, especially strangers. Manners, however, come more naturally when you know the people you deal with or know they could know who you are. Anonymity is not good for manners or happiness.

Manners are more than conformity, but they require some conformity. Manners are less learned than mimicked, less taught than exemplified. The models come from family *and* community; family alone does not do the trick. When the community has a shrinking supply of acknowledged manners, there is less worth imitating. And there is an ample supply of bad role models. Recall that the philosopher Alasdair MacIntyre in *After Virtue* argued that coherent, communicable moral standards could exist only in vibrant communities. We are now close to living After Manners.

Etiquette 2.0

TECHNOLOGY POSES NEW challenges to respectful manners. There is not yet any common etiquette for using cell phones, "crackberries," laptops, and ear-bud thingies in public. What is interesting is why we hate techno-rudeness so much. Techno-boors are oblivious to others and to public space in a way that feels menacing and destabilizing. It's like living in a zombie world. A rude zombie world.

The new technology, first of all, is easy to get hooked on. It gobbles up huge chunks of our days. Instant messaging, text messaging, cell phone talking, gaming, and e-mailing have an addictive quality. People touch their portable devices like rosary beads. They are compelled to check their e-mail when they could be talking to you face-to-face. Parents who roamed their neighborhoods at will when they were little kids now freak out if they can't have instant access to their own children by cell phone. They also pacify their children with video and computer games and television and, worse, portable electronic games like GameBoy. Addicts are not generally known for swell manners.

The perceived subconscious anonymity of technology also enables rudeness. I receive comments via e-mail almost every day that people would never, ever, say to my face. Coworkers send e-zingers to one another, and parents send nasty-grams to their children's teachers. Children may be the worst. I recently saw a letter from a camp director that addressed an especially nasty version of e-rudeness. When one of the campers discovered that a kid he didn't like was returning to camp, he set up a Facebook page called "Everything We Hate About 'Bobby.' " Of course, "Bobby" found out about it. Does technology cause bad behavior? No. Does it make it marginally easier? Yes.

But there are deeper issues. Recall Pig Man and his cell phone. "Because cell phone talkers are not interacting with the world around them, they come to believe that the world around them really isn't there and surely shouldn't intrude," wrote Christine Rosen in an essay called "Our Cell Phones, Ourselves." "And when the cell phone user commandeers the space by talking, he or she sends a very clear message to others that they are powerless to insist on their own use of the space. It is a passive-aggressive but extremely effective tactic."

Cell phones are not the only portable technology used for passive-aggressive public-space bullying. The laptop is a mighty sword, too. Power fingers and monster thumbs can create a racket in the lap of an aggressive user. Wireless technology allows people to hook into the Internet umbilical all over, so coffee shops, airports, parks, and bookstores are populated by laptop hooligans. An expert can commandeer a large space. This kind of behavior also signals an egomaniacal message like "I'm very, very important. I am more important than you. I must be connected at all times."

Personal digital assistants—such as BlackBerries—have a much smaller zone of conquest but are even more addictive. Their contribution to social evil is different and more subtle. Like GameBoys, iPods, and their ilk, PDAs allow people to retreat into private social oblivion while in social space. It is a statement of power to use a BlackBerry in a meeting; the top of the food chain is allowed to, the bottom is not. Everyone thinks their job, their e-mail, their social plans, are so important that commandeering public space is okay when *they* do it. Again, Christine Rosen:

> The group is expected never to impinge upon—indeed, it is expected to tacitly endorse by enduring—the individual's right to withdraw from social space by whatever means he or she chooses: cell phones, BlackBerrys, iPods, DVDs screened on laptop computers. These devices are used as a means to refuse to be "in" the social space; they are technological cold shoulders that . . . impose visually and auditorily on others. Cell phones are not the only culprits here. A member of my family, traveling recently on the Amtrak train from New York, was shocked to realize that the man sitting in front of her was

watching a pornographic movie on his laptop computer—a movie whose raunchy scenes were reflected in the train window and thus clearly visible to her.

For some weird reason, our group rules now seem to favor the individual pod person over the group.

Social Alone

EVEN WHEN TECHNOLOGY use isn't so passive-aggressive, it can be alienating and rude. Social obliviousness empowered by technology has been called "absent presence." We tend to treat this as an excused absence. For example, when a person is on a cell phone in a store, it seems to be acceptable for that person not to thank or exchange pleasantries with the cashier. Well, that isn't acceptable. It is not permissible to let a door swing shut on someone carrying a heavy bag of groceries just because you're listening to music on your iPod and didn't notice. Possession of portable technology is being treated like the right to bear arms. If you are plugged in, you have the right to declare that you don't acknowledge my existence. Usually we think of passive antisocial behavior as being expressed through gestures like tattoos, extreme piercings, biker regalia, ghetto fashion, or the punk look. I'm beginning to believe "absent presence" and techno-aggression are more pervasive threats to social well-being and far more destructive of social capital. For all the positive potential of new technologies, in some ways *Bowling Alone* author Robert Putnam now needs to look at whether we are, paradoxically, "social alone."

Most everything, in the end, is harder alone.

Much of what we hate in everyday life are the things that make us feel alone, invisible, disregarded, or dismissed. That's how we feel when someone is using a BlackBerry in the middle of a conversation or talking loudly on a cell phone in a line for a movie. That's how we feel when we see manicured people in private skyboxes at baseball games or when we shield kids at a football game from drunken, cursing fans. That's how we feel when a clerk at a chain store ignores us. It all makes us want to withdraw and tune out even more. This makes it harder to see the best in people and society—harder in everyday life, harder as consumers of media, harder as citizens. We live defensively. We end up hating us. We respond by withdrawing more. We give less to others and to community, which just breeds more alienation. Appointing enemies and reverting to clannish xenophobia creates more belligerence. There is no script for liking us more. But there are obvious but difficult directions for improvising.

Chapter Nine

AUTHENTICITY, THOUGHTFULNESS,

AND MANY THINGS

SOME AMERICANS HAVE a clear script for their lives, but fewer do than in times past. Some are lucky enough to have inherited articulated beliefs from their family that still fit their own lives. Many are religious. Most secular Americans have a more ad hoc moral point of view, formed on the run through life. Both religious and secular people tend to have better-defined political philosophies than moral ones. But we need both. In our private and public lives we need a compass. We can't wing it. We need a tolerant, morally empathetic yet tough outlook in a society as wildly diverse as America, where moral, religious, and political world-views collide each day. We can't retreat; we can't be Amish; we can't choose to wear blinders. That is not only wrong morally, but it is wrong emotionally. Focusing on others generates more happiness than focusing on your own dear self. That is an emotional fact, not a theory. It's the narcissistic paradox. Looking in the mirror too long is depressing; looking out the window isn't.

So we need to fix how we look and what we see. We need to discover how we might hate us a bit less. That means steering our own lives away from the phony and the hateful. I am more comfortable carping than preaching so answers don't come easily. But I do have two ideas. They

229

might better be called difficult projects. They aren't political platforms or programs of reform; in a country of three hundred million people, the problems I have written about aren't amenable to intentional, organized solutions. My two projects are not achievable. The success is in the effort. And any enduring contributions this book might inspire solely belong to insights readers may have.

Two Difficult Projects

PROJECT ONE: To hate us less and like us more, it is necessary to find and nurture authentic commitments in private and community life. This means constantly making thoughtful and unselfish choices about matters both essential and seemingly trivial.

Project Two: In making thoughtful choices, it is necessary to cultivate a guiding "moral temperament"—a philosophic perspective, an outlook, a clear script. The purpose of a moral temperament is not just personal satisfaction but also to guide your treatment of other people and communities. That is what makes it moral. It must be a temperament in order to guide "thoughtful and unselfish choices" effectively in real time, as they come at us. It should help sort through the conflicts we face in life, including as citizens and voters.

The moral temperament I am going to sketch is unfamiliar to most Americans as an official philosophy. It has no famous advocate in this country. It isn't liberal or conservative. Frankly, it doesn't suit the psychological bent of most people who write about social and political theory for a living because it is not grandiose and systematic. It isn't idealistic. But it does fit the realities of American culture today—diverse, mobile, materialistic, and cranky. The inelegant name this thinking goes by is "value pluralism." (I'll mostly just call it pluralism.) It is a pragmatic outlook on the world, a perspective. Its most influential advocate was Sir Isaiah Berlin, a philosopher, historian of ideas, and essayist who was perhaps England's most well-known intellectual when he died in 1997. I should add that I studied with Berlin as a graduate student and embarrassed him by writing my master's thesis on his political ideas. It took me twenty-five years to truly understand the wisdom of Berlin's pluralism in today's America. I'll try not to embarrass his legacy yet again.

I am not going to get heavily into public policy and hot-button issues. Dwelling on the agenda of the polarized elite is no longer productive. In today's culture of belligerence, it is a recipe for interminable, futile argument—for becoming part of the noise. But I am not arguing for a retreat from politics, community, and civic engagement in the name of finding your private authentic self. Quite the contrary. I fully intend for my difficult projects to be unselfish and community oriented. Their goal is to frame things in a way that helps us contribute more as parents, colleagues, aunts and uncles, siblings, bosses, teachers, neighbors, friends, bar stool philosophers, and, yes, bowling team members.

As much as we hate the belligerent blowhard who cuts off a conversation with the surly and disgusted announcement "You just don't get it," we don't want to be that guy, either. It is challenging to acknowledge our own bad behavior. But it is necessary and responsible. We give and take in the world.

A Valid Life

MY FATHER-IN-LAW LED his life better than anyone I have known intimately. He practiced medicine in the area where he grew up for his whole career. He was a beloved doctor in the old-fashioned way. He knew everyone in town. Married for fifty-one years, he doted on his children and grandchildren. He always enjoyed life and his head was never turned by someone else's success or luck. He gave more than he took, but somehow he ended up with the most. At his funeral, the former rabbi at his congregation came back. He began the service by saying plainly that my father-in-law was the best person he had ever known. I agree.

His final illness came as I was writing this book. When the prognosis was unclear but bad, he told me, "I don't want to be an invalid. But I also don't want to be invalid." His voice was weak and his breathing difficult. He couldn't say much more. But I knew exactly what he meant. "You mean you don't want to go on if you can't contribute and keep earning your way on the planet? I know you. You don't want to be a 'me-firster,' right?" He nodded with his jaw set hard. "Me-firster" is a term he used raising his kids. I found myself saying that as long as I had access to his mind, I would be a better father, husband, sibling, and professional. So would his own son. My wife would be a stronger mother, a richer person. I pointed out that the subtle distinction he drew between being an invalid and being invalid was actually quite brilliant, proof that his mind was still first-rate. Proof that he was still valid, that he could give and not just take.

That settled the conversation for the moment. But the tenaciousness of my father-in-law's example of what it means to be valid in life stuck with me. Of course, all lives but the most twisted are valid in some sense. But leading a life where the self-knowing drive to remain valid endures when life is on the line takes effort, honesty, the love of others, and a long view. It is a tall mountain.

Mount Authenticity

THE MECHANICS OF forging and sustaining the authentic—the valid—in your own life are common sense but take effort. In the simplest terms, it means thinking about things that are usually not thought about at all: how much television you watch, how much time you spend on the Internet, how you get the news, how you consume advertising, what you read, whether you read, how you think about major purchases, how you think about your political views, where you shop, how you make time for friends and family, and, of course, where you get lunch. It means steering deliberately instead of flying along on automatic pilot. It means identifying and evaluating the "pictures in your head" that may have been put there by advertising, Hollywood, or a sixth-grade teacher but that don't reflect your chosen sensibilities and ideals.

Some of these choices are obviously very significant; some may seem trivial. But in today's crazy busy world, *any* decision that involves a time commitment is serious. For parents, a long commute, tiring hours at work, errands, chauffeuring children on weekends, and constantly "staying in touch" via portable technology can gobble away the years. It can feel like all you have to show for the grind is a stack of bills and a sore back. For young people, the thrill or pressure of new jobs, the constant data stream of instant messages, text messages, e-mails, phone calls, and MySpace notes, paying off student loans, consuming entertainment, loading iPods, getting a hard body, dating, partying, and reliving it all online the next day can chew up days like a meat grinder. Time devours.

Because we make so many decisions in a single day now, cultivating a thoughtful moral temperament is necessary to making thoughtful choices. It functions like character and manners. This doesn't mean walking around like Socrates constantly debating the good and the just. It simply means making the *effort* to train your intuitions and embrace the moral challenge of life.

I've quoted *Zen and the Art of Motorcycle Maintenance* by Robert Pirsig often, and it might seem like an odd book to draw from so much. Writing in the midseventies, he had all the open-mindedness of the sixties, mixed with the ferocious, naïve, and creative rationalism you see in a brilliant computer programmer or physicist and salted with an old-fashioned respect for craft. He was a sympathetic critic of Phase One of America's late-twentieth-century transformation and an informed prophet of Phase Two. A central theme of the book is his search for a concept he calls "quality." Quality is a first cousin of what I mean by authenticity. So read this sentence with that in mind: "My personal feeling is that this is how any further improvement of the world will be done: by individuals making Quality decisions and that's all." Substitute "authentic" instead of "quality" and that is my position, too.

Authentic decisions. They add up to a valid life, not a picture of a life, not an unexamined life. My father-in-law's life wasn't valid because of what it looked like from the outside or because of his stature, but because of the long stretch of decisions and actions he made with character and consideration about things large and little. His example and his thoughtfulness inspired others and made them intuitively feel cared for; in turn my father-in-law flourished because of what he got back. Frank Bascombe could not live like that. Nor could Jerry Rubin (the hippie king who turned to serial self-help) or Sheila (the woman who founded "Sheilaism"). My career introduced me to many famous, wealthy, and powerful people, some of whom I know well; few were satiable, though the pictures of their lives were perfect.

There are certain conditions that need to be met before making authentic decisions. Another passage from Pirsig expresses the most important—effort:

> When you try to climb a mountain to prove how big you are, you almost never make it. And even if you do it's a hollow victory. In order to sustain the victory you have to prove yourself again and again in some other way, and again and again and again, driven forever to fill a false image, haunted by the fear that the image is not true and someone will find out.

You have to think about the climb and not the summit. On a basic, almost universal level, Pirsig means that egotistical endeavors are rarely excellent or satisfying. They often fail outright. The America of Omni-Media and OmniMarketing teaches just the opposite, that only the end result and the image of success count. But that is a soul-scorching path through life. If you climb a difficult mountain simply because you want the picture on the office wall, you either won't make it to the top or the experience will be hollow and unimportant. If you go fishing because you love to fish, you will have a good day no matter if the fish are biting; if your goal is not fishing but catching, a slow day will be a bad day.

For our purposes, trying "to climb a mountain to prove how big you are" is similar to trying to find your true self or worldly status to solve your life's problems. This is a doomed venture not just because it is selfish but because it's looking for happiness in all the wrong places. This is frustrating because society seems to promise that you can get to the summit of Mount Self going solo. But you can't. You can only climb. So much of our well-intentioned, high-toned modern soul searching is like an internal version of striving for material success, believing that you can get to the top of Mount Happy and Healthy, displaying yourself to the world in a way that will bring instant stature, respect, and love; that acquiring something—even something "spiritual"—can be an enduring part of your happiness and worth, be it a flat-screen television, fancy job title, tattoo, gun, tenured professorship, great body, wealth, fame, blond hair, a bigger house than your neighbor's, or a well-received book. It's like the hedonistic treadmill. Someone will always have a bigger television, car, bass boat, job, and house, or a better book. So "you almost never make it," as Pirsig said. If those are the goals you seek, you will "have to prove yourself again and again in some other way, and again and again and again." You'll worry about being exposed.

So if you want to climb Mount Authenticity, think only about the climb, about making decisions for authentic reasons. Those will, in turn, be unselfish decisions. Think about climbing well and being a good climbing partner to others. Don't fixate on the summit.

Pictures of yourself on top of the mountain are a corrosive, tenacious problem in life. Recall how Chris Eads, the pastor in Sterling, Virginia, described how many of the parents in his congregation felt they needed to have fancy cars, manicured backyards, and top-notch consumer durables to be good parents. He said that compulsion came from the picture these people had in their heads of what a good parent looked like. It caused them to lose focus on what a good parent does— the climb: having time to spend with children, making sure they know their relatives, eating dinner together, and turning the screens off.

Preparing to Climb

OTHER PREPARATIONS ARE necessary before the climb. You need to answer big questions. Is this kind of authenticity a worthy goal? Is this a measure by which you want to judge yourself and your actions? Are you in fact willing to be judged? Many will say, "No, thank you." Being judged today is perceived as a violation of privacy. Calling someone judgmental is to insult them, which is silly as we're either judgmental or brain-dead. It is an essential part of being human. The point is to judge humanely and try to live up to your own judgments and self-corrections.

Some who answer no to these questions will be religious people who have their own clear codes. Some will be soloists or ironists who find this whole line of thought corny, antiquated, and stern. Some will be selfists. But obviously, my answer is yes. A quest for authenticity sounds touchy-feely and may appear inconsistent with my unsympathetic criticism of the selfism mentality. I hope the differences among Jerry Rubin, Sheila, and me are clear by now. Emphasizing the climb is not the same as preaching that "life is a journey," a passive, "Que Sera, Sera" bromide that seeks to avoid judgment, effort, and moral reckoning. It matters intensely that you end up near a place worthy of respect, in a dead-white-man kind of a way.

The Burden of Choice, the Lure of Escape

THERE IS A dark, archconservative path away from selfism that tempts me abstractly. It is the notion that the only real alternative to the excesses and anxieties of the Me Decade ethos is some kind of strict catholic regime, the kind of thing Fyodor Dostoyevsky's Grand Inquisitor darkly preached in *The Brothers Karamazov*. Believe what your elders believed. Trade freedom for certainty. Entertain no doubts. At some point, *everyone* aches to believe blindly and devotedly in something, to be relieved of the burdens of choice, doubt, and free will.

With a social climate as toxic and menacing as today's is, I also deeply sympathize with the natural impulse to withdraw. I fight this impulse every day of my life. The crazy, poisonous texture of the times reinforces an ancient impulse toward a path of happiness that is purely private, a solo journey that leaves the rat race to the rats. I think it is wonderful for monks, nuns, artists in garrets, and hermits to follow this path with true devotion. For the rest of us who aren't willing to drop out entirely, the half measure of living in a private, unengaged relativism is half-cocked and selfish. Put plainly, the righteousness of finding your own dear self does not trump obligations of parenthood, family, citizenship, work, and craft.

This doesn't mean you have to run for city council, be a supermom, or become a hyper-charitable entrepreneur. It simply means, for example, that you can't explain away being a lazy teacher because you're putting your energy into "working on yourself." You may not ignore the needs of ailing friends or relatives because you have "issues" with sick people or hospitals. You may not screw people over at work because it will lead to greater personal riches. Being true to yourself does not mean doing exactly what *you* want to do. You must race without being a rat.

Climb or Fall

THE COLD REALITY of American life today is that if you don't actively make the climb, you will either be lost or trapped. OmniMedia, Omni-Marketing, and the culture we hate will fill the vacuum and make a new you, and the old you won't even notice.

We don't live in a primitive, closed, or ancient society where our role, position, status, duties, faith, and fate are set in stone. That is a plain fact of modern life. There is no alternative to forging your own path; you either do it thoughtfully or you don't. If you do it thoughtfully, it takes commitment and perseverance. It is a perpetual goal. Every day is a mix of thoughtfulness and routine, of guilty pleasures, blind spots, and considered choices. It is, of course, much easier to proceed thought-lessly, but it will be devastating in the long run. You will drown. Your life will disappear. There's a Talking Heads song that expresses this, "Once in a Lifetime":

> *And you may ask yourself*
> *What is that beautiful house?*
> *And you may ask yourself*
> *Where does that highway go?*
> *And you may ask yourself*
> *Am I right? . . . Am I wrong?*
> *And you may tell yourself*
> *MY GOD! . . . WHAT HAVE I DONE?*
> *Letting the days go by/let the water hold me down*

What have you done? The days do go by and the water will hold you down. Time drains and is gone. What can keep you afloat and directed? The modern answer is that you are your own buoy—your precious, nur-tured, indulged self. But that can't possibly answer "Am I right? Am I wrong?" What can keep you afloat is the water itself—the world, other people, community, history, your legacy—all that you give to the world that comes back to hold you up. So you'd better both forge and create authenticity soberly. The hyper-individualistic approach is lethal. It makes the existential and moral mistake of believing the self can swim without community, without history, without effort, and without moral obligation.

Put another way: If you do take the me path, don't expect anything from the world because you aren't giving anything to the world.

Charles Chaput, the Roman Catholic archbishop of Denver, has said this is the essence of becoming a grown-up today:

> Much of American culture right now is built on an adolescent fiction. The fiction is that life is all about **you as an individual**—your ideas, your appetites, and your needs. Believe me: It isn't. . . .
>
> Adulthood brings power. Power brings responsibility. And the meaning of your life will hinge on a simple, basic choice. Will you engage the world with your heart and brains and faith, and work to make it a better place—not just for yourself and the people you love but also for people you don't even know whose survival depends on your service to the common good? Or will you wrap yourself in a blanket of noise and toys and consumer junk, and stay a child?

Adult engagement is absolutely vital. It requires getting past the culture of narcissism and rejecting the solipsism of truthiness and putting forth a sustained effort to invest in social capital. This is what the ascent of Mount Authenticity is all about. Staying in the proper frame of mind for the climb, and *being a good person to climb with,* is what moral temperament is all about.

Against the Current

A TEMPERAMENT THAT can do battle with the demon forces of why we hate us faces challenges. It has to steer our private choices and commitments to minimize the hateful threats of OmniMedia, OmniMarketing, character deficiency, and the decline of manners. More important, it has to lend perspective to our citizenship and help us not become belligerent boors fighting interminable arguments with people for whom we have no tolerance or empathy.

A moral temperament for these times must swim against the two great currents in contemporary thought: lily-livered relativism and toxic orthodoxy. The cacophony of worldviews in today's America leads some to a laissez-faire retreat: "To each his own; who am I to judge?" Others judge with undeserved certainty and aggression: "My way or the highway." The synthesis of these imperfect impulses is moral empathy that has the courage to judge mercifully in the face of uncertainty and the humanity to empathize with the unsympathetic.

There is one great American hero who embodies this wisdom. He comes from literature: Atticus Finch from Harper Lee's *To Kill a Mockingbird.* Atticus was an old-fashioned country lawyer who had the independent courage to defend a black man, Tom Robinson, falsely accused of rape in the segregated Alabama town of Maycomb. He also had empathy for Tom Robinson's accusers and even the racist lynch mob that threatened his own life. He told his daughter, Scout, "You never really understand a person until you consider things from his point of view . . . until you climb into his skin and walk around in it."

That is the emotional heart of value pluralism.

Atticus Finch was unwavering in his judgment of the white people of Maycomb who wanted to see Tom Robinson hang: They were racist, scared, and sinful. He understood them and didn't hate them, but his empathy didn't stop him from judging them. Atticus was willing to die for what he believed in. But he wasn't willing to hate.

The Pluralist Temperament

A GREEK POET named Archilochus supposedly said, "The fox knows many things, but the hedgehog knows one big thing." Isaiah Berlin turned this aphorism into a famous essay, "The Hedgehog and the Fox," that helps reveal the intellectual heart of pluralism.

Hedgehogs "relate everything to a single central vision, one system less or more coherent or articulate, in terms of which they understand, think and feel—a single, universal organizing principle." Foxes "pursue many ends, often unrelated and contradictory . . . seizing upon the essence of a vast variety of experiences for what they are in themselves without, consciously or unconsciously, seeking to fit them into, or exclude them from, any one unchanging, all-embracing . . . at times fanatcal, unitary inner vision." The fox has the empathy and mental agility to do as Atticus Finch did and climb into another person's skin and walk around in it. Hedgehogs do not.

Hedgehogs are more inclined to think they know what is best for you, while foxes are more inclined to respect differences. Hedgehogs see the world from what the philosopher Hilary Putnam called the "God's-eye view." They can justify most anything in the name of that "one big thing"—violent revolution, inquistions, civil war, or mass layoffs. Hedgehogs tend to be zealots; foxes are pragmatists. Hedgehogs are at greater risk of belligerence and fanaticism, foxes of insipidness and complacency.

Today's American hedgehogs are most easily spotted by their volume, sanctimony, and inability to see the gray: Al Sharpton and Rush Limbaugh, Michael Moore and Bill O'Reilly.

Value Pluralism

THE FOX'S PLURALISM is as notable for what it is *against* as what it is *for.*

The pluralist renounces the need to explain everything and trusts unanswered questions more than certainty. Pluralism opposes any form of what philosophers call "monism," a belief system that says there is only one source of truth and one true and right way to describe and judge the world. Malignant forms of monism have caused most of the wars, persecutions, and atrocities in history. The "one great thing" gave fervor to the Crusades, jihads, the Inquisition, the guillotine of the French Revolution, colonial conquests, the Holocaust, Stalinism, and the atrocities of the Khmer Rouge. To know this is to know the power of irrational belief and of the group over the individual. The pluralist is always wary of self-certainty, of talk that smells of oppression, violence, or sacrifice in the name of progress or the greater good.

The pluralist believes that history and humanity produce many true and great things. The essence of human nature is to discover, create, and pursue these Many Things. The great religions and philosophies of the world all contribute to the fox's grand Many Things even if they believe in One Thing. There isn't one winner.

As strongly as I believe in the truth, profundity, and utility of value pluralism, I am not suggesting that monists and true believers—Catholics, radical socialists, born-again conservatives, or utilitarians—renounce their path and walk with me into the promised land of value pluralism. Spiritual and intellectual pluralism is exactly what makes the world humane, passionate, and balanced. Flattening the world of ideas and faiths is abhorrent. But vigilance against closed minds and righteousness is necessary. This is an awkward, conflicting position.

What I am suggesting is that we all would do well to consider this different kind of pluralism. Walking around in another person's skin, the core of the pluralist temperament, is one of the most necessary and moral skills in our diverse, unattached, and mobile society. Most Americans believe in an open society with many faiths and moralities, but many have lost the tolerance, security, and civic virtues needed to flourish in this pluralism. Too few realize that conviction need not be based on absolute truth and certainty to be strong and honorable.

The Pluralist

ISAIAH BERLIN IS the patron saint of value pluralism. Born in Riga, Latvia, in 1909, he was Jewish and brought up speaking Russian and German. He moved to England in 1921, went to Oxford, and stayed there for the rest of his life except during World War II, when he was a diplomat in Washington, D.C. He started his academic career in the dry field of analytic philosophy but veered off course and wrote one of the earliest English biographies of Karl Marx. That started him on a path of writing about historical figures. He often detested his subjects, but he had an astounding ability to see the world through their eyes and speak in their tongues. His life was pluralism incarnate.

Berlin saw Jews killed in the Russian revolution, in pogroms, in the Holocaust, and in Stalin's Soviet Union. He saw Russian intellectuals killed and persecuted in the name of Communism. His intellectual mission was not to advocate Berlinism or value pluralism. It was to fight the epic, evil "isms" of the twentieth century: Communism, Fascism, Nazism, and Stalinism, not as an ideologue but as a humanitarian. He cared about the moral heart of a philosophy, not the technicalities. In his writings, he exposed the key intellectual impulses that threaten human freedom: the belief that *I* know what is best for *you* and the need to believe in the "one great thing" that justifies sacrifices of life and liberty in its name. Here is Berlin's enemy:

> One belief, more than any other, is responsible for the slaughter of individuals on the altars of the great historical ideals—justice or progress or the happiness of future generations, or the sacred mission or the emancipation of a nation or race or class, or even liberty itself, which demands the sacrifice of individuals for the freedom of society. This is the belief that somewhere, in the past or in the future, in divine revelation or in the mind of an individual thinker, in the pronouncements of history or science, or in the simple heart of an uncorrupted good man, there is a final solution.

Yet Berlin understands the allure of the hedgehog's way, the opiate of pure belief. It "has always provided a source of satisfaction to both the intellect and the emotions." This is why you don't have scads of value pluralists and foxes on university faculties and in student cafés. Value pluralism is not comforting and intoxicating. It is sobering. Deflating, even.

It is important to understand both this human need to believe in a great thing and its danger. "Absolute faith corrupts as absolutely as absolute power," wrote Eric Hoffer, author of *The True Believer*. Berlin suggests it is better to believe in human beings than systems or abstractions. Resist the single lens and the tidy solutions and embark on the difficult project of trying to understand not just what others believe, but why. This means cultivating something beyond tolerance, something like a genuine fondness for human pluralism and the radical differences of what we wacky humanoids create on earth. This means understanding that most different kinds of believers—religious and political—are not out to get you; they are not against you, but for themselves.

This is vital for improving American politics today. At the moment we have an exaggerated view of our own precariousness. We worry that America is about to be exterminated by illegal immigration or Islamic terrorism. We think other factions in our own country want to destroy our faction, so we retreat further, fearfully. Community and civic ties are so frayed that many people and groups feel endangered. Every conflict is magnified and every disagreement is do or die. We bet the pot on every political position we take. We ignore common sense and tolerance. Everyone who doesn't support gay marriage isn't homophobic or prejudiced. Everyone who opposes any kind of prayer in school isn't a heathen or antireligious bigot.

Believing things is what people do. Creating arrangements under which the maximum number can freely believe the maximum range of ideas is what constitutions, governments, and citizens ought to do. For pluralists, that is the whole ball of wax, a moral imperative.

But beliefs do collide. Ultimate values are not consistent or compatible. Values often conflict and do not share a common moral vocabulary, language, or assumptions. Our job, the pluralist's job, as Archbishop Chaput said, is to grow up and resist the human urge for all good things to fit together neatly and then make sound choices in imperfect conditions. Berlin writes in "Two Concepts of Liberty":

> "To realize the relative validity of one's convictions," said an admirable writer of our time, "and yet stand for them unflinchingly, is what distinguished a civilized man from a barbarian." To demand more than this is perhaps a deep and incurable metaphysical need; but to allow it to determine one's practice is a symptom of an equally deep, and more dangerous, moral and political immaturity.

Not giving in to that "metaphysical need" for comfort is the core of the second difficult project—cultivating a moral temperament. And so is the mature ability—and it is learned, not inherited—to stand "unflinchingly" behind convictions that you hold despite having no metaphysical certainty in their validity. This is the pluralist's great leap of faith.

America today is pluralistic as few societies ever have been. In *The American Kaleidoscope: Race, Ethnicity, and the Civic Culture,* Lawrence Fuchs wrote, "No nation before had ever made diversity itself a source of national identity and unity." One of the central social challenges today is maintaining that unity and preventing our diversity from becoming dangerously Balkanized along ideological, religious, racial, ethnic, or economic lines. This is a greater threat to civil society than any single ideology taking over. While our ideology and partisanship have become less tolerant and more belligerent in recent years, we have become more empathetic on matters of civil rights and ethnic, racial, and sexual diversity. That said, value pluralism is not "multiculturalism" or "diversity worship," both of which support a relativistic morality.

Pragmatists and Pluralists

PLURALISM HAS BEEN a subplot in Western thought since the Enlightenment. John Stuart Mill introduced his *On Liberty,* the classic defense of utilitarianism, with this quote from a German philosopher: "The grand leading principle, towards which every argument unfolded in these pages directly converges, is the absolute and essential importance of human development in its richest diversity."

In America, the school of philosophy called "pragmatism" and associated with William James and John Dewey shares the spirit of pluralism. "My philosophy is what I call a radical empiricism, a pluralism," James wrote. "It rejects all doctrines of the Absolute." Defined simply, pragmatism holds that usefulness and practical consequences are the best tests of beliefs and ideas. Unpractical and harmful ideas should be dismissed.

Pragmatism also abandoned the God's-eye view. Meeting the spectrum of human needs, and the conflicts they render, is the pragmatist's moral and political mission.

Like pluralism, pragmatism is not something that makes undergraduates swoon. Young idealists like big, gaudy ideas and theories. They want answers. They want to be right. They fall for Plato, Rousseau, Hegel, Marx, Nietzsche, or the existentialists. Pluralism and pragmatism are too sober and fretful. Idealists tend to believe, the leading contemporary pragmatist Richard Rorty wrote, "that moral idealism depends on moral universalism." The only universal in pluralism is that ideals are plural. The only universal in pragmatism is that what works and what helps human needs is good. That's not very sexy.

Pluralism Against Relativism

A COMMON BUT incorrect attack on pluralism and pragmatism is that they are necessarily relativistic. If there are many ultimate values, aren't they all equal? How is rational choice possible between them? There are certainly relativists who would be happy to be called pluralists—the sixties bred them like rabbits. Disagreement about relativism and truthiness is what separates value pluralists and other foxes.

Put simply, the pluralist is willing to make value judgments despite the lack of universal truths. To refrain would be inhuman and inhumane. The existence of many ultimate values is, the value pluralist argues, empirically accurate. That very fact dictates some moral imperatives. Thus pluralism is antithetical to relativism. Values and beliefs *must* be morally and politically judged by two measures: first, by the room and respect they give to *other* ideals and beliefs, and second, by their practical, earthly results, by their real human effects. Christianity that says all heathens are to be vanquished is immoral no matter how devoutly it is held. A Communist who says all rights of speech, worship, and property must be relinquished in the name of equality is immoral, period. A Muslim who believes in the fatwa against Salman Rushdie is immoral. The relativist will not be willing to make such judgments. The pluralist won't hesitate.

This is a fundamental distinction. Knowing full well that, without a God's-eye view, there is nothing like moral certainty for choosing well, the value pluralist still chooses. Theoretical consistency is not everything. Fully rational choices are not always possible but always desirable. Making choices that have positive effects in the world trumps philosophical and theological tidiness.

Our modern impulse toward relativism comes largely from the desire to escape judgment. But it isn't fatal to fail a moral judgment. We all

fail repeatedly and constantly in life. We're human. But it is fatal to refuse to exert moral effort and to retreat from being judged. That atro-
phies the soul.

Tragic Conflicts

SOCIAL AND POLITICAL maturity is tested when we are called on to
make difficult choices for ourselves and society. There is no honest way
to smooth over the strong conflicts between competing goods that we all
face. Does your opposition to abortion absolutely demand that it may
not be available to *anyone* in society? Is your view of the separation of
church and state one that demands no school can observe any type of
prayer or moment of silence? Is your belief in the sanctity of life so certain, precise, and detailed you object to tax dollars funding stem cell research?

When grave issues collide, the conflicts can be tragic. In an ancient
Greek play, Antigone had to choose between duty to her city and duty to
her brother. There was no possible resolution or compromise; either
course led to failure and shame. Pluralism focuses on these choices to il-
lustrate the variety of competing ultimate values, but also the sobriety
necessary to see the world as it is and to choose as an adult, not as a
childish wishful thinker.

The difficult choices we must act on, and not just opine about, are
about competing personal values. Do you work extra hours to earn more
money and a chance at a better job knowing that it means sacrificing
time with your toddlers? Do you avoid a call from your demanding boss
while on a crowded train because you know it will irritate your neighbors? You can't trick yourself into believing these choices entail no sacrifice; they are "zero sum" options. You can either decide thoughtfully or
not. You cultivate character, manners, and temperament so there is a
habit or instinct of thoughtfulness.

In practice we decide thoughtfully some of the time and automatically some of the time. That's fine, that's the climb. So we try to marshal
our thoughtfulness for the big choices necessary in modern life, choices
that were once not possible. To be religiously observant is a choice, even
for those who have faith. It entails sacrifices: no soccer on Saturday, for

example, or no premartial sex, or no drinking. To move away from your family is a choice. To seek wealth is a choice. Our goals are many and conflict with one another.

Berlin's point is to be wary of anyone claiming these conflicts can all be worked out, that all the true goods in life must be in harmony. The steadfast inability of the American system to recognize this in an honest way and treat the citizenry as adults is perhaps its greatest failing. By pretending that obviously irresolvable conflicts can be resolved, politicians hemorrhage credibility: Taxes can be cut with no loss of services or increased debt load; the health needs of the elderly can be paid for without diverting resources from other generations. Voters respond prudently to this civic immaturity. They withhold trust and divide power between the factions.

In our own lives, three things become extremely important: choosing thoughtfully for yourself, as an adult; striving to exercise the virtues related to your choice; respecting and considering the choices others make. In a world with so many options, part of this means limiting your options, an un-American inclination. There are objective virtues within the smaller worlds we choose. In my life there are virtues related to being a journalist, a manager, and a member of a family. I have no illusions that I act on the relevant virtues very often, but I do try hard to do so. I haven't always. I also do not kid myself that the idea of virtue is a myth and that there are no such things as authentic or quality choices.

So those are my two small ideas, the two difficult projects. Roll them into one and we have something like: Strive to make thoughtful choices using a sound moral temperament.

Rotisserie Baseball and the Well-Examined Life

SO HOW DO you make such choices? For most, the simple beginning is to catch yourself in the act of mindlessness. This takes some discipline and perspective, but it isn't navel gazing and it isn't especially cerebral. It eventually becomes instinctual. Results are unpredictable; effort matters most.

I know this because I am busy but lazy. This is not an optimal state in a multitasking universe. So why do I choose to spend one Saturday of every spring and then fifteen to thirty minutes every day until early October playing Rotisserie baseball? Because of truth, virtue, and the American Way.

For those who haven't had the pleasure, Roto is a complicated baseball wager similar to fantasy football. At the beginning of the season, the league, usually twelve players, gathers for an auction where you may spend $260 assembling a roster of fourteen hitters and nine pitchers from the major leagues. You then compile the statistics of those players throughout the season, though you can obsessively make trades and other roster moves all summer. Whoever has the best stats at the end of the season wins money and glory. Roughly 99 percent of the world thinks this is infantile and pointless.

But for us founding fathers who began the Capital City Day Dreamers league in 1990, it is now a tradition and a meaningful one, albeit in a small way. Auction day is one of the truly fun days of the year. People fly in from Arizona, Michigan, New York, New Jersey, and Arkansas. Some of us see one another only once a year and so we catch up and laugh. It generates priceless social capital. So, sure, it is insignificant compared to global warming and curing cancer, but it is quietly important.

Rotisserie baseball also meets my demands for authenticity. It is certainly true to the little boy part of "mine own self" and is sincere and passionate. It is moral because it is sustaining a small community, a group of men who have a loyal bond. It takes both effort and virtue. Winning takes skill. There is no relativism here; winners are winners. The guys who think they are smart on auction day rarely triumph. You must be well prepared and coolheaded during the draft. Then you need to manage your roster, make wily trades, and get lucky with injuries. You must also be loyal and steadfast toward the players on your roster if you expect to generate good Rotisserie karma.

The idea here is similar to my custom of buying lunch only from people I know. Limiting choice and being loyal for the sake of being loyal is fun.

I also have a poker game with very close friends that I could have described instead of Roto. An even better example is the mother-daughter book club that my wife and daughter have belonged to for ten years and counting. Creating and cultivating these small groups—small but meaningful communities—is essential today. The trick is to avoid Balkanization and create kinship that isn't defined through opposition to other groups. It is often said groups need a good enemy to cohere. There's an old joke Jews tell about themselves that every town has two synagogues, the one I go to and the one I wouldn't go to in a million years. But enriching communities can have all sorts of people in them. They don't need to be only kinships of the similar. It takes effort to keep a group together in America today, to nourish loyalty, routine, ritual, and belonging. It is easy to let go of group activities that take effort and patience in the shuffle of a busy life.

Rotisserie baseball, poker games, and book clubs may seem like puny responses to a powerful problem. Perhaps. But the big, bad world isn't going to change for you, so you must try to repair your own small world and take responsibility for it. Obviously, we have opportunities to join and serve larger communities than a poker game: a school board, a local charity, an election campaign, a congregation, or a hospital's volunteer corps. Some are lucky enough to have work that is a calling, a contribution, and a community. The most important community, in the end, is the smallest: the family. But, again, success is in the process and the attitude, not in the final results or the pictures of success, whether they are grand or humble.

Liking Us More

HATING US LESS also demands making thoughtful choices from a thoughtful temperament precisely in areas where we hate us most: media, politics, consumerism, marketing, and so forth. It almost becomes necessary to parent our own lives because there are so many bad influences out there. We need to be careful who we associate with in both real life and OmniMedia life.

In politics, in being a citizen, this entails thinking hard about what tolerance and intolerance mean. Blanket tolerance is inane; without discretion and standards, without some intolerance, tolerance itself is cheap and easy. But we also need to think hard if we're really so convinced of the righteousness of our positions that we should literally hate those who disagree on important, passionate issues. When we find our-selves intolerant of ideas or people, usually distant, who seem threaten-ing but pose no realistic harm, it's time for a hard second look. Too many liberals today, for example, harbor an intolerance of very religious people that is uncalled for. And too many religious people and conser-vatives harbor exaggerated ill will toward liberals. They call each other "scary." This is wrong. Neither side is scary. Discretion and tolerance don't need to exclude each other. One of Frank Bascombe's friends in Richard Ford's *The Lay of the Land* has as his epitaph, "He suffered fools cheerfully."

Our hair-trigger intolerance is especially misguided when you con-sider how tolerant we are of the people who really do cause us harm, the purveyors of the prevailing culture. We let them into our living rooms every night. We don't need to.

We can change who we let into the living room. We can't change the world, but we can change our OmniMedia world. Media consumption is at the top of the "things we can sort of control" list. Remember, all media is optional. In "reality," you cannot easily eliminate your child's learning disability, the driver who rear-ended you, or your mother's illness. But you can always turn off the TV. You can't go out and buy new psycholog-ical and emotional hardware and software. You can turn the computer off. Trust me. My wife and I worked in broadcast news for years but wouldn't let our kids watch television. They survived.

This doesn't mean you have to be a Luddite hermit, just a more thoughtful consumer. If you are going to watch the news, do you truly want to watch a shout-fest on cable, or something else? Do you really want to click around or watch reality TV, cooking shows, or network dra-mas for a couple hours most nights? Do you really want to drop three hours playing online poker or surfing knitting sites? Do I really want to cruise baseball statistics online alone in my office for long stretches to win at Rotisserie baseball? Sometimes the answer is yes. The point is to consider how you portion out your time and mental energy. It is impor-tant to consider the side effects on others. Rotisserie baseball takes time away from my family, and I can't pretend it doesn't. These decisions are like calculating dosages; in small doses, most things (Rotisserie baseball, online poker, and surfing knitting sites) are harmless or even beneficial. Large doses may be a different story. All activities exclude other things. Modern life is full of addictive little time sinks: television, e-mail, the computer, iPods, and much more. Media usage is especially worth some thought—not angst, just a little pondering. The important point is that thinking about such things may matter almost as much as the big decisions.

Unity in Diversity

IT IS NOT a sign of a terminal social disease that we do hate us. Who knows what our social self-loathing bodes? Perhaps a growing consciousness of our discontent will be an opportunity for society. I know it is for individuals. We hate politics, for example. Liberals hate politics for different reasons than conservatives, but at some level there is a shared disrespect for the phoniness and stagecraft. It would be helpful if we could harness common antipathies constructively instead of destructively. That isn't a job only for leaders, public figures, intellectuals, and storytellers; it's also a job for people who argue, who teach, who are role models, colleagues, employers, students, and voters. That means resisting the powerful calls to move apart, to fight, to demonize, or to withdraw. In *The Disuniting of America*, Arthur Schlesinger said the question is, "How to restore the balance between *unum* and *pluribus*?"

Obviously, there isn't room for harmony in every area of social conflict. Some issues become symbolic battlegrounds and stay that way for a long time: abortion, immigration, flag burning, gay marriage, and gun ownership. That is politics. But these don't have to be the issues that make the most noise and define the times. And the noise from those fights should not worry or distract us too much, because society does still agree on a *process* for balancing, not resolving, conflicts through democracy, elections, representative government, and the law. That process in America does not yet face a crisis of legitimacy. I don't see one ahead. But there is a social crisis—a crisis of phoniness, demonization, belligerence, and Balkanization. There is a lack of cultural pride that limits our capacity to address the practical and spiritual problems of our times.

The processes of democracy cannot repair that directly. That takes something more.

Americans are wary of the prevailing culture. As I have spoken to people over the years about why we hate us, I have found few people who don't express profound suspicion of prevailing culture as it is manifest in television, computer games, music, MySpace, marketing, or politics. Different people fight different devils, but everybody is fighting. I have heard this articulated passionately by all kinds of people all over the country, especially people who deal with children. Sometimes it's just lip service, but that doesn't mean the concerns are phony. There is a unity in this diversity of discontent.

I believe and hope that there is a unity about why we hate us and that it might someday be channeled to shift the tone and direction of American public culture. Americans who seem at odds in so many ways share basic worries and hopes. This is obscured in the noise of politics, the flood of media, and the pace of everyday life. It has been further obscured by the relentless social change and stress of the past decades. Lacking deep community that can make change more tolerable, we find it difficult to walk in another's skin. Americans feel attacked and have hunkered down. We emphasize differences and diversity, not a deeper unity. That is a paradox of pluralism.

That's the way it is. It is not the way it must be.

Selected Bibliography

I have tried to put enough information in the main text to make all quotations, articles, and specific references easy to find. I also drew heavily and gratefully from several books that I did not cite or quote from directly, and I want to acknowledge them. I have listed them here, along with the books cited, as something of a "why we hate us" reading list.

Baker, Wayne E. *America's Crisis of Values: Reality and Perception.* Princeton: Princeton University Press, 2005.

Bell, Daniel. *The Cultural Contradictions of Capitalism.* New York: Basic Books, 1996.

Bellah, Robert N., Richard Madsen, William M. Sullivan, Ann Swidler, and Stephen M. Tipton. *Habits of the Heart: Individualism and Commitment in American Life.* Berkeley: University of California Press, 1996.

Berlin, Isaiah. *Concepts and Categories: Philosophic Essays.* Edited by Henry Hardy. Princeton: Princeton University Press, 1999.

———. *Four Essays on Liberty.* Oxford: Oxford University Press, 1979.

———. *The Hedgehog and the Fox: An Essay on Tolstoy's View of History.* Chicago: Ivan R. Dee, Publisher, 1993.

Bernays, Edward. *Propaganda.* Brooklyn: Ig Publishing, 2005.

Blumenthal, Sidney. *The Permanent Campaign: Inside the World of Elite Political Operatives.* Boston: Beacon Press, 1980.

Boorstin, Daniel J. *The Image: A Guide to Pseudo-Events in America.* New York: Vintage Books, 1992.

Broder, David S. *The Party's Over: The Failure of Politics in America.* New York: Harper & Row, 1972.

Brooks, David. *Bobos in Paradise: The New Upper Class and How They Got There.* New York: Simon & Schuster, 2000.

Bryce, James. *The American Commonwealth.* MacMillan: New York, 1891.

Callahan, David. *The Cheating Culture: Why More Americans Are Doing Wrong to Get Ahead.* Orlando: Harcourt, 2004.

De Zengotita, Thomas. *Mediated: How the Media Shapes Your World and the Way You Live in It.* New York: Bloomsbury, 2005.

Dionne, E. J. *Why Americans Hate Politics.* New York: Simon & Schuster, 1991.

Dreher, Rod. *Crunchy Cons: The New Conservative Counterculture and Its Return to Roots.* New York: Three Rivers Press, 2006.

Duany, Andres, Elizabeth Plater-Zyberk, and Jeff Speck. *Suburban Nation: The Rise of Sprawl and the Decline of the American Dream.* New York: North Point Press, 2000.

Easterbrook, Gregg. *The Progress Paradox: How Life Gets Better While People Feel Worse.* New York: Random House, 2003.

Edsall, Thomas Byrne. *Building Red America: The New Conservative Coalition and the Drive for Permanent Power.* New York: Basic Books, 2007.

Eisen, Arnold M. *Taking Hold of Torah: Jewish Commitment and Community in America.* Bloomington: Indiana University Press, 1997.

Emery, Michael, Edwin Emery, and Nancy L. Roberts. *The Press and America: An Interpretive History of the Mass Media,* 9th ed. Boston: Allyn & Bacon, 2000.

Fiorina, Morris P., Samuel Abrams, and Jeremy C. Pope. *Culture War? The Myth of a Polarized America,* 1st ed. New York: Pearson Education, 2006.

Ford, Richard. *The Lay of the Land.* New York: Alfred A. Knopf, 2006.

Frank, Robert. *Richistan: A Journey Through the American Wealth Boom and the Lives of the New Rich.* New York: Crown Publishers, 2007.

Frank, Robert, and Philip Cook. *The Winner-Take-All Society: Why the Few at the Top Get So Much More Than the Rest of Us.* New York: Penguin, 1996.

Frankfurt, Harry G. *On Bullshit.* Princeton: Princeton University Press, 2005.

———. *On Truth.* New York: Knopf, 2006.

Fuchs, Lawrence. *The American Kaleidoscope: Race, Ethnicity, and the Civic Culture.* Middletown, Conn.: Wesleyan University Press, 1990.

Fukuyama, Francis. *The Great Disruption: Human Nature and the Reconstitution of Social Order.* New York: Free Press, 1999.

Gerth, H. H., and C. Wright Mills, eds. *From Max Weber: Essays in Sociology.* New York: Oxford University Press, 1946.

Gitlin, Todd. *Media Unlimited: How the Torrent of Images and Sounds Overwhelms Our Lives.* New York: Metropolitan Books, 2001.

Glassner, Barry. *The Culture of Fear: Why Americans Are Afraid of the Wrong Things.* New York: Basic Books, 1999.

Goetz, David L. *Death by Suburb: How to Keep the Suburbs from Killing Your Soul.* San Francisco: HarperSanFrancisco, 2006.

Gray, John. *Berlin.* London: Fontana Press, 1995.

Greenberg, Stanley B. *The Two Americas: Our Current Political Deadlock and How to Break It.* New York: Thomas Dunne Books, 2004.

Hallowell, Edward M. *CrazyBusy: Overstretched, Overbooked, and About to Snap—Strategies for Coping in a World Gone ADD.* New York: Ballantine Books, 2006.

Hendra, Tony. *Father Joe: The Man Who Saved My Soul.* New York: Random House, 2004.

Himmelfarb, Gertrude. *One Nation, Two Cultures.* New York: Vintage Books, 2001.

Hoffer, Eric. *The True Believer: Thoughts on the Nature of Mass Movements.* New York: HarperCollins, 2002.

Hunter, James Davison. *Culture Wars: The Struggle to Define America.* New York: Basic Books, 1991.

Hunter, James Davison, and Alan Wolfe. *Is There a Culture War?* Washington, D.C.: Pew Research Center and Brooking Institution Press, 2006.

Keen, Andrew. *The Cult of the Amateur: How Today's Internet Is Killing Our Culture.* New York: Doubleday, 2007.

Kennedy, William. *Roscoe.* New York: Viking, 2002.

Kierkegaard, Søren. *The Present Age.* New York: Harper & Row, 1962.

Klein, Joe. *Politics Lost: How American Democracy Was Trivialized by People Who Think You're Stupid.* New York: Doubleday, 2006.

Klein, Naomi. *No Logo: Taking Aim at the Brand Bullies.* New York: Picador, 2000.

Lane, Robert E. *The Loss of Happiness in Market Democracies.* New Haven: Yale University Press, 2000.

Lasch, Christopher. *The Culture of Narcissism: American Life in an Age of Diminishing Expectations.* New York: W. W. Norton & Co., 1978.

Lee, Harper. *To Kill a Mockingbird.* New York: Warner, 1982.

MacIntyre, Alasdair. *After Virtue: A Study in Moral Theory.* Notre Dame: University of Notre Dame Press, 1981.

Martin, Judith. "Who Killed Modern Manners?" In *The Essential Communitarian Reader,* edited by Amitai Etzioni. Lanham, Md.: Rowan & Littlefield, 1998.

Morgan, Peter. *The Queen: A Screenplay.* New York: Hyperion, 2006.

Nivola, Pietro, and David W. Brady, eds. *Red and Blue Nation? Characteristics and Causes of America's Polarized Politics.* Washington: Brookings Institution Press, 2006.

Pirsig, Robert M. *Zen and the Art of Motorcycle Maintenance: An Inquiry into Values.* New York: William Morrow & Company, 1974.

Plissner, Martin. *The Control Room: How Television Calls the Shots in Presidential Elections.* New York: Free Press, 1999.

Postman, Neil. *Amusing Ourselves to Death: Public Discourse in the Age of Show Business.* New York: Penguin, 2006.

Putnam, Robert D. *Bowling Alone: The Collapse and Revival of American Community.* New York: Simon & Schuster, 2000.

Reeves, Byron, and Nass, Clifford. *The Media Equation: How People Treat Computers, Television, and New Media Like Real People and Places.* Stanford, Calif.: CSLI Publications, 1996.

Rieff, Phillip. *The Triumph of the Therapeutic: Uses of Faith After Freud.* New York: Harper & Row, 1966.

Rorty, Richard. *Achieving Our Country: Leftist Thoughts in Twentieth-Century America.* Cambridge: Harvard University Press, 1998.

Rosen, Christine. "Our Cell Phones, Ourselves." *The New Atlantis* 6 (2004), thenewatlantis.com/archive/6/rosen.htm.

Roszak, Theodore. *The Making of a Counter Culture: Reflections on the Technocratic Society and its Youthful Opposition.* Berkeley: University of California Press, 1995.

Rousseau, Jean-Jacques. *The Confessions.* Translated by Angela Scholar. Edited by Patrick Coleman. New York: Oxford University Press, 2000.

Rubin, Jerry. *Growing (Up) at 37.* New York: M. Evans, 1976.

Sabato, Larry J. *The Rise of Political Consultants: New Ways of Winning Elections.* New York: Basic Books, 1981.

Salinger, J. D. *The Catcher in the Rye.* Boston: Little, Brown, 1951.

Schlesinger, Arthur M., Jr. *The Disuniting of America: Reflections on a Multicultural Society.* New York: W. W. Norton, 1998.

Schor, Juliet B. *The Overworked American: The Unexpected Decline of Leisure.* New York: Basic Books, 1991.

Schwartz, Barry. *The Paradox of Choice: Why More Is Less.* New York: HarperCollins, 2004.

Skocpol, Theda. *Diminished Democracy: From Membership to Management in American Civic Life.* Norman: University of Oklahoma Press, 2003.

Tannen, Deborah. *The Argument Culture: Moving from Debate to Dialogue.* New York: Ballantine Books, 1998.

Taylor, Charles. *The Ethics of Authenticity.* Cambridge, Mass.: Harvard University Press, 1991.

Trilling, Lionel. *Sincerity and Authenticity.* Cambridge, Mass.: Harvard University Press, 1972.

Veblen, Thorstein. *The Theory of the Leisure Class.* New York: Dover, 1994.

Weinstein, Arnold. *Nobody's Home: Speech, Self, and Place in American Fiction from Hawthorne to DeLillo.* New York: Oxford University Press, 1993.

Wolfe, Alan. *One Nation, After All: What Middle-Class Americans Really Think About God, Country, Family, Racism, Welfare, Immigration, Homosexuality, Work, the Right, the Left, and Each Other.* New York: Viking, 1998.

Wolfe, Tom. *Mauve Gloves & Madmen, Clutter & Vine, and Other Stories, Sketches, and Essays.* New York: Farrar, Straus and Giroux, 1976.

Acknowledgments

I suppose this book might be considered somewhat sour. Now comes the sweet part.

My gratitude extends far beyond those I can thank here, especially to my past teachers and current close friends. Gail Ross, my agent, and her editorial director, Howard Yoon, were very generous and helpful, as was my editor, Sean Desmond. They made it fun. I doubt I would have gotten this book written if Morris Fiorina and David Brady hadn't arranged for me to spend time at Stanford University and the Hoover Institution. While at Stanford, I was able to resume tutorials with my favorite teacher and friend, Arnold Eisen.

I am grateful to Martha Hodes, whose careful reading of the proposal and an early draft of the final chapter was extremely useful. Martin Plissner, who hired me at CBS News in 1985 and who knows more things than anyone, helped me with the politics chapter. I am deeply indebted to Elizabeth Scalia and Jeffrey Goldberg, who were kind enough to provide argumentative, smart, and funny comments on the whole manuscript. Marc Fisher helped early in the writing process and then took on the whole book. His brilliant editing and advice were essential. Lauren Clark and Arnie Seipel provided careful research. Don't blame these nice people for what you hate about the book.

ABOUT THE AUTHOR

Dick Meyer was a reporter, producer, online editor, and columnist at CBS News in Washington for more than twenty-three years. He is now the editorial director for digital media at National Public Radio.